Startup Kudos

By Rami Alame

ISBN: 978-1-7375999-0-6

A Story of Struggle, Passion, Success, & Endless Journeys

By Rami Alame

© Rami Alame

Something that happens along the way, is we somehow lose clarity and drown in small problems, forgetting about our dreams, goals, and aspirations. One of the reasons children and teenagers are so full of life is because of the endless opportunities. Yes, dreams and a lack of pressure from society can make you full of life. What is called energy at a young age, praised, and pushed; transforms to lack of responsibility and criticized in adulthood. I was born with several deficiencies, but lack of passion is not one of them. I decided I would be a soccer player, a writer, a singer, a lawyer, a businessman, a lover, and everything in between. This is both the blessing and the curse of being an entrepreneur.

Success is relative and is best when shared. You must accept sharing the spotlight, rewards, and everything in between with others. When dealing with potential projects, I like to build with people I synchronize with, and God knows I have had my fair share of failures, disappointments and setbacks from people who refused to see what was in front of their eyes. Dealing with people is difficult, and it takes an enormous amount of work to find the right person to work or partner up with.I also like to pick businesses that create value and add to people's lives, making things easier in their respective fields or industries. Take Lexyom Inc., for example. I always say Lexyom is not in the legal business, servicing people, but it is a peoples' company providing legal services. Blaxity Inc. is not just providing a dating service; it is providing people the backbones of a relationship 2.0. Remy Remez is not about selling clothing; it is about the craftsmanship of limited sale items that create a sense of belonging, warmth, and differentiation, that leads to feeling more confident, more determined, and happier along the way.

I tried to relate experiences and stories that would help you get a glimpse at how a start-up functions, how entrepreneurship is built and lived, and, more importantly, how to circumvent boundaries, traditional concepts, and stagnation. Indeed, I found the solution to many things in entrepreneurship, but that is not to say it will be like that for everyone. I found many similarities between a human being's life and a start-up. In the book, I try to go through a kind of chronological evolution that will concurrently exteriorize two main points: One, that structure is needed in what is so many times described as chaotic, and two, that there are specific things that do predetermine success.

I do not mean things are engraved in stone, they can be changed and transformed. Success depends on different variables. Sometimes, even the person involved cannot assess these variables that are present deep in the subconscious, the education, and the culture.

You will experience the ups, the downs, the struggles, and the stories I share for the first time in each chapter to give you a glimpse of the journey. You will ultimately learn exceptional skills in management, marketing, deal-making, and more critically, the day-to-day buildings of a start-up, with hands-on tools and techniques that will rocket launch your business.

The story starts in 1986, with a kid born and raised in adversity, shaping this sense of adaptation. That is one of the main pillars of entrepreneurship, but what is entrepreneurship? It is the concept of venturing into something where success, stability and structure are in no way guaranteed, but the possibilities are limitless. What I tried to do throughout my journey was to appreciate what most people depreciated.

The book goes through a chronological approach to building a start-up. Through that, I wanted to give you a sense of structure to building your dream, an approach to the different aspects and components to make it easier to understand struggles and externalities. I will share my views on relationships 2.0 and government as well. I believe that these two concepts will undergo a significant disruption over the next few years, indirectly shaping what entrepreneurship will look like in the future

Table of Contents

Prologue   9

1. Basic Instincts   12

Self Preservation   16

How does it manifest?   17

Sexual   20

What is it?   21

How does it manifest?   21

Social Survival Instinct   27

What is it?   27

How does it manifest?   28

2. Real Life Neuromarketing   35

First information and bias   36

Priming yourself for success   37

Neuro-marketing in designing successful websites   38

3. Hustle Before Starting   45

13 Secrets To Closing A Sale   49

1. Asking questions   49

2. Five Basic Reasons For A Customer To Say No   50

3. Buyer's buying psychology   52

4. Be a helper   52

5. Believe in what you do   53

6. Persuading the prospect   53

7. The price   54

8. Believers are closers   54

9. The salesman as a person   55

10. The use of reasons   56

11. Identify problems and find solutions   57

12.Take suggestions but don't make them final decisions   57

13. Self image   58

4. The Legal Guru   59

16 Steps To Take Alongside Legal   61

1. Define your mission   62

2. Define your end goal   64

3. Define your "who"   65

4. Define your "where?"   72

5. Protect your brand (and intellectual property)   75

6. Plan your funding   79

7. Select your type of entity   82

8. Register with your state in the u.S. Or your country or in an active startup ecosystem   86

9. Select your tax treatment   89

10. Obtain your EIN from the IRS   90

11. Create a separate bank account   92

12. Determine your industry-specific regulations   93

13. Determine your liabilities and insurance needs   94

14. Set up an accounting system   97

15. Set up your basic contracts   99

16. Keep it simple   101

5. Start Today   104

1. Find the problem or need you are solving   105

2. Find the right name for your business   106

3. Build/source the best product/service   107

4.Build an amazing team   107

5.Build an amazing website/platform to sell   108

6. Start selling, selling, selling   109

proven sales strategies   117

6. The Art Of Attracting People & Building A Team   146

7. How To Take Advantage Of The Startup/E-Commerce Boom To Control
Your First Market   161

8. Growth Hacking Digital Marketing   165

1. Self marketing   172

2. Social media   173

3. Email marketing   225

4. Search engine marketing   243

5. Influencer marketing   250

Key metrics to track   285

9. Raise Money Fast.   296

10. Control Your Design Theory   310

Warm Colors   315

Red (primary color)   315

Orange (secondary color)   319

Yellow (primary color)   322

Cool Colors   326

Green (secondary color)   326

Blue (primary color)   330

Purple (secondary color)   332

Neutrals   336

Black   336

White   339

Gray   343

Brown   346

Beige and tan   349

Cream and ivory   352

User Experience   356

11. Relationships 2.0   361

The Four Ps   362

1. Positivity   **362**

2. Passion   **365**

3. Purpose   367

4. Productivity   370

12. A Country Is A Startup   374

The Evolution Of The State   379

The Startup Theory   382

Step 1: vision, mission, goals   382

Step 2: giving the tools to small districts   382

Step 3: install centralis   383

Relationship 2.0   385

Prologue

I was born clinically blind. Each one of us has an optic nerve that goes to the back of our head, feeding our brain data received from our eyes through electrical impulses; It is also called the second cranial nerve or cranial nerve II. It is a web of nerves, just like roads that lead to the part of the brain that analyzes and concludes. In my case, these roads suffered a congenital disaster that led to darkness. Until the age of three, I could not see a thing. Doctors had concluded that there was no end in sight as no medical solution was available at the time. Think of a baby boy roaming around, discovering the world in darkness at an age that Sigmund Freud eloquently describes as the basis of life. The development that goes on during the first years of your life determines the rest, even if many fails to acknowledge it. This has fueled the endless debate on whether things are genetically inclined or acquired. I tend to lean quite drastically towards the latter.

One Sunday afternoon, as the sun was diving into the deep waters projecting its lasts rays on the beautiful city of Limassol, my father Was Watching me play on the carpet. He noticed a bizarre behavior that would be so random regularly but, considering my case seemed extraordinary. I was evading chairs, tables, and obstacles. He started observing my behavior and took me to the ophthalmologist the next day for a check-up. It turns out that this was the start of something the doctors could not explain and summarized later as an adaptation that modified the brain structure, which allowed me to see. From that moment on, I had to go through seven major eye surgeries to reach some kind of equilibrium.

When human beings are faced with an imminent urge to dosomething - to adapt to a hostile habitat, especially at a young age, when fear and social boundaries have not yet kicked in, our body tends to adapt and transform. I like to portray it as what started as a negative, turned with "adaptation" into a positive. I developed all my senses and even felt I had elaborated an acute 6th sense that became a significant component in my decision-making process and remains important up to this day.

As I was growing up, I used to sit in the first row in class, but I still couldn't see anything on the board, so I memorized everything I heard. When students would go write on the board, I would remember them by their scent (I mean that in the least creepy way possible).

Tough days, struggles, and risky surgeries taught me the strength of the mind, the importance of determination to reach goals, and achieving all you want to achieve with passion and adaptation. Please do not focus on making things right; focus on making them fun and interesting. That does not mean that you will not have weak moments, oh boy did I have a few, but life does not wait for anything or anyone.

I mean, look at minorities. Look at the Jews, at the Armenians after the genocide, at all the minorities that had to adapt, create rules and systems to survive. I genuinely believe that every one of us can train our brains to think like a minority, to think that we deserve more, and that we need to fight, survive, and grow. This creates the wave of energy that ignites a sense of adaptation that will serve as a booster to growth and creativity.

Coming back to work, yes, I do it for the money. It serves as a measurement tool, but I realized quite early that no money metric could dictate who I am or what I do in life. Nevertheless, it remains an essential metric in a capitalist economy. A runner must time their runs with a timer, and it cannot be done otherwise. However, they don't run for the timer. They run for the fun and thrill.

Some people are excellent at soccer, and some are amazing at singing; I close deals and open businesses. This has been my passion since day one, and it has given me so much pleasure that I would not want it in any other way, shape, or form. I think it comes partly from a mixture of my Lebanese and Polish roots, as both people have so much in common and have been shaped so similarly. It amazes me every time. Think of these small countries surrounded by big powers always feeling threatened. This is the strength of minorities and underdogs; they hustle to survive and make it through. This is how I was brought up; with this deep urge to hustle and survive. I believe that big winners come from underdogs. Put yourself in an underdog position. Be hungry, hustle, and run through actions, plans, and dreams.

I get my adrenaline from closing deals, negotiations, impact, and growing things from zero to a hundred in the fastest and most robust way possible. With several businesses co-built and growing up in one of the most challenging circumstances, I came to the conviction that it all starts with basic instincts.

"I will tell you a secret, something they do not teach you… the gods envy us; they envy us because we are mortal. After all, any moment might be our last. Everything is more beautiful because we are doomed. You will never be lovelier than you are now. We will never be here again"

ACHILLES TO MYRMIDONS

1. Basic Instincts

A lot of people enjoy art forms, I create angles, ideas, and products. That is how I get excited. I play it very loose when working. I do not carry briefcases, schedule meetings, or close doors. You can't be imaginative or entrepreneurial if you have too much structure. I prefer to come to work each day and see what develops. There is no typical day or week in my life. I wake up around 6 AM every day, spend the first hour reading and then go to work. I try to have as many interactions as possible and few last for more than 15 minutes. I like to do things in the spur of the moment to make sure I can take out as much as possible from whatever I am doing. It never stops, and I would not want it any other way.

Awkward phrasing:
Execution was a struggle as creativity does run in -1 with execution, and today I would choose execution every hour of every day. Carlos Ghosn attributes nearly 80% of success to execution, and well-crafted business structures and products.

Remember we play with the tools the gods gave us

Although it was not a field I was passionate or knowledgeable in, I went into law. My father is a lawyer, and so we often discussed law related topics at home, but I never had a strong urge to go into law. I will discuss in the next chapter how I was primed and lured into it. I was always into business, finance, and innovation to the point that I would run to the Kiosk to buy Businessweek (which later became Bloomberg Businessweek); I was only 12 years old.

Fast forward to today - I was going to a meeting in Downtown Dubai at 9:00 AM, the meeting was with a few investors interested in putting some money into Lexyom. Usually, I make sure to plan my schedule to arrive 5 minutes late, not too late - so that I remain credible but just a little late to raise the adrenaline on the what-if scenarios being built in their heads. It is about planning and relying on the basic instincts human beings have, especially when it comes to opportunities and deals. I arrived at the meeting and looked around to make sure I was sitting in the best spot, which would affect my negotiation tricks and abilities. I vetted the place beforehand, so I knew exactly how to take the lead during the meeting. The meeting started, and Joe A asked about Lexyom and how it was doing with the pandemic, (remember its 2020). He was trying to throw the first hook but remember that throwing an early hook can have a counter effect, especially if you have a fierce opponent facing you. The first can turn against you if you are not in control of the situation. I answered: "We are doing amazing; the pandemic has helped us triple our headcount and double our revenue" and Boom! Joe, trying to hit our valuation with the question directly was an amateur move and it put him in a weak position as I started hitting them with numbers and successes.

I see many people who talk the talk, making sure they sound convincing, always smiling, etc. But what is be1neath all of that? Because you can convince people to a certain extent, but you will have to deliver eventually. This is what Joe did not do when hitting me with his first hook. I probably will not have him on my board or as my investor, because I want wise people surrounding me who make sure to push me to succeed.

I try to learn from the past, but I plan for the future by focusing exclusively on the present, because that is where the fun is. If it can't be fun then tell me, what would be the point? The meeting continued, and I made sure to stick to my numbers. Still, I lost interest because there was no excitement anymore, there was no thrill, and the meeting ended up lasting less than 20 minutes. I excused myself and told them I would get back to them should we be pursuing the conversation.

Another basic instinct is giving out information. We, modern humans, like to share information, and sharing can be risky and a deal-breaker at many levels. Don't get me wrong, you should share. This is something I love to do – sharing stories, information, chitchat, and even making people intrigued about my life and my activities. However, I don't share private information or give others leverage. I once met with clients who started chitchatting, and as we were signing, one of them threw out a question. He asked me about my thoughts on the overall economic situation. From this question, which was not innocent at all, he hoped to gain some information on how I perceived the economy and how I saw my financial situation. My answer was another "Boom!" I told him that I saw great potential in everything. I evaded and misled him even though our situation was indeed terrible at the time.

My biggest motivation growing up was my grandfather, who was a very hard-working man. He kept good control of his environment and his assets but he did not care about the money. It was a way to keep score, that is all. He taught me to tackle things head on and get the job done, then analyze whether I could improve, all that while having fun in the process. My grandmother was also a huge inspiration to me and made me look at life differently, especially with regards to women. I have a massive amount of respect for women, and I consider them much more creative and smarter than men. Women have a sense of their surroundings much more than men, simply because they are more in touch with themselves and their emotions. Only their self-doubt weighs them down and makes them lose some life battles. I appreciate women so much that I have at least a 60% to 40% Female to Male ratio across my ventures; not that I focus on the percentage that much, but still, it happens instinctively.

Humans all have three primary survival instincts: Self- Preservation, Sexual, and Social. Our Enneagram type is a strategy used to meet the needs of these three instinctual drives. Our personality tends to have an imbalance with the three rather than use them equally. Which one do you think you most identify with? Before understanding how our type interacts with our instinct, it is crucial to understand what each instinct is in its natural state.

Today, at the end of 2020, I am the CEO at Lexyom. I own three ecommerce businesses and have made many industry-agnostic investments. I went from studying financial law to working in Downtown Manhattan for a major law firm, to a start-up lawyer, servicing many prominent start-ups across the Middle East, France, and the United States from 2014-2018. Then, to a businessperson with investments in E-commerce, to a co-founder and CEO of a Legal Tech start-up called Lexyom which operates across the MENA and GCC. This journey was fueled with instinct and a sense of self-preservation.

Self Preservation

Self-preservation is the survival instinct of physical self-protection. As a living species, our bodies are the catalyst for our lives. It's the most basic, ubiquitous survival instinct. If our bodies fail, we cannot live. This instinct is concerned primarily with one's own physical body and its health, stability, protection, and ultimately that it continues to survive.

On a rainy day in New York City, I was sitting in my high-rise apartment looking at the Hudson. Clouds had covered the tops of the building, and I had just broken up from a relationship that was very dear to me. I remember sitting there feeling like the world was breaking down, nothing was fair, and thinking possessively, albeit my constant determination to fight that feeling. I did think, what will happen, who will she be with? What will happen to me? How will I make it through? This is when I stood up and went down to the liquor store to get some booze and get my mind of all of this. As I was walking there, my brain started reacting in a certain way bringing different ideas to the forefront. Anger kicked in, some arrogance, some reactivity, frustration; and I found myself picking up the phone and calling them to go out, picking up the phone and calling my friends to distract myself, and it worked. This is a small example of how self-preservation kicks in backed by different emotions; the brain ignites to instinct. As with most things, we exaggerate, and the funny part is that we ended up being genuine close best friends with my ex, and all the drama I had lived through that night seems so subtle. What seemed unequivocally dramatic turned out to be significant, relative to variables and factors it was surrounded with.

How does it manifest?

1. Physical well-being

The self-preservation instinct is focused on the body itself and its wellbeing. It includes health, strength, diet, fitness, and endurance. This facet of self-preservation is like a management system for your body. It seeks to find a root cause for problems in the body, and it can test the body's endurance to harm or stress.

Possible examples of thoughts:

Is this food healthy? Why do I feel so tired today? When can I get back to the gym so I can feel more energetic? Could I climb to the top of this mountain? Could I survive in the forest for one month?

Concrete examples:

Buying only organic because it's better for you, high focus on working out or fitness, health and medicine, diets, fasting, boundaries.

2. Self-regulation and skills

The primary tasks and errands required by life to keep one healthy are a facet of preserving the self. It also includes the skills necessary to take care of oneself, such as maintenance, repairs, and the ability to adapt to new circumstances should they arise. These are the most fundamental survival skills according to whatever circumstances a person is in. A person will not necessarily find pleasure in focusing on these things, but they will nonetheless focus. The sense of building something also goes along with these skills, whether it be making furniture or building a business. The lack of this skill can make a person see goals without having any patience or knowledge of how to reach them. In general, there is a sense of practicality in these skills.

Possible examples of thoughts:

Can I take this apart/fix it? How does this work? What work needs to be done to get what I want? How can I autonomously create my own life? Did we do the laundry? Are my affairs in order? Will I be able to settle in a new place? How do I make this more convenient?

Concrete examples:
Business savvy, investment skills, home improvement, errands, administration, mechanics, sports, transportation, logistics, craftsmanship, surgery, survivalist skills.

3. Foundations and resources
This facet of self-preservation focuses on life's tangible aspects, such as a home, earth, food, shelter, etc. Much of this manifest into a focus on money needed to gain resources. There is also a focus on making things permanent and secure. In general, some people may not like massive changes to their lives or uprooting something that was once a stable anchor. However, people can also test their ability to survive by jumping out of everyday situations. Either that or they will seek "adventure" in terms of lifestyle (travel). What separates this behavior from SP-blinds is the inner motivation to build endurance and skills, rather than the SPblind tendency to not register foundations and resources as something that needs to be worked for specifically. The lifestyles sought after by SP [Self Preservation] people can vary wildly between frugal and straightforward to opulent depending on the enneagram type and individual scenarios. The idea of foundations also brings the drive to preserve things, disregarding an interest in concrete, old, or historical things.

Possible examples of thoughts:
Is owning property better than renting? How much money do I have this month? Where is the closest grocery store? Why am I stuck here when I want to travel and see the rest of the world? Why isn't there enough nature in this city? Do I have any savings?

Concrete examples:
Finance, eco-friendly initiatives, saving money, mutual funds, property, land, the earth, animal care, monuments, history.

Self-preservation is crucial. Making sure we have a clear sense of how to protect ourselves while getting out of our comfort zone and making sure we can defy our fears, boundaries, and norms wherever we go. The first step is the hardest. If you have a business, open an Instagramaccount and invite your friends.

Self-Preservation is how I started. My first venture was organizing parties for friends, and this came from self-preservation. I wanted to protect myself against marginalization and discovered early on that the biggest weapon to fight being marginalized, is honesty and boldness. Getting out there and expressing yourself is what will protect you against society. People can be a tsunami in your life, and if you cannot stand out there, you will fail.

Sexual

Sex is one of the biggest drivers in life. It is a cornerstone in our decision making, our life path and whatever we do. I want you to think of a time in your life where you fully dissociated yourself from sex; I doubt you will find it. I'm not saying that it is the ultimate goal but it does shapes the way we do things. I remember I was around 12 and we went on a summer trip to Cyprus with my parents. We had friends there we would hang out with. We visited a woman called Yanoulla, an old lady friends with my grandmother who worked at the fish market. The family was so welcoming, warm hearted and caring. Her husband, Harris, was a huge fan of Liverpool FC and we would tease each other, me being an avid Manchester United FC Fan. We arrived at her home which was a ground floor apartment, and the balcony was on the street overlooking Limassol's sandy beach. I started running around and playing with small things as all kids do; until Soulla [Her daughter] arrived with her children, Chris, and Harris Jr. At the time, Chris was the coolest person ever to my brother and me. He started talking about how he went clubbing and met so many fit girls. I remember my brother and I were in awe at his stories. This was my first interaction with puberty. We would talk about girls and one night we went into Chris' father's room. He showed us cassettes, not CDs, Not MP3s, Video Cassettes. It was porn.

While reading this, I'm sure your brain will take you through the experiences that shaped your puberty; you will remember the small interactions; the small secrets; the rooms; warmth and passion. You will remember the people you interacted with discovering and exploring when the unknown was just an increased heartbeat. As we grow, we always want to continue being sexually relevant and play the seduction and attraction game. I discuss this in my concept of relationship 2.0, in which I go through an analysis of our physical needs to remain relevant, and how it impacts Monogamy turning it into a "Monogamish" concept. For businesses, it's the same. Understanding attraction and seduction makes you understand ideation, product creation, customer support, and scaling your business.

What is it?

The sexual survival instinct is the instinct of attraction and seduction. Beyond the physical drive to have sex, this instinct is the drive to attract sex. As a species, mating is essential for the survival of humanity. However, it is often not easy to ensure a mating partner. We have a choice in who we mate with, and humans have developed attraction strategies to ensure that they are able to seduce a mate's interest. Sexual selection has ensured that our most attractive qualities are genetically passed on through the ages. For example, the female peacock is attracted to large, colorful plumage, and so the males evolved to grow larger and more elaborate. In people, this instinct is an overidentification with the attraction strategies and mating elements (beyond the act of copulation itself). To understand, when you are marketing products, you need to come back to human beings' basic instincts

How does it manifest?

1. Arousal vs. Repulsion
The sexual instinct seeks to be aroused and to elicit that response in others. It wishes to be energetically "turned-on" by people or things. For this chapter, sx_actives are those who give so much importance to the physical and are closer to basic instincts. While sx_passives are more on the reluctant, refusal side either because they block or are fearsome.

Sx_actives tend to be a slave to the things that arouse them, moving intensely toward these things in the manner of a drug addiction. When humans are sexually aroused, studies have shown that they are less likely to be disgusted by their partner's smells or even less sensitive to physical pain. It is nature's way of ensuring that the intense and boundary-destroying act of sex is a deep need in us and that we are not deterred from mating by other instinctual boundaries. However, when one is not sexually aroused, the idea of sex with an unwanted mate is repulsive and can produce a response of disgust. This is also nature's way of ensuring we mate with the right person. We are either "turned on" or "turned off." While Sx_actives do not necessarily wish instinctively to repulse or be repulsed. In a way, repulsing another can be confirmed that they are affecting them. If there's no response, they do not adequately send attraction signals as people's reaction to sex is either turned on or off.

Possible examples of thoughts:
Is this arousing me? Do I crave it? Do they desire me? How deep can I penetrate this? Why aren't they hooked on me? Will they be turned off if I do this?

Concrete examples:
Pushing a person's boundaries, trying to get a rise out of someone, invading their comfort zone, locking someone into you.

2. Transformation via seduction & display
The sexual instinct aims to fuse chemically with another, this fusion transforming both parties. In a sense, this need for fusion on both parties can be objectifying. It is not a caring social fusion, but rather a chemical essential to infect and be infected, to have the other person grow inside you and alter you, thus each person transforming into something else. Achieving this fusion via seduction and display manifests in two ways:

A. Loss of self - the orifice - feminine
Some animals such as cicadas and male praying mantises work vigorously to mate, just so they can die after. The thing about giving oneself completely over to fusing with another, is that you completely lose yourself in the process. Metaphorically, this is the feminine aspect of this instinct (we all have both feminine energy and masculine energy, regardless of gender). It is the open hole, the receptive socket for self-transformation. "Make me one with you." Often, the depictions of the sexual instinct in subtype literature focusses only on the aggressive/ masculine tendency of this instinct. But both the feminine and masculine are present in all of us, and Sx_actives, in particular, can tend to wear more androgyny. This is the aspect of sex that is creative, open, receptive, and soft and is a complete opening of all boundaries. This can soften certain enneagram types who usually have

emotional and mental walls up. This brings the walls down in a way that Sx- Passives would be opposed to.

b. Aggression/Display - The Phallus - Masculine

In most animal species, the male species display themselves to attract a suitable female partner. The peacock has its feathers, and other birds have their intricate nests and special dances. Humans have their creativity, or the thing that makes them stand out amongst the crowd. These displays can sometimes be counterintuitive from a survival standpoint, but they aim to attract a mate. For example, the peacock's feathers slow him down and make it harder to escape predators. By using his instruments of sexual display to attract the female, the act threatens the self-preservation in the peacock. However, the display is essential for its attraction strategy because it's the hook that gets him noticed by potential mates. Humans can advertise their uniqueness, their talents, exposing the underbelly of what's beneath them, metaphorically, the exposed phallus.

Note: In humans, both masculine and feminine strategies are present in all of us regardless of gender or sexual orientation. One may be more of a focus than others. However, in both these strategies, there is intense psychological nudity stemming from making oneself vulnerable.

Possible examples of thoughts:

Are we one? Am I penetrating? Am I leaving my scent or my mark on this person? Do they want me? Will they find someone else to be hooked on? Why aren't they addicted to me? What can I become? What can I transform into?

Concrete examples:

Letting yourself be taken, emotional/psychological nudity and openness, displaying an emotional or physical scar, deliberate androgyny as an attraction strategy, allowing yourself to be changed or transformed by another, having a particular attraction strategy, fluid boundaries.

3. Chemistry

The sexual instinct needs to feel the chemistry of being hooked by something and have it returned. Sx_actives can feel like a hunter waiting for their prey, or prey, waiting for their hunter. They are sending out pheromones wherever they go, aiming to leave their "scent" on others. Their biggest fear is being undesirable or losing that chemistry. Not being captivating or exciting enough to attract a mate is devastating. To use the peacock example again, the male peacock can put a great deal of mental and physical energy into their display, and still, the female might not find him attractive enough to mate with.

The synergy craved in sex is a sense of simultaneously giving and taking (although the giving is not altruistic). It can be paralleled abstractly in vampire literature where the vampire bites and drains blood, but the victim gains some sort of pleasure. This is usually eroticized. During intercourse or other kinds of mutual sexual activity, both people crave the other as an object to "take" and enjoy "being taken" by the other.

Both people are objectifying each other but getting what they crave in the process. This chemical synergy of objectification on both sides locksboth people into a chemical flow.

Note: This kind of chemistry is not the same as love or connection; however, humans can mix love with sex. The Sexual instinctual drive is a separate domain. Connection and bonding are more in the social instinct domain. Love and intimacy are not instincts.

Possible examples of thoughts:
Is there energy building up between us? Are we magnetically drawn to each other? Can we sustain this? If it is gone, what else is out there?

Concrete examples:
A heat between you and another that registers as sexual, a sense of addiction or obsession, possession, turning off most people to attract the one that likes your scent.

Understanding this will help you further understand human behavior and relate to the things that are happening to you. So, lets say you are trying to build a business. You will be surrounded by and interacting with different types of people. The more you understand this theory, the faster you can determine the types of people surrounding you. So, let's say you are dealing with a cross-gender interaction [Male - Female] or [Male Dom - Male Sub]; in all cases, you will have sx_actives and sx_passives, and you should channel your conversation accordingly. In some meetings, the physical part, the look, the smirk will make all the difference, and other times it would be just the opposite as it would trigger irritation and anger.

It would generate negativity if done in the wrong way, and I am not telling you that it should always be calculated; sometimes, it is a feeling and an instinct that can make all the difference. Remember what I told you about looks and things you are born with.

"We play with the tools & weapons the gods gave us."

No matter what you look like, there are indeed people who have succeeded and have a look like yours. However, your physical appearance is irrelevant, what you do with it and how you turn it into an asset is the most important thing. Look at major celebrities who sometimes have weird looks or weird features and they use it to their advantage.

"What was once the subject of discrimination and sometimes mockery is the new cool today."

Make inner peace with who you are. Life is too short to wait on the side-line. Hit it with the most you can and be happy and expose yourself. Most importantly, do not fear being shamed or mocked, just look at the success of stupidities on TikTok, and know that it is perfectly okay. Norms are changing, and people will look at your content even if you are a lawyer and are making jokes; it is okay; you are human and you are allowed to be fun, have fun, and create fun.

Back to the sexual aspect, do understand that it makes a massive difference if you know the dynamics, and with time, you will find this chapter crucial in your growth.

After organizing parties and events, I started getting into design, art, and technology, mainly through my interest in electronics and gadgets. I started selling Nokia phones and other electronic devices, and then went to trading stickers and other artist related items. I remember a guy called David. He was a smart guy who would always be one step ahead in hustling and manoeuvring to the point I focused my observation on the different tricks he used to do. Don't get me wrong; he was a fraud and stole from me on several occasions but trust me, you learn from these people on how to improve your game and know your limits. The last day I saw him was in his home. I convinced him I could get him some collectibles so I could gain access and get my stuff back. I have interacted with many people, but there are certain experiences that are stuck with me as I move forward in my life.

Social Survival Instinct

What is it?

The social survival instinct is the instinct of connection. A connection is a gigantic domain, and so this instinct is multi-faceted and adaptable, which is part of its innate skill. The prehistoric human brain became larger very quickly, which resulted in offspring's being born out of the womb less developed than other species.

Social addiction is one of the most draining influence on a person's life, it can make them or break them. As a piece of advice, surround yourself with people who love you, whom you can trust. Family is a concept that has grown and evolved over the years to include friends and people who shape what your life will be. My grandfather would always tell me "Our family we have, our friends we choose". This is an especially important concept for both parents and children reading this. Let your children go out in society and interact to build relationships because otherwise they will lack the experience and the knowledge to choose who they want to be with and/or surrounded by. Therefore, children who go through a difficult childhood end up stronger and more prepared for the complexities of life. They develop a simplicity in meeting and interacting with people through adaption and this is one of the most important traits that define an entrepreneur alongside their choice to fight for their life.

Many species' offspring are born almost fully formed, and the period of infancy is much shorter. However, because the human brain is so large, offspring were born early with a long period of helplessness before adulthood. This meant that the young needed a strong bond with a caregiver to protect them for several years. The red-alert response we get when we hear a baby crying is the social protection drive in all of us.

This drive to form connections with other human beings develops deeply in humans to the point where we can live in vast societies cohesively. Few other species can do this. Bees and ants are examples of other very socially cohesive creatures. In humans now, this insect is an over-identification of relationships with other humans in various ways, whether they are deep or cursory.

How does it manifest?

1. Connection and Care

Our brains have built-in mechanisms that register threats to our connections as pain (the dorsal anterior cingulate cortex and anterior insula). This facet of Social is a two-way street that begins in childhood and stays with us as an archetypal duality: the parent and the child. Even as adults, we not only long to be cared for, but we instinctively long to care for others. This is the instinct of closeness and "common ground." All bonds, whether they are friendships, relationships, or familial, have a common ground space. It is a collection of commondenominator activities, interests, feelings, etc., that two people (or a person and a group) share.

The two social stacks will find common ground in different ways, depending on their blind spot. This sense of connection and care leads humans to feel rewarded when they are altruistic without any personal motivations behind it.

The darker side to this is registering the people one should not or cannot connect with. Sx-actives can be particular about who they do or do not connect with, and they can have an adverse reaction to a person or group that they see as a threat or someone to stay away from.

Examples of this are:

racism, prejudice, exclusion, seeing the other as unclean (ex. hygiene, home cleanliness), seeing differences as a threat, etc. Part of protecting "us" is being a unit that unites against the dangerous "other." This skill is useful when used against a person who is a threat and becomes problematic when turned into prejudices.

Possible examples of thoughts: Who are we? What do we have in common? What connects us? Are we an item? How close are we? Are we close enough that I can call them after 9 PM? Will anyone be there for me? Does that person have germs? Why isn't she responding to my text? Why can't I find anyone to hang out with? Did my boss get me a birthday card? Why can't we spend quality time? Do I have these people under control?

Concrete examples:
Asking a person how they are, active listening, friendships, and close bonds, family, power-seeking, group leading, group control, teaching, lecturing, imparting, social media, providing, making a difference, making an impact

2. Mind reading

Unlike other species, humans can interpret the actions of others as having consequences and motivation. We can even personify inanimate objects as having their own "minds" and "souls." For example, "That willow tree looks so sad, and the wind seems angry." Our brains also have built-in mechanisms (the dorsomedial prefrontal cortex and the temporoparietal junction) to essentially make assumptions about others' feelings and their goals and aims. Seeing other humans as individual minds with different thoughts and motivations is instrumental in our success in connecting with others, knowing what they need, and reducing the pain of social rejection.

This mind-reading process is called MENTALIZING, and studies have shown that this region of the brain is active even when we're doing nothing. We mentalize in the background all the time. To do this well, humans and animals have all kinds of unspoken rules and contracts for behavioral expectations, and it can be devastating/disorienting when these are broken. These vary depending on location and period of life.

Possible examples of thoughts:
Does the cab driver want me to get into the car? Is this person waiting for me to pay? Is that person going to cross the street? Is my mother mad at me? Am I the only one with my windshield wipers on? Is what I'm saying too harsh? Is this polite? If that person is standing up, does that mean I should too? Should we bring a gift?

Concrete examples:
Knowing how to respond in any human interaction, from paying at the grocery store to a job interview to create either a positive (or deliberately

negative) bond/response. Partially, this is why you disagree with people at times, you do not connect or converse with people, and you do not even know or understand why.

I met a person, Mr. M, a designer, whom I appreciated and respected even though I did not interact a lot with him. During one of the few sitdowns at a Starbucks in Downton Dubai, he mentioned frustration at a close friend he was living with. It was not an actual problem they were having but rather a sort of Mentalizing issue. When you are in a divergent mindset or on a divergent path, you can disagree; you can fight for what seems superficial at first but soon turns out to be a profound valley that separates your two destinies.

For your start-up, your team, your idea, you need to think of the best way to channel that energy in one direction, and even if it is hard to let go of people, you need and have to do so to pursue your journey to success. Choose the people you feel a good vibe and connection with, and people you can easily and concretely agree with on many levels.

3. Harmony & Social Role (You vs. Me)
This aspect of the social instinct also has two facets: the self and the other– the "me and you" instinct. We all have a sense of self (the medial prefrontal cortex in the brain) that includes our thoughts, feelings, likes, dislikes, etc. However, this absolute sense of self has been heavily shaped by society and our surroundings our entire lives.

Many of the things we think, our viewpoints or ideas are shaped heavily by our external circumstances and the influence of others. When we transport ourselves to another social ecosystem elsewhere in the world or into history, we see that a sense of "normalcy" always exists. Still, it may be completely different than what it currently is for us. Our understanding of self, in a sense, is also a communal "us."

Self-control (ventrolateral prefrontal cortex) allows us to harmonize with others, the reward being acceptance by others.

"We are approval addicts"

This means that our ability to shape the way we see fit what is required of us externally involves a sense of self-control and mediation of what's inside vs. what is outside. Our attempt to harmonize our internal "us" with the external "them" is part of where our social "role" comes from. It allows us to put ourselves forward and be valuable to the group. Included in the social role is the pecking order, hierarchy, and social status. These are all ways to measure who we are in comparison to others.

Possible examples of thoughts:
Who am I? Is this person problematic? Are they using appropriate terminology when describing identities? Am I offending anyone? Should I post this photo? Is this the right thing to wear? How should I say this? How do our political views differ? What makes me? How do people see me right now? Who's in charge here?

Concrete examples:
Getting along with others, forming alliances, living harmoniously with other humans, forming lines, having a sense of self that you consciously present to others, knowing how you come across, knowing how to behave, protesting, unionizing, understanding social protocol (one can reject social protocol, but Social would be aware of this deliberate rebellion, rather than Social blinds not registering the situation), consciously accepting or rejecting what others expect you to be, feeling social humiliation.

The Social instinct aims to create bonds of all kinds with fellow humans. Some of those bonds will have love, and others will not; for example, friendships, romantic partners, business partners, parents, children, crossing guards, etc.

Not all people with heavy social insects are necessarily socially extroverted. This means that many people still enjoy spending much time alone to recharge. And some introverted people are happy to be amongst people all day. Introverted Socials might focus on a smaller number of connections or find fewer active ways to keep those connections alive such as texting, long-distance friends, less time spent together, etc. Social can also manifest in smaller ways, like trying on a new outfit that puts you in a new "genre" or considering your relations from a detached viewpoint.

Being an introvert or extrovert does not necessarily mean that one has a positive attitude toward people or humanity. Many socials can be more on the positive side of how they view life. However, any social type can be antagonistic towards people, humanity, social norms; they can protest, rebel, break the rules, be a tyrant, etc. It's the preoccupation with these issues and reactivity to them that speaks volumes. Social can go pro-social or anti-social. In either case, there's still a focus on how to do social properly.

To continue with the distinction between social extroverts and "one-toone," I should state that social instinct is not the instinct of "groups." In a sense, yes, human instinct has allowed us to form gigantic cohesive groups, which is one of the main reason's humans rule the earth. However, people will not necessarily want to spend time in groups at a more granular level than one-to-one interactions. If anything, extroverts will be more particular about who they spend time with and what contexts, whether it be group or duo. Extroverts can end up curating specific people that they care about the most.

To summarize this chapter, we went through the basic definition of a human being, their basic instinct, and how we interact with and understand each other. It will help you understand the human being at the source of anything you do- whether it's business, marketing, management, product design, and any aspect of your life. It all comes down to understanding the traditional concepts.

In 2010, I started heavily working in legal and joined several law firms as
an intern and junior before making it through to the United States joining
New York Law School and discovering New York and its beauty. I had
a few side-hustles, selling items on eBay, but to be honest, I was more
captivated by the city to the point that I had focused more on discovery
and creativity. I started going further into music, going back to my DJ
roots, and often visiting museums and fairs.

Remember how I told you I started working as a start-up lawyer in 2014.
Imagine a 27-year-old lawyer living the good life in New York City—living
on 120, Greenwich in the Financial District of Manhattan, apartment
PH3, with a morning view of the freedom tower, a fantastic job, and
exceptional prospects on the horizon. Well, as they say, you do not choose
life, but life chooses you. I received a call to go back to Beirut, where
my grandfather was sick, and his situation was deteriorating. I talk more
about this later, but three months later, my grandfather passed away, and
three days after that, I had opened my law firm servicing start-ups and left
everything behind in NYC.

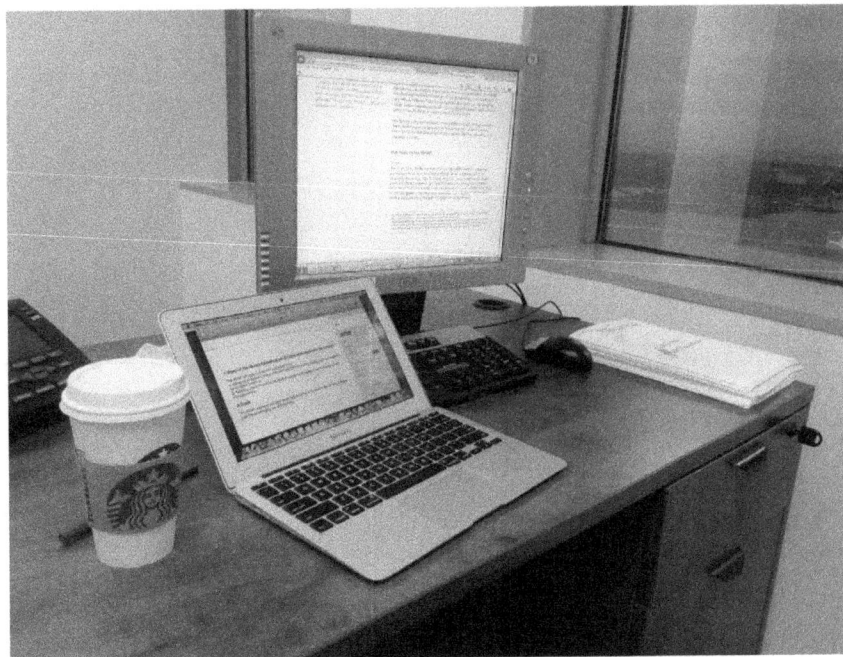

Corporate lawyer life in New York 2014

Sometimes, our instincts prevail, and in this case, it did. I remember after the funeral sitting in my office, alone and thoughtful. It was a dark time that made me further trust my instincts. I am originally an introvert who turned into an extrovert. I pushed myself to be so.

2. Real Life Neuromarketing

I started getting into Neuro-marketing when I discovered the brain's power in art during my stay in New York. I remember beginning to do searches on the brain and ability of neurons to generate and create concepts. In 2018, I had another interaction with neurons in San Francisco during Batch 23's acceleration program for 500 start-ups, to which Lexyom was admitted. One night my friend Kevin and I bought weed and headed to our friend's place in Palo Alto to have a casual home barbecue at our friend's. We arrived in Palo Alto went down the train to the amazing small train station and unique green surroundings.We walked a bit to the restaurant area of town where we were supposed to meet at a Mexican Pub. We met there and started eating and drinking. We then went back to his home, where we sat in the garden and started smoking. Kevin and I realized that unknown to us, the joint was not mixed with tobacco as we thought. As we smoked, we started feeling disconnected and started detaching from our bodies. We separated and moved past the state of numbness. It was my second experience with detachment, and I trusted myself; it was one of the most challenging experiences I've had.

As we left, I felt my body had detached from my brain, and I could not feel myself moving. I was in the middle of the road, but I was not; I was here but there. We grabbed a cab and drove to the hotel. I remember feeling challenged to make sense of my reality. Was it a virtual world, a reality, or what else? From that day onwards, I started focusing on NeuroMarketing as I had unveiled the brain's power and what it could achieve with focus, determination, and scope.

Neuro-marketing, sometimes known as consumer neuroscience, studies the brain to predict and potentially manipulate consumer behavior and decision-making. Until recently considered an extravagant "frontier science," Neuro-marketing has been bolstered over the past five years by several ground-breaking studies demonstrating its potential to create value for marketers. "Neuro-marking" loosely refers to the measurement of physiological and neural signals to gain insight into customers' motivations, preferences, and decisions, which can help inform creative advertising, product development, pricing, and other marketing areas.

Growing up with this different life view, this observation made me see people and situations differently. I would assume this comes from my rooted feeling of discrimination from a young age. I was born to a family as a first child, who were very well surrounded, sometimes oversurrounded. I was born when cousins and relatives had not yet married, and no children were my age. Moreover, my grandparents had child, i.e., my father, who was in his late 30s while they were in their 50s. You must understand the dynamics surrounding this child and how they are brought up to grasp their ins and outs. Being too pampered sometimes creates this gap when the pampering stops; it creates a gap, and most of the time, this gap cannot be filled by anyone other than the initial people who gave it, i.e., in most cases, parents.

Neuro-marketing predicts and potentially even manipulates consumer behavior and decision-making. To do that, marketers dig deep into human psychology, neurology, and in-depth analysis of human beings' behavioral aspects. This is why we discussed basic instincts and the reasons behind certain behaviors in Chapter 1.

First information and bias

We humans usually rely on the first information we receive, no matter how reliable. The first piece of information has a lot of effect on the brain. This is called the anchoring bias. The same thing happens when you are given a certain truth that is continuously promoted and pushed to you through media. For example, a US citizen might fear a terrorist attack more than anything else, while a surfer in Australia might fear a shark attack. This is the concept of availability heuristic bias.

Moreover, the further you are given a piece of information, the more your brain searches for information or data to confirm that initial piece of knowledge. This is the concept of confirmation bias.

This brings us to the Bandwagon effect. If everyone agrees to something during a meeting, you are more likely to agree to it as well. Companies should try to push for groupthink, which is the opposite of Bandwagon, pushing minorities to express themselves so that it can be evaded if there is a mistake. This is also fueled by the Ostrich bias, which is dismissing negative information in favor of the initial discrimination.

So, your start-up decisions should not be based on bias and should not be based on selective perception, especially since it is very easy to be blinded by your will to succeed, your prejudices, and your background. You need to lay back and think before acting; decisions require thought and unbiased behavior to succeed. Focus on making your decisions based on elaborate thinking, complex arguments, and, most importantly, reliable facts. This concept in Neuro-marketing is called System 1 vs. System 2 decision making.

Simply put, System 1 and System 2 thinking may be defined as two modes of thought: System 1 is fast, intuitive, and emotional; System 2 is slower, more deliberative, and more logical. And it would help if you had both in your start-up life to succeed. Sometimes you might need to make decisions instinctively & swiftly. You may also need to make an informed decisions on investments and new market openings.

Priming yourself for success

As you saw, decisions can be complex and lead to unpleasant results if not done correctly. A powerful concept in Neuro-marketing is "PRIMING," and it is, in my opinion, the most important concept that should guide our professional lives. What is priming, and how does it work? To start with, I would urge you to watch the movie "Focus" and see how Will Smith playing Nicky, pushes someone to choose the Number 55 without him even noticing he was being prepped.

Scan this Link and watch the two videos.
One of the more intriguing concepts in Neuro-marketing is priming, i.e., influencing an individual's behavior by introducing various subtle cues. This often occurs subliminally, i.e., the individual is entirely unaware that he has received cues of any nature or that his behavior has been affected and manipulated in any way.

If you can prime yourself through daily cues to be successful, you will be able to drive your brain and the synapses in your head to gear towards success and successful opportunities. Start by adding interesting details to your routine. Wake up to pictures that radiate success and positive energy. Practice saying positive words, dismiss negative words, surround yourself with successful people, read success

stories, and expose yourself to any content that shows success. Priming for success is what I did by starring Lexyom. Following my grandfather's passing on February 2nd, I decided to accept it swiftly. So, whether it was accepting or refusing, I do not know, but what I do know is that by February 3rd, I was reading content on successful businesses. By February 5th, I took a shared office and launched my business, leading to a round of investment 12 months later at a valuation that exceeded 3 million USD. But pay attention; this is an endurance run, not a sprint. You should be able to do it daily and continuously without interruption; otherwise, you will not be able to reap the rich result.

So priming is something we use at Lexyom, internally & externally. Internally we have regular meetings where we promote what we have achieved and what we can achieve in KPIs and successes. Externally we are working on many aspects of priming to our customers that include giveaways, small messages and focus on making our customers feel immersed in the Lexyom experience. We are also building a strong community that makes Lexyom clients feel that they belong to a community, a group, a tribe.

Neuro-marketing in designing successful websites

This is a juicy part; it will help you design and succeed with your new website or platform. The best websites out there are designed with principles. These principles will shape what we call the user experience, which means taking the customer from point A to point purchase/subscribe/any action you want the customer to do. Part of Priming is building an experience, there are six main principles when it comes to building a successful website, and these are principles you should think about profoundly:

Leverage scarcity to persuade a visitor to buy now:
Make a limited offer or promote a limited edition item. People want what they can't have. Likewise, when something is in short supply, prospective buyers inherently feel a sense of urgency to act before availability runs out. This is the scarcity principle. It works whether it is supply-driven (e.g., there is a limited quantity available to sell) or deadline-driven (there is a time limit set on the availability or the price of an item). If a buyer feels they can come back to your site at any time to purchase a product or service, they feel no urgency to make that "buy now" decision. But, if alerted that an item's stock is low or that the sale price is ending, you immediately create a "buy now" urgency that didn't exist before. Why? Because people have a natural aversion to loss–they instead act too hastily, knowing full well that they haven't given the matter proper consideration, rather than risk missing out.

Online retailer RueLaLa has built an entire business model around scarcity. The site curates fashion-centric boutiques that are "open" for only a few days. Each boutique has its countdown timer to remind visitors that time is running out constantly. Then, for an extra powerful one-two punch, the site also indicates in prominent colored type when the supply of a specific item is running low. Scarcity sells.

Use A Decoy to Steer Visitors Toward a Certain Product:
People like to have options. The human brain is designed to compare things. We have a hard time making a choice when there's only one option because, as psychology and behavioral economics professor Dr Dan Ariely explains, "most people don't know what they want unless they see it in context." Enter the decoy.

Also known as the asymmetric dominance effect, the decoy effect uses an alternate (less desirable) choice as a benchmark against which to compare the real product or service you wish to sell.

For example, you may have two home gyms you wish to sell on your site One has only basic features and sells for $599. It's a reasonable choice. The other includes features like a built-in heart monitor and additional accessories and sells for $1100 — a big jump for most consumers. To minimize the shock of that price difference and encourage more consumers to select the $1100 model, you can add a decoy option. In this case, you might add a third model with features that are mostly similar to the $1100 home gym but sells for $1400. Regardless of the visitor's initial preference, the decoy gym's inclusion will encourage the buyer to consider the benefits of buying the $1100 model more carefully, comparing it to the more expensive decoy and eliminating the lower-priced option as a choice.

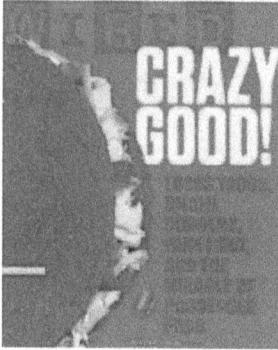

Wired All Access
☆☆☆☆☆ ☑ (92 customer reviews)

Cover Price: $59.88
            Price: **$5.00** (s0.83/issue) & shipping is always free.
You Save: $54.88 (92%)
    Issues: 6 issues / 6 months auto-renewal

Subscription

All Access (Print + Digital) $5.00 (6 issues)	Digital Access $19.99 (12 issues)	Print Access $19.99 (12 issues)

Use Anchoring to Help Visitors Justify Their Selection

People tend to rely too heavily on the first piece of information presented when making decisions. This becomes the "anchor" against which subsequent products will be compared. Sound illogical? It may be, but you can use this anchoring bias to help visitors justify their purchase selection. "Once an anchor is set, other judgments are made by adjusting away from that anchor, and there is a bias toward interpreting other information around the anchor. For example, the initial price offered for a used car sets the standard for the rest of the negotiations, so that prices lower than the initial price seem more reasonable even if they are still higher than what the car is worth."

Make Visitors Feel Indebted to You

In 2002, researchers tried an experiment with tipping in restaurants. They wanted to see what would happen when the server supplied a piece of candy along with each check. They tried a series of scenarios where servers put a small amount of chocolate on the check, gave a larger quantity of candy, or gave no candy at all. They learned that the gift of candy increased the average tip from 15% to just over 18%.

The trick at work was reciprocity. People are driven to repay debts of all kinds — no matter how small. When one person does something nice for another, the person feels a desire to return the goodwill. Marketers can use this impulse to spur site visitors to action. By giving your site visitors something of value, with no expectation of anything in return, you can begin to harness the power of reciprocity.

Offer exclusive information, free samples, or even a free in-home trial — anything that has real value and is obviously and exclusively for the recipient's benefit. That last point is critical — nobody wants to feel like they are being manipulated or receiving a gift with "strings attached." What can you offer to people to entice a sense of reciprocity? Free advice? A buyers' guide? Instead of requiring users to fill out a form to download a white-paper or e-book, maybe you could test, giving them a portion of the content for free.

You might find that this strategy results in a higher download request rate, primarily due to the power of reciprocity. Be the first to give something of value, and your customers will be more likely to provide you with something in return.

Offer Things You Don't Expect to Sell

It may seem odd trying to sell a product or service on your website that you don't expect anyone to buy on the surface. Yet, according to a door-in-the-face compliance technique, this strategy will help you sell lower priced options.

Here's how it works: you start with an unreasonably large option, for example, a VIP conference pass with back-stage access for $1300. When the site visitor signals their disinterest by leaving the page or hitting a "no thanks" button, he is presented with another offer at a lower price — maybe a regular ticket at $500. According to social psychologists, he's more likely to buy the $500 ticket after rejecting the more expensive option than if he were presented with the lower-cost access upfront.

The second (lower priced) option uses the contrast principle, making it seem like a very reasonable price compared to the first. This principle is used very effectively in fundraising and volunteer services.

Throw Out a Lifeline With The Hurt & Rescue Principle
In this method, the marketer allows the prospect to see that they have a problem and then offers a way to fix it. One excellent way to do this is through online quizzes.

For instance, a fitness site may offer a quiz entitled "Do You Have These Six Risk Factors for Diabetes?" The test can include questions about diet, family history, and level of physical activity. If the reader's answers indicate that they are at high risk for diabetes, this provides a perfect opening to sell a disease prevention fitness program or e-book.

But don't think that the hurt and rescue principle works only for websites geared toward a consumer audience. This technique can be instrumental in the B2B environment.

Use your web copy to point out to visitors how much money they are losing, the time they are wasting, or the stress they are experiencing, and then offer them a solution. Or, as the folks at the persuasion site ChangingMinds.org put it, "A drowning person will clutch at a straw, so push them in the water, and then throw them a rope."

Hurt and rescue sound negative, but it's nothing more than emotion based selling. Show that you understand your customers' pain points, and you'll be more effective in persuading them to consider you their solution.

With Lexyom, when it comes to providing litigation services and representation, we tend to use this strategy to reach our goal, showcasing what you would lose should you not have a lawyer representing you.

By designing your sites around people's desires and unconscious behaviors, you can better influence buyer decisions. Use these and other neuromarketing principles to make your sites more comfortable and pleasant to use and win loyalty.

On February 5th, the day I started Lexyom, was the start of one of the most challenging years I have gone through. I started working harder and harder every day, and by March, I had two associates and was already working hard on marketing Lexyom [Ororus at the time]. My office had no windows, except the only window I needed: a whiteboard. This whiteboard will prove to be a critical success in what would happen later. I used to write down all the problems I could think of in my field and the ideal solution to these problems irrespective of the restraints, whether tech, industry standards, or even ethics. This excess work and focus made me more prone to overthinking other things, and I would go through a spiral of thoughts and overthink many topics, including game theory, science, life, etc., and I channelled these thoughts towards work and chess.

Santiago Ramon Y Cajal, the father of Neuroscience, discussed how the brain and nerves adapt to a certain rhythm you put your brain on. Say you are working fast, moving fast, learning quickly for a specific time. The brain will adapt and follow this pattern. This does not mean that there is an absolute rule to move fast to make your brain move quickly. Instead, it is an equilibrium that combines pace, memories, and creative content you gather to reproduce creativity and other factors.

I have used Neuroscience and Neuro-marketing many times, whether it comes to my work. When I learned about priming, for example, I had a grade against my father because he so smartly primed me to become a lawyer. I had so many subliminal cues throughout my childhood regarding being a lawyer, but not once did my father say, "why don't you become a lawyer like me?" He played it smart. Even you are primed for something. Look back at your childhood and think about what you can learn about yourself and what you were primed for. This will help you better understand your strength and benefit from your strongpoints in building your career.

———————————●◗●◖●———————————

"Neuromarketing is the next big thing and thinking about how the brain functions and analyzes is crucial to succeed in any venture today."

3. Hustle Before Starting

Athough I was a top student most of the time. I liked to hustle, and I remember buying and selling Nokia phones, trading POGs, and selling tickets to music events later on. I even went as far as opening my own casino at home. Yes, we had a full

empty unfinished floor, which I filled with plastic tables and chairs and opened it to the public. At a point, I was having more than 100 players per night and making 3k to 5k just by taking small blinds off the tables. Even when I was making my money, I made sure to set the mood with dimmed lighting, music, sandwiches, and soft drinks; why? Because this is what gets you recurrence. Yes, it is all about hustling before starting. Going to market is going to the streets and feeling the challenge to sell and make money.

I like to set the mood, and I enjoy designing beautiful experiences and environments. I always was very picky, and as an adolescent, I liked to test people, not to be malicious but to test and experience things. My brother was more aggressive and more careless when it came to studying. When I turned 13, I underwent a colossal operation done by an amazing MD; Professor Annese Spielmann- a unique and talented Doctor. When it was decided I should undergo the operation, I remember my parents were told that there was a 20% chance of success, and I still remember my grandmother saying, "let's go for it. I would rather see him live a full life or not at all." Of course, this is a bit drastic, but my grandmother was quite radical. My grandmother came from a wealthy family but was married forcibly at a very young age, i.e., 14 years old. She got pregnant at 15 and was abused by my biological grandfather. She ran away and was rejected by her parents due to social constraints. She continued her studies to become a Doctor. She was granted honors recognition by the Lebanese President Charles Helou back in the 1960s when women were still unable to compete with men effectively. She was adamant and lived life to the utmost extent, working hard, traveling, healing others, impacting, and not missing anything.

When she raised me, she taught me to hustle, work hard, and deliver results. There are three unseen laws of hustling:

1. Do something that moves you to make sure you are enjoying yourself in the process.
2. Keep your head up and look for opportunities wherever, whenever.
3. Seal the deal and make it real because as long as you are not making it real, it will remain an idea, and other people will move, and you will remain on the side-line.

Despite our best intentions, our talents often remain buried and elusive, hidden underneath doubts, maybes, and wishes of our rented dreams. The best thing we can do to remedy this tragic waste of potential is to expose ourselves to challenging projects and environments in our work and life and focus on the unexpected strengths that will rise to the surface when we do so.

The second step is to realize that in small doses, stress helps us grow. It helps with our future skills, knowledge and complex problem solving skills. Once you have accepted that small amounts of pain are the most significant growth agents, you can begin to think about your future more boldly.
Do you have a great but somewhat risky idea with terrific potential but isn't a sure thing? It turns out; it's not the number of hits or home runs we get that matters; instead, we can manifest our success by merely stepping out on to plate more often.

The third step is to develop your own Personal Opportunity Portfolio [POP], a guiding plan for organizing and making sense of all your hustle efforts and following through to achieve your goals. There will be bumps along the way, and sometimes we will fail and need to regroup.

Sometimes a plan will have unintended outcomes that you need to step back and make sense of. The indirect nature of hustle makes each journey significant. Doing the wrong thing (falling in love with the wrong type of person, taking a job for the wrong reasons, trying to become someone you are incapable of becoming) is often a necessary step toward finding the right path. All roads lead to Rome, as they say.

Indeed there are multiple approaches to getting ahead and moving forward in your career plan, and all of them will be enhanced once you have learned how to hustle.

13 Secrets To Closing A Sale

There are 13 Secrets to Closing a Sale and Get Others to Say: Yes! All you are asked to do is believe in your product, question your product, and have the correct voice inflection.

1. Asking questions

Start by asking the right questions. Who should your product be sold to? Why should it be sold? By asking these questions, you can pretty much guarantee a constructive and successful outcome, and will know whether it's worth investing time and energy in selling this product/ service. When I started Remy Remez, it was all about asking the right questions. I wanted to sell clothing because I had a passion for it and saw that I could build a beautiful brand. My initial struggle, like in any inventory-based company, was the "Inventory." This is why my first question was, "What products do not have sizing? What products can remain in stock for a long time without losing intrinsic value? Where should I source my product?" All these questions brought me to the necktie business, which is full of opportunities. One day, as I was reading about brands, I discovered that Ralph Lauren had started with neckties and built his empire out of it. This shows one thing: When you ask the right questions, you converge with the most successful ideas out there.

For example, if your company is in the process of manufacturing a new variety of mobile. You need to have questions like, who is your target audience? Are they runners, mothers, workers? What are the key features to be added?

2. Five Basic Reasons For A Customer To Say No

Firstly, let's list down the five reasons; **"no need, no money, no hurry, no desire, and no trust."**
This is something that even "Zig Ziglar" took seriously. You have to know why a customer would even want to buy your product. A customer will have a million reasons to say no, and it is your job to give them the reason to say yes!

Customers are kings of the market. No matter what, you have to please the king first to be successful in the market. There are times when customers don't need product.

For example, a customer already owns a motor vehicle, which means he does not need to buy a new one. Your company has launched the latest model of the same motor vehicle. Now, as a salesperson, you have to convince the customer to make an upgrade. Tell him about the new safety features, better mileage, more power, etc.

The same goes for the other four reasons as well. If the customer tells you that he has no money, make payment schemes available which will help your customers pay in instalments.

If the customer says he is in no hurry to buy a product, make him feel as though he will regret missing out if he doesn't buy it now. You can use the same for no desire as well. This can be done by offering limited deals etc.

In terms of the trust - yes, customers do take this seriously. If a customer does not trust you or your product, they will not buy from you. Therefore, the first thing you need to do before introducing your product is to win your customer's trust. And how do you win that trust? Well, there are several ways to win trust.

1. Build or source an amazing product.
2. Build an amazing website/app/social media pages.
3. Add testimonials as fast as possible.
4. Add celebrities/ influencers or anyone who a has a social holding to promote your product.
5. Have a legal entity and add legal information, address, and policies in your platform's footer.
6. Add as many pictures as possible of your product or service.
7. Descriptions/technical aspects to explain to skeptics.
8. Build a comfortable journey that shows you are professional, bringing the best experiences to your customer.
9. Add videos, videos, and more videos.
10. Add an "About us" page where you describe your company and where you came from. It helps to have your customers relate to you.
11. Add cash-back guaranteed or satisfaction guaranteed icon and refund policy.
12. Add a reliable payment gateway.
13. Add people, websites, sources like the New York Times, or any Journal or source that has mentioned you or potentially talked about you.
14. Add a blog where you have content about your industry and your product/service.
15. Add production details about the product - How is it made? How is it offered?

The above steps will create feelings of trust between you and your customers and help your business.

3. Buyer's buying psychology

———•◉•———

"People buy what they want, when they want it more than they care about the money it costs."

One of the examples would be the situation of onions in India. The onions price in India had gone up to 120rs/kg, which is more expensive than usual. However, the people did not stop buying onions. This will relate mostly to daily needs and luxurious goods. For example, if a rich man wants to buy a new house in another city, he will buy it at any cost. This is because he has the money, and it is his need to buy the house. As a salesman, you need to take advantage of the situation and do your best to get maximum profit.

4. Be a helper

Try acting like a helper rather than a salesman. Changing your psychology as a salesman is always helpful as it will bring in new ideas of selling. As a salesman, your priority is that you want your product to be sold.

For example:

if a customer walks into a store looking for some new cutlery, make sure to ask questions. Is it a gift or for the customer? What is the customers budget and taste? Then try and be helpful and give the customer what he wants. The more you help your customers, the more you will sell.

"You can get everything you want in life if you just help enough other people to get what they want."

5. Believe in what you do

It does not make sense to be a salesman if you don't believe in yourself or the product. Every salesperson needs to have the drive to be able to convince the customer. That is only possible if you have strong self-confidence and believe in your ability to showcase your offering.

'You must believe in what you are doing; that you are interested in serving your client and that you do feel you are offering the best product or service at the best price, which will do the most for your client and their needs.'

Let me explain the quote with an example. You have been asked to sell an insurance policy to an electronics shop that covers damaged goods. The policy will surely benefit the shopkeeper. But why the policy is the best for him is what you have to prove. This must be done with full belief in your product and yourself.

6. Persuading the prospect

The client is more interested in your final judgment. He does not believe in the logic you put behind selling the product. It is similar to when you watch a movie; all you are thinking about is the climax.

As a customer, if I want to buy a smartwatch, I would like to know what use the watch can be to me and how it stands out from other watches. What is not so important is how it will look good on me, or it suits me well, those are all secondary thoughts.

One more thing to add to this is always compare two products while selling something. Then all the customer is waiting for is your verdict on which product is better.

————•◉•————

"The prospect is persuaded more by the depth of your conviction than he is by the height of your logic."

7. The price

'I hope you are concerned about the price….because that's one of the most attractive advantages. Would you agree that, as a practical matter, a product is worth what it can do for you and not what you have to pay for it? Your company has the choice between providing coaching as cheaply as possible and selling it as a get-by service or providing coaching that teaches you how to create long-lasting results, profits, and growth.'

Pricing plays a vital role in sales. As a salesman, you need to acquire the power to convince the customer about its price. Price is something that you should not focus on but rather focus on the service it will provide.

8. Believers are closers

The best sales results come only when you feel for the product. Only then can you praise the product to its highest values. It's the customers who you sell the products to, so if you entice the customer about the product with how much you believe in it, you will make them believe in it and buy it.

————•◉•————

*Selling is essentially a transference of feelings…
believers are closers; c stands for conviction.*

For example, if I were asked to sell football t-shirts of Lionel Messi, I would instantly look for football fans. Then make them connect with the product by telling them about how great Messi is. By praising Messi, this will cause an emotional attachment to the product, which will help me close the deal. It is about the feeling, the relating, and the emotional aspect.

I collect Porsches. I know the feeling when I am steps away from buying a Porsche, how things materialize, how they just become all about closing the deal, and no longer about money or cost.

9. The salesman as a person

How you are as an individual plays a significant role in your sales techniques. It also affects the customer's buying psychology. If a customer finds a salesperson genuine and honest, they will more than likely make a sale.

* * *

"A calm, confident, positive, reassuring salesperson working from a base of honesty and integrity is the most effective tool to calm the fear of the prospect and get the sale".

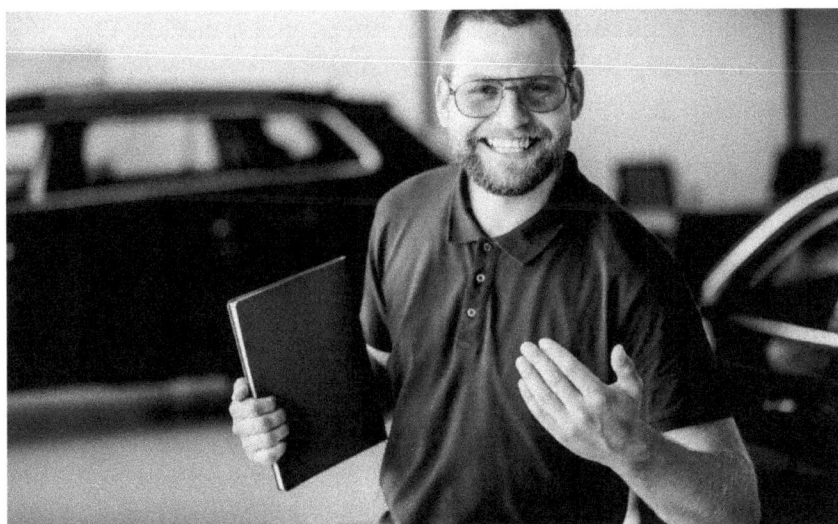

A customer needs to find some trust and connect before buying a product. The salesperson can only pass on the trust and connection. E.g., "Why do people refuse to buy policies online"? -" Because they don't feel safe, right." Yet, if they had to buy a policy on a face-to-face basis, they would feel more secure. With this, there is a 98% chance they would take the policy.

10. The use of reasons

Customers will always find reasons for not buying a product. If you want to be a good salesperson, you need to learn the art of using reason to sell your products.

"Take the reason why he could not buy and use it as the reason why he must buy."

What does the quote say? It says, 'you need to make the customer believe that the reason he is giving for not buying the product is the actual reason he should buy the product'.

There is a day-to-day example of this situation. People often refuse to eat ice cream during winter, saying they will get a cold. As ice cream sellers, you have to inform the customer that ice cream is a heat generator. Once it is in the body, it keeps the body warm. Promote it as part of a warm activity like watching a movie with friends. This is what Häagen-Dazs did with their winter ads.

What does the quote say? It says, 'you need to make the customer believe that the reason he is giving for not buying the product is the actual reason he should buy the product'.

There is a day-to-day example of this situation. People often refuse to eat ice cream during winter, saying they will get a cold. As ice cream sellers, you have to inform the customer that ice cream is a heat generator. Once it is in the body, it keeps the body warm. Promote it as part of a warm activity like watching a movie with friends. This is what Häagen-Dazs did with their winter ads.

11. Identify problems and find solutions

'Move to the prospect's side of the table, identify the problem, get involved in the solution, and your closing percentage will increase.'

'All is only well in heaven and not on earth.' There can be problems every day, and there can be a continuous patch of bad sale days, but you cannot just sit and cry about your problems. If you want to succeed, you need to find solutions.

For example, your company has held a flea market. You have been having a problem with giving clear information about your product, causing a problem in closing your sales. The solution? You need to take a break and relax before you get back to it. This will surely increase the closing percentage as you will feel revitalised and ready to sell.

12. Take suggestions but don't make them final decisions

It's good to take suggestions from the world. Although, it becomes a problem when you start working only according to those suggestions.

'Your business is never really good or bad out there. Your business is either good or bad right between your own two ears.'

You should always do what you think is right, so if something goes wrong, you know you can only blame yourself and correct it.

E.g., if you are a tobacco seller and people tell you it's a bad business to do, you need to block your ears. If the government does not have an issue with tobacco, it is not the wrong business.

13. Self image

Your self-image will affect the product you are selling. E.g., If you are a serious kind of person, you shouldn't try to sell tickets to a stand-up comedy show.

'Improve your self-image, and you will improve your sales performance.'

You need first to identify what your personality and traits are. Then improvise on them to sell a particular product.

An example of this would be a fashion designer. Most fashion designers wear the flashiest of clothes. Why? So that people notice them, inspiring them to check their brands. So, you can follow this path or do the opposite to make sure you are differentiating yourself from others. Remember, your attire is not final, nor is it something you have to stick to.

4. The Legal Guru

What you need to know in legal is crucial because it will determine how you will succeed in the medium and long term. Some start-ups need legal from day one, along with compliance and licensing if they are involved in different aspects of Fintech, Regtech, or other regulated industries.

Taking you back to 2005, I was always passionate about business, finance, and trading, but never about law. Nevertheless, as we have discussed in "priming" and the movie "Focus,"; I later discovered that I was primed for law. For a long time, I was pushed towards legal without knowing, and I became interested in legal without noticing it. My father would discuss his cases with such enthusiasm and such interest that it seized me. He would take me with him to the office to see him in action. I was fascinated by the lawyers there, their activity, the concept that they were defending people, rights, and concepts.

My father has a very lawyerly figure with white hair, a big body, and a way of dressing and speaking that inspires you to become a lawyer and adopt this profession. As I was graduating from high school, I decided to pursue studies in hotel management. I applied to Ecole Hotelière de Lausanne [EHL]. I was accepted and was so excited to go live there.

My beloved cousin was there. I was so excited to join him I thought of taking his apartment or sharing it with him. However, my life would be turned upside down on March 3rd, 2005. My grandmother was diagnosed with cancer and had only six months to live. All my plans changed, and I decided to stay in Lebanon for my grandfather and family. My father asked me if I wanted to give law school a shot and that's what I did. I still remember failing my first year epically and sitting on that warm July day thinking about how I got to where I was.

That same day, I discovered Facebook through my cousin, who had received an invitation to join Facebook with his EHL Email account. I set myself to redo my full academic year and succeed irrespective of whether I would continue. I ended up loving law and graduating, pursuing my LLM at New York Law School and starting Ororus Advisors, and then Lexyom.

16 Steps To Take Alongside Legal

I always thought of corporate law as a means to an end. When you are molded with business concepts and understand the real value of projects in life and what is underneath all you are doing, legal becomes a tool you need to use smartly. I discovered my true passion for start-ups, entrepreneurs, and the life of excitement back in 2014 when I started working closely with exceptional entrepreneurs. This was when I discovered the thrill of building projects and building new concepts and great ideas. I remember sitting with an entrepreneur who wanted to create this start-up that would scrap data and analyze it, bringing reporting to the next level. I sat with her for hours discussing the concept. How to discard, and at each cross-point, I could pinpoint data breaches, violations, and how we could evade them. The process was so smooth because I could start my analysis from the business side and move to the legal aspect on top of it.

When I came to start Lexyom, I went through these 16 steps that I will enumerate. We got accepted to an accelerator in Beirut called UK Lebanon Tech Hub. I remember it was a nice June morning, and I went to my firm's office, picked a few things, and walked to the accelerator. I called my best friend Mark, who was still awake in Canada. I said, "Mark, we got accepted to an accelerator," he replied, "Oh! What the F… is that? Explain". And I went on to explain the whole concept detailing what we were doing to get support and investment. I remember during the first lecture, the amazing mentor Cyrille clearly visualized everyone and, at the end of the session, said, "Guys, whoever is sitting past the 5th row is out of the program as they are not that serious about it". Guess where I was sitting? Yes, the first f***ing row.

A week later, we were asked to set our vision, mission, and goals. We had an office underground with glass walls we could write on. We Imagine us writing on these glass walls, step by step, how we would build Lexyom [Lexium at the time].

There are 16 steps you need to take between legal and business for start-ups when thinking about your legal framework.

1. Define your mission
2. Define your end goal
3. Define your "who?"
4. Define your "where?"
5. Protect your brand
6. Plan your funding
7. Select your type of entity
8. Register with your state if in the US / Country
9. Select your Tax treatment
10. Obtain an EIN from the IRS / Fiscal ID
11. Create a separate bank account
12. Determine your industry-specific regulation.
13. Determine your liability and insurance needs
14. Set up an accounting system
15. Set up your contracts
16. Keep it simple

1. Define your mission

Creating a clearly defined mission statement is the first thing you should do when starting a business or entrepreneurial venture. Many resources go in-depth about writing a mission statement, but it's ultimately a very personal process.

To come up with your mission statement, start with reflection.

Ask yourself these critical questions and reflect deeply:
------- Why do you want to start this business? What are you trying to accomplish?

What will it mean for your life?
What will it mean for your co-workers?
What will it mean for your customers?

How will you create change with your business?
Why does this business have to exist, and why do you have to be the person to start it?

After you've gone through the reflection phase, articulate your findings. Write down some of the answers you discovered during reflection. Your mission statement is not something that just lives in your head. Actually write it down and read it back to yourself aloud. Then revise it. Then, revise it again.

There are no formal requirements for what a mission statement has to say or include. It can be short, or it can be long. The important thing is that it communicates what is driving you to start this particular business. The whole purpose of a mission statement is to communicate your business's intention to yourself and others.

Your mission statement will act as your north star and guide your later legal decisions. It will inform the type of entity you select, your tax treatment, who you work with, where you work, and more. We will discuss those particular decisions a little later as well.

Our Vision at Lexyom is to "Make Legal the First Universal Known Language"

At Lexyom, our mission statement is to:
"Increase access to high-quality legal services for start-ups, entrepreneurs, freelancers & artists."

We want to increase access, meaning we want to make legal services more affordable. We also focus on our clients: start-ups, entrepreneurs, freelancers & artists, who are often underserved in the legal industry.

One thing to keep in mind about mission statements: even though they are your north star in guiding your business, they are not necessarily set in stone. **Your mission statement can evolve as your business grows.** Once you've successfully defined your mission, it's time to start looking into the future.

2. Define your end goal

Once you've set a clear mission statement, it's time to look into your business's future and define your end goal.

The First Flyer I did at Ororus Advisors, 2016

Defining your end goal is slightly different from defining your mission statement. It's more specific and more concrete. Picture your business in one year, five years, ten years, and at the end of your career. Where do you see your business? down the road? ---- Do you want to have lots of outside investors?

Do you want to be publicly traded on a stock exchange?
Do you want it to remain small and fit into your existing life?
Do you want to sell the business and spend the rest of your days on a beach?

It might seem too early to think about your exit but defining your end goal will affect all of your later legal decisions. For example, suppose you want your business to become publicly traded. In that case, you likely want to set yourself up as a C-Corp (a subchapter C corporation) right from the get-go (we will go into more details about selecting an entity type in future chapters). Another way your end goal can have legal impacts on your business is if goals differ from your business partners.

If that's the case, you could face legal complications down the road. Your end goal will also affect where you conduct your business and even what state you register your business in. There are advantages to registering in different states, but those advantages are only worth it if you have a specific end goal in mind. For example, registering a business in Delaware can be advantageous for large corporations, but it probably doesn't make sense for a small local business.

The point is that many legal decisions will ultimately trackback to your end goal.

What are some examples of end goals for small businesses?

Getting A Getting Acquired - Sell your business to a larger corporation.
Going public - Some businesses start with the end goal of becoming traded publicly by listing the business on a stock exchange. Creating an Enduring Brand - Maybe your ultimate goal is to have your business outlast you.
Staying Small - Many people start small businesses with the intention of keeping them small and close to the family.
Providing Supplementary Income - Perhaps you want to keep your business on the side while maintaining employment elsewhere.

All of those are legitimate end goals for a business. No one end goal is better than the other. It's just essential to find out what works for you and your future to have that as a baseline for all of your legal decisions going forward.

Next up in the Legal Checklist for Start-ups, we'll discuss why it's crucial to define the people associated with your business.

3. Define your "who"

The next step to think about when you are starting your business is what we call "defining your who." This is when you identify the people who will be involved with your business. Defining your who is not in itself a legal concept, but it will absolutely affect your legal decisions.

The "who" of your business can be broken down into three different parts:
• Partners
• Employees or Independent Contractors
• Other Collaborators (Investors, Lenders, Vendors, Service Providers, etc.)

Let's take a look at each of these parts in depth.

Partners

The first group of people you should identify is **potential partners.** We talked about this earlier in Defining Your End Goal. If you're thinking about going into business with a partner, you both must have a similar end goal. Otherwise, different directions can be taken and tensions can arise.

You'll also want to make sure that a partnership is right for you personally. If you are considering bringing on a partner, make sure you are comfortable giving up some level of control. Also, try to identify what each of you brings to the table so you can break up responsibilities and set realistic expectations. Another vital aspect is your ability to synchronize with your partner and enjoy working close to them. The relationship should be fun, exciting, filled with positive energy. So make sure both of you have positive energy across your daily life so you can push each other further. This is part of the priming we have discussed as well.

If you start your company with co-founders, you should agree early on about your business-related details. Not doing so can potentially cause significant legal problems down the road (a good example of this is the infamous Zuckerberg/Winklevoss Facebook litigation). In a way, think of the founder's agreement as a form of "pre-nuptial agreement." Here are the key deal terms your written founder agreement needs to address:

- How is the equity split among the founders?
- Is the percentage of ownership subject to vesting based on continued participation in the business?
- What are the roles and responsibilities of the founders?
- If one founder leaves, does the company or the other founder have the right to buy back that founder's shares? At what price?
- How much is the time commitment to the business expected of each founder?
- What salaries (if any) are the founders entitled to? How can that be changed?
- How are critical decisions and day-to-day decisions of the business to be made? (By majority vote, a unanimous vote, or are individual decisions solely in the hands of the CEO?)

- Under what circumstances can a founder be removed as an employee of the business? (Usually, this would be a board decision)
- What assets or cash does each founder contribute to or invest in the business?
- How will the sale of the business be decided?
- What happens if one founder isn't living up to expectations under the founder's agreement? How will it be resolved?
- What is the overall goal and vision for the business?
- If one founder wants to leave the business, does the company have the right to buy back its shares? At what price?

Employees or Independent Contractors

The next group you need to think about when defining yourself is people who will work for your business—namely, employees and independent contractors.

It is common for businesses to pay their workers as independent contractors when they should be treated as employees. If you try to save tax money by classifying an employee as an independent contractor, it can come back and bite you. If you are caught, you'll have to pay back-taxes and penalties.

In short, if you have someone who is working for you most of the time, and your business mostly supervises them in regards to time, place, and manner of their work, then they are most correctly and appropriately defined employees rather than independent contractors.

When you are thinking of who will work for your business, think about the day-to-day activities that you can't (or don't want to) handle. Next, consider if this will be a person who you will bring on full or part-time as an employee, or if this can be taken by a contractor (or a combination of the two).

If a person is working:
- Regularly from time x to time y
- Doing predefined regular tasks
- Paid at the end of each cycle

Then this person will be considered an employee even if you sign an independent contract agreement with them. Make sure, if you insist on signing an independent deal with them, on them doing the work:

- Irrespective of the time they attend. Do not add a time.
- State the scope in the agreement to be project-based, not tasks based.
- Add the remuneration to be based on targets or milestones rather than cycles.

Another aspect to consider is ESOP [Employee Stock Option Plan]. This is a legal structure that allows you to give your employees stocks on a later stage based on a particular KPI or target that you want them to achieve. ESOP has many forms, and it would vary based on each country and each state in the US, if you are operating in the US, or have plans to set your business in the US.

For us-based businesses only

You can accomplish employee ownership in a variety of ways. Employees can buy stock directly, be given it as a bonus, receive stock options, or obtain stock through a profit-sharing plan. Some employees become owners through worker cooperatives where everyone has an equal vote. The most common form of employee ownership in the U.S. is the ESOP, or **employee stock ownership plan.** Almost unknown until 1974, ESOPs are now widespread; as of the most recent data, 6,460 methods exist, covering 14.2 million people.

Companies can use ESOPs for a variety of purposes. Contrary to the impression one can get from media accounts, ESOPs are rarely used to save troubled companies—only at most, a handful of such plans are set up each year. Instead, ESOPs are most commonly used to provide a market for the shares of departing owners of successful, closely-held companies, motivate and reward employees, or take advantage of incentives to borrow money to acquire new assets in pre-tax dollars. In almost every case, ESOPs are a contribution to the employee, not an employee purchase.

ESOP Rules

An ESOP is a benefit-in-kind plan, similar in some ways to a profit-sharing plan. In an ESOP, a company sets up a trust fund, into which it contributes new shares of its stock or cash to buy existing shares. Alternatively, the ESOP can borrow money to purchase new or existing shares, with the company making cash contributions to the plan to enable it to repay the loan. Regardless of how the plan acquires stock, company contributions to the trust are tax-deductible, within certain limits. The 2017 tax bill limits net interest deductions for businesses to 30% of EBITDA (earnings before interest, taxes, depreciation, and amortization) for four years. At this point, the limit decreases to 30% of EBIT (not EBITDA). In other words, starting in 2022, businesses will subtract depreciation and amortization from their earnings before calculating their maximum deductible interest payments.

Newly leveraged ESOPs, where the company borrows a large amount relative to its EBITDA may find that their deductible expenses will be lower. Therefore, their taxable income may be higher under this change. This change will not affect 100%-ESOP owned S corporations because they don't pay tax.

Shares in the trust are allocated to individual employee accounts. Although there are some exceptions; generally, all full-time employees over 21 participate in the plan. Allocations are made either based on relative pay or some more equal formula. As employees accumulate seniority with the company, they acquire an increasing right to the shares in their account, a process known as vesting. Employees must be 100% vested within three to six years, depending on whether vesting is all at once (cliff vesting) or gradual.

When employees leave the company, they receive their stock, which the company must buy back from them at its fair market value (unless there is a public market for the shares). Private companies must have an annual outside valuation to determine the price of their shares. In private companies, employees must be able to vote their allocated shares on major issues, such as closing or relocating. Still, the company can choose whether to pass through voting rights (such as for the board of directors) on other issues. In public companies, employees must be able to vote on all matters.

Uses of ESOPs

1. To buy a departing owner's shares: Owners of privately held companies can use an ESOP to create a ready market for their shares. Under this approach, the company can make tax-deductible cash contributions to the ESOP to buy out an owner's shares, or it can have the ESOP borrow money to buy the shares (see below).

2. To borrow money at a lower after-tax cost: ESOPs are unique among benefit plans in their ability to borrow money. The ESOP borrows cash, which it uses to buy company shares or shares of existing owners. The company then makes tax-deductible contributions to the ESOP to repay the loan, meaning both principal and interest is deductible.

3. To create an additional employee benefit: A company can simply issue new or treasury shares to an ESOP, deducting their value (for up to 25% of covered pay) from taxable income. Or, a company can contribute cash, buying shares from existing public or private owners. In public companies, which account for about 5% of the plans and about 40% of the plan participants, ESOPs are often used in conjunction with employee savings plans. Rather than matching employee savings with cash, the company will match them with stock from an ESOP, often at a higher matching level.

Major Tax Benefits

ESOPs have several significant tax benefits, the most important of which are:

1. Contributions of stock are tax-deductible: That means companies can get a current cash flow advantage by issuing new shares or treasury shares to the ESOP, which means existing owners will be diluted.

2. Cash contributions are deductible: A company can contribute cash on a discretionary basis year-to-year and take a tax deduction for it, whether the contribution is used to buy shares from current owners or build up a cash reserve ESOP for future use.

3. Contributions used to repay a loan that the ESOP takes out to buy company shares are tax-deductible: The ESOP can borrow money to buy existing shares, new shares, or treasury shares. Regardless of the use, the contributions are deductible, meaning ESOP financing is done in pre-tax dollars.

4. <u>Sellers in a C corporation can get a tax deferral</u>: In C corporations, once the ESOP owns 30% of all the shares in the company, the seller can reinvest the sale proceeds in other securities and defer any tax on the gain.

5. <u>In S corporations, the percentage of ownership held by the ESOP is not subject to income tax at the federal level (and usually the state level as well)</u>: That means, that there is no income tax on 30% of the profits of an S corporation with an ESOP holding of 30% of the stock, and no income tax at all on the profits of an S corporation wholly owned by its ESOP. However, note that the ESOP still must get a pro-rata share of any distributions the company makes to the owners.

6. <u>Dividends are tax-deductible:</u> Reasonable dividends used to repay an ESOP loan, passed through to employees, or reinvested by employees in company stock are tax-deductible.

7. <u>Employees pay no tax on the contributions to the ESOP, only the distribution of their accounts, and then at potentially favorable rates:</u> The employees can roll over their distributions in an IRA or other retirement plans or pay current tax on the distribution, with any gains accumulated over time taxed as capital gains. However, the distributions' income tax portion is subject to a 10% penalty if made before the normal retirement age.

Note that all contribution limits are subject to certain limitations, although these rarely pose a problem for companies.

Caveats

As attractive as these tax benefits are, there are limitations and drawbacks. The law does not allow ESOPs to be used in partnerships and most professional corporations. ESOPs can be used in S corporations but do not qualify for the rollover treatment discussed above and have lower contribution limits. Private companies must repurchase shares of departing employees, and this can become a significant expense. The cost of setting up an ESOP is also substantial—perhaps $40,000 for the simplest of plans and up from there. Any time new shares are issued, the stock of existing owners is diluted. That dilution must be weighed against the tax and motivation benefits an ESOP can provide. Finally, ESOPs will improve corporate performance only if combined with opportunities for employees to participate in decisions affecting their work.

Other Collaborators

Another group to think about when you are defining your who, is other collaborators.

The most significant types of collaborators are lenders and investors. If you collaborate with people who will be providing funding for your business, you need to think about what type of relationship you want. At this stage, you may not know precisely who your investors will be, but you can start to think about what kinds of investors you would want.

For example, if you're seeking venture capital funding, do you want an investor who gives you money and gets out of the way? Or do you want someone who will serve more as a mentor and advisor to your business, with a board of directors and hands-on involvement in the day-to-day operations?

The last group we will talk about in defining your "who" is vendors. Vendors could be the suppliers of raw materials, landlords, service providers (such as attorneys and accountants), and even technology providers. Vendors are much like independent contractors or employees, but they are often other businesses instead of individuals.

When considering outside collaborators, think about your strengths and weaknesses. What skills are you lacking? Does it make sense for someone (a partner, employee, or other collaborators) to fill that gap?

Why is this important? Because when you introduce partners, it affects the type of business entity you select. If you have people working for your business, it will affect your tax decisions.

4. Define your "where?"

The next thing is to define your "where?" This doesn't just mean figuring out where you want to work, there are more intricate details that you'll have to work your way through. Your "where" can be broken down into three parts:

1. Where do you want to work?
2. Where do you want to register your business?
3. Where will your customers be?

Let's take a look at each part in more detail.

Where do you want to work?

First, where do you want to work? We're not just talking about what city or state you want to work in, we're talking about your specific location. The main options here include retail space or office space.

If you are selling hard goods, then you will more than likely need retail space. Operating your business out of a retail space opens up your business to potential liabilities if someone gets injured in your store, so you'll want to make sure proper legal protections, like insurance, are in place.

You'll also need to think about a commercial lease and negotiating that lease. Another factor that you'll need to consider for any retail location is the advantages and disadvantages of that space. For instance, do you want to be in an area with a lot of pedestrian foot traffic?

If so, the monthly rent will probably be much higher than a place off the beaten path. When selecting a retail space, it is essential to weigh the pros and cons and estimate your business's eventual impact.

If you are in the service business or another professional industry, you may opt for office space. There are a few factors to consider when selecting an office space that will affect your legal and financial decisions.

For instance, do you need a space for a large group or just a few key individuals? How much do you want to grow your team? This decision will be affected by defining your who, which we talked about in the previous section.

If you're going to have an office, will a virtual office suffice? Virtual offices are a great way to keep expenses low while maintaining the benefits of a physical office. A virtual office is a place where you can receive mail or rent out conference space while working remotely from your home or other office locations.

Speaking of other office locations, co-working spaces are growing in popularity. Co-working spaces can offer an excellent environment for collaboration and lead to random interactions with other small businesses. Many co-working spaces also have private offices within the larger co-working space so that you can have a personal office's privacy with the benefits of a co-working space.

If you do want your own private office, you need to consider a potential liability if someone is injured at your office. You'll also have a commercial real estate lease to consider. If you have a long-term commercial real estate lease, it is not uncommon for landlords to ask for a personal guarantee, especially for new business owners. If your landlord requires a personal guarantee, it is imperative that you fully understand the agreement and what it means for your personal finances.

Where should you register your business?
The second part in defining your "where" is figuring out which state or states in the country you want to register your business.

We previously mentioned that you might want to register in Delaware if you are interested in starting a large corporation. Many businesses register in the state of Delaware because of their specialized business courts and other advantages for large corporations. But if you have no intention of growing that large, you may not need to go through all the trouble to register in a different state. Registering in your state is likely to be sufficient. The same thing applies if you are based in the UAE or any other country. You might need to register in your own country or another country, depending on what you are looking for in industry and scalability matters.

In most instances, registering in the state where you live and work makes the most sense. But with all major business decisions, it is never a bad idea to consult with a professional.

We will talk about how to register your business in Step 8. You can check Lexyom for consultations on how and where to register your company.

Where are your customers?
The third part of defining your "where" is to determine where your customers are. If you are a small retail business, your customers may only be in your state. However, because of the internet it is becoming more common for businesses to interact with customers in other states and even in other countries.

If you sell a product or service across state lines, you could become subject to those other jurisdictions' laws.

For example, if you're selling a product out of Country X to people in other countries or states, there is a possibility that you could get sued in those other states because you're choosing to do business in those countries or states. The law will say you're purposefully availing yourself of business contacts in those other countries or states.

We'll later talk about determining your industry-specific regulations. If you're doing national or international business, you'll need to think about how laws in those areas could potentially affect your business.

That wraps up Step 4 in the Legal Checklist for start-ups: determine your "where?" Next up, we talk about protecting your brand and intellectual property.

5. Protect your brand (and intellectual property)

The first four steps in the Legal Checklist for start-ups included a lot of big-picture thinking. While all these things are important and will affect your legal decisions down the road, none of them are specifically attached to a legal concept.

That all changes with step number five, which is **protecting your brand and your intellectual property.**

What is Intellectual Property?

Intellectual property is one of the most critical legal issues any new small business faces. It's also one of the most misunderstood areas of the law. So, what is intellectual property?

Intellectual property, or IP, is any unique creation of your own mind that the law protects from being stolen.

The law offers three main types of protection for your intellectual property:
1. Trademarks
2. Copyrights
3. Patents

But before we dive into each of these types of protection, let's quickly discuss some common misconceptions about IP protection.

Misconceptions

The most common misconception about intellectual property is that you have no protection unless you register for a trademark, copyright, or patent.

That is not the case. Your ideas are protected by common law even if you do not register for a trademark, copyright, or patent.

However, it can be challenging to prove your intellectual property without these. For instance, someone could claim that they came up with a name or idea before you. Plus, you can only receive statutory rewards in a lawsuit if you have registered for intellectual property protection.

Ultimately, it is prudent to protect yourself and your business by registering for intellectual property protection.

Many states offer some level of intellectual property protection. Still, the most common way to protect yourself is by registering for intellectual property protection with the U.S. Patent and Trademark Office - the

USPTO.

Let's talk about each of the three categories of protection: trademarks, copyrights, and patents.

Trademarks

A trademark is something that usually protects the name or the logo of your business.

If your business is called XYZ Corp., you could register a trademark so that nobody else can start a business called XYZ Corp. **in your specific line of work.**

It is essential to highlight that trademarks are only specific to your line of work. The USPTO has separate "classes," and your brand is only applicable within that class. For a full list of classes directly from the USPTO, visit this page.

For example, if you are an auto mechanic and you want to be called XYZ Auto Mechanic, you can register for a trademark in Class

37(construction and repair). But that doesn't mean a that beauty company can't register its products called XYZ Beauty Products in Class 3 (cosmetics and cleaning products).

If your business offers several different products and services, or you think it overlaps between categories, you can often register for a trademark for several categories. Keep in mind; you will have to pay a filing fee for each separate class.

As mentioned above, trademarks can protect your business's name and how the name is written and visually represented. That could include a specific font, style, and color, or the actual logo for your business.

On the USPTO's website, you can register for a trademark (even without a lawyer's help). When you register a trademark, you will have to pay a filing fee. Trademark filing fees vary and are calculated on a "per class basis."

Copyrights

The second type of protection for your intellectual property is copyrights. Copyright traditionally **protects things like the written word.** If you write a book, you have a copyright on that book.

One of the most prominent uses of copyright law, especially for start-ups, is to **protect computer** code. If you are a tech computer or a software company, you must defend your proprietary computer code with some intellectual property protection.

A patent is another option to protect computer code, but the emerging trend is for copyright law to govern and safeguard any code you write.

The two basic requirements for copyright protection are (1) fixation and (2) originality. To be copyrightable, it must be an original work of authorship and fixed in a tangible medium of expression. Technically, registration is a legal formality, and you can have protected work without registering. Still, you can't assert a civil claim for copyright infringement against someone else unless you have registered, and with a few exceptions, you can't get an award of statutory damages or attorney's fees without registration.

Patents

The third type of intellectual property protection is a patent. Patents are typically used for scientific or technological innovations.

To receive patent protection, a specialized lawyer will need to file for the patent for you. To represent you in what's called "prosecuting a patent," lawyers not only have to pass the bar exam, they also have to give the patent bar exam. And to do that, your lawyer would need to have a scientific background before going to law school.

If you are looking for protection for scientific or technological advancement, a patent may be the way to go. To get started, contact a qualified attorney in your state.

Intellectual property protection is such an important issue for small business owners because your intellectual property is the most valuable thing your business owns.

This section scratches the service of intellectual property law. We will make sure to revisit this topic in other articles.
Next up, funding your start-up.

6. Plan your funding

We've all heard the saying, "It takes money to make money." And in the case of most start-ups and small businesses, it's true. You are going to need some amount of money to start your business. Initial start-up costs can range from a couple of hundred dollars for single-person companies to hundreds of thousands of dollars for big tech start-ups and brick-and-mortar stores.

In this section of the Legal Checklist for start-ups, we're going to walk through the various methods you can use to fund your business, plus provide some insights into the potential pros and cons of each.

The three main ways to fund a new business are:
1.   Self-Funding
2.   Loans
3.   Outside Investors
Let's look at each one individually.

Self -Funding
Self-funding is the simplest and cleanest way to fund a new business venture. When self-funding, you have no interest to pay (like you would with a loan), and you don't have to hand over any control or ownership (like you would with outside investors).

As a self-funding business, you are in the driver's seat.
The biggest obstacle to self-funding is having the available capital. Another issue is that self-funding could limit how quickly you expand, which could lead to missed opportunities.

If you have enough cash on hand to avoid these pitfalls, self-funding is the smoothest path forward.

When it comes to self-funding (and all other forms of funding), you must separate your personal and business expenses. We will talk more about that in Step 11: Create a Separate Bank Account. It may also help to consult with an accountant to determine the best ways to use your own funds.

Small Business Loans
The second way to fund your business is through a loan.
In the US and abroad there are several different types of loans for small businesses. The most well-known is an SBA loan, which stands for Small Business Administration loan.

SBA loans are guaranteed up to a certain point by the federal government. This means that lenders can give them out with reasonable interest rates because they have a high level of confidence that they will be paid back. If the lender can't get the money back from you, they can get a certain amount back from the government.

One common and very dangerous misconception about SBA loans is that you will get off scot-free if you cannot pay it back because the government will cover you. This is not the case; the bank will still come after you. Only after the lender exhausts all collection efforts will the government step in. The banks will get their money, and they will most likely get it from you.

The major downside of SBA loans is that they are hard to qualify for. You have to have excellent financials, credit, and you might even have to put up collateral (such as your home) as part of the loan.

If you don't qualify for an SBA loan, there are many different types of private loans to fund your business that the government does not back. Since they do not have a government guarantee, they usually have higher interest rates.

Many companies and programs provide Loans to SMBs and start-ups in any active ecosystem, so make sure to check them out.

The downside of any loan (personal or professional) is that you must pay it back (with interest). That means that your business will owe monthly, quarterly, or annual payments to the lender. Repayment schedules for small business loans vary. Repayments typically start a year or so after the loan is granted, and repayments can last a few years or decades, depending on the amount.

If you're unable to pay back a loan, the lender can attempt to collect the debt you owe. Collection methods vary from state to state, so consult with a professional in your state and make sure you understand the consequences of delinquent payments. Also, make sure you know who is liable to make those payments. Depending on your business entity type, your personal assets could be at stake (we'll talk more about that in the next section).

Outside Investors
The third way to fund your business is through outside investors. It's essential to make this decision early because if you use outside investors, you should consider forming your business as a subchapter C corporation, also known as a C corp.

Make sure for a Delaware C Corp to file Form 83[b], and then Form D through regulation 506[d] with the Security & Exchange Commission [SEC] to file an exemption for private placement.

There are a lot of factors to think about when considering outside investors.

First, how many investors do you want? With every new investor comes a new chef in the kitchen. For instance, venture capital investors often want a seat on your board of directors, meaning they'll oversee your job and essentially be your boss.

Think long and hard about whether those investment funds are worth giving up control over your business.

The flip side of that argument is that having a sophisticated member of your board of directors could be an excellent mentorship opportunity for you. It can be a great way to learn from their experiences and to seek guidance for your business.

If you bring on investors, it typically means handing over your business shares in exchange for capital, making your business's partial investors owners.

There are also a host of laws and regulations governing outside investments in your business. If you go this route, do your homework and consult with a securities lawyer licensed in your state.

Now that we've talked about the three main ways to fund a business, remember that you can do some combination of all three. You can self-fund a portion of your business and make up the remainder through loans and investors.

Next, let's dive into the various business entities you can choose from.

7. Select your type of entity

Selecting your type of business entity is one of the most crucial early decisions for all small business owners.

The business entity is the legal **structure of your business.** This decision determines, how the government taxes your business, how your assets are protected (or not protected) in a lawsuit, and what types of investments you can accept for your business.

Many of the previous sections have been building up to this decision. We talked about defining your "who," defining your "where," and . Those earlier decisions now come to fruition when selecting your type of entity.

Here are the primary entity types that are generally available in most states:

- Sole Proprietorship Corporation
  - C Corp
  - S Corp
- Limited Liability Company (LLC) Partnership
  - General Partnership
  - Limited Liability Partnership (LLP)
  - Limited Partnership (LP)
  - Limited Liability Limited Partnership (LLLP)

Let's walk through each one to help you decide which is best for your business.

Sole Proprietorship

A **sole proprietorship** is the most basic type of business entity. A sole proprietorship means you are the only person in charge of your business, and you have **no liability protection.** This means your personal adders are on the line if you get sued.

One of the benefits of a sole proprietorship is that there is **no double taxation.** In other words, you don't get taxed at the business and the individual level. Another benefit is that it is straightforward to set up.

However, it is an old-fashioned way to do business. If you are serious about your start-up's future, you will want to consider another option.

Corporation

The second most common type of a business entity is a corporation. In many ways, this is the opposite of a sole proprietorship. With a corporation, you have liability protection, meaning that if you are sued for negligence or breach of contract, you generally have a level of security over your personal assets.

One of the downsides of corporations is that there are all sorts of corporate formalities and extra paperwork. Plus, traditional corporations are typically double-taxed, meaning you are taxed at the corporate level and the individual level. That particular type of corporation is called a subchapter C corporation, commonly known as a C corp.

A more recent development called a subchapter S corporation is like a C corp, except you are generally taxed at the individual level. The IRS does not tax you at the corporate level.

On the other hand, a C corporation has greater flexibility in the number and type of investors it can use for funding. So, if you are planning on seeking venture capital or even hope to be publicly traded someday, you might consider a C corporation. As with so many other decisions, it all depends on your end goal.

Limited Liability Company (LLC)

There is also something called a limited liability company (LLC). It is a state law concept available in many, if not all, states.

LLCs provide liability protection and pass-through taxation. LLCs are becoming a more common way to organize your business. They are not as complicated as corporations, and they do not have the double taxation that you see with a C corp. They also won't leave you completely vulnerable as a sole proprietorship would.

If you do not intend to take on many investors or seek investments from companies or foreign nationals, an LLC is 66666+9 the way to go. Again, keep your end goal in mind as you make this decision.

Partnership

There are also partnerships. The first two types of partnerships that we'll talk about are designed for equal partners, meaning that everything is split equally. **General partnership** is the more traditional type of partnership. This is equivalent to having a sole proprietorship, meaning that both partners are entirely in charge of liabilities.

There is also something called a **limited liability partnership (LLP).** It is like a general partnership in that both partners are in it together, and there is no differentiation between the levels of responsibility and benefits. The benefit of a limited liability partnership compared to a general partnership is, of course, limited liability.

You may want to set up a partnership where the partners have differentiated levels of responsibility and benefit. Those are called limited partnerships. In a limited partnership, you have a general partner who is in front, doing the work, taking on the responsibility; and you have a limited partner; sometimes these are just investors backing the business, but don't want to be involved in the day-to-day operations. A limited partnership (LP) is the fundamental way to separate the roles of the partners. What it's lacking is liability protection.

A **Limited Liability Limited Partnership (LLLP)** is a new type of partnership. You can still differentiate between partners and roles in an LLLP, but it's limited liability, so if the business gets sued, you and your partner's personal assets will not be at risk.

It is important to note that you're not limited to partnerships just because you're going into business with a partner. You can also be an LLC or a corporation. There are both single-member and multi-member LLCs. Tax usually plays a part in the choice between a partnership and a multi-member LLC. If you have narrowed down your choices to these two options, consult a tax professional.

Here's a quick rundown of the different business entity types:
- Sole proprietorship - Just you. No liability protection and no double taxation.
- Corporation - More complicated than a sole proprietorship. It has liability protection. C corps are often better for larger businesses but do have double taxation. S corps do not have double taxation.
- Limited Liability Company (LLC) - Single-member or multimember offers liability protection without double taxation.
- Partnerships - Can be broken down into two categories: equal level of responsibilities or differing levels of responsibilities. From there, you

can choose to have liability protection or forgo it.

Choosing the right entity type for your business is crucial and requires some thought. Do your homework and consult a licensed professional.

8. Register with your state in the u.S. Or your country or in an active startup ecosystem

The next step in the Legal Checklist for start-ups is to register with your State. Make sure to check lexyom.com for the best place to register. Our YouTube Channel is also highly informative.

DISCLAIMER: Colorado is a state that has seen a spike in interest from international companies.
Refer to Step #4 in the Legal Checklist for start-ups: Define Your Where. In that section, we talked about making sure you know where you want to register your business.

Want to know a secret? **You don't need to pay a lawyer to do it for you.** Let's walk through the straightforward process of how to do it online in Colorado.

Start by going to the Colorado Secretary of State's website and navigating to the business section.

If you haven't already done so, you can search for the availability of your business name. This checks whether somebody else has a registered business with the same name in the same state.

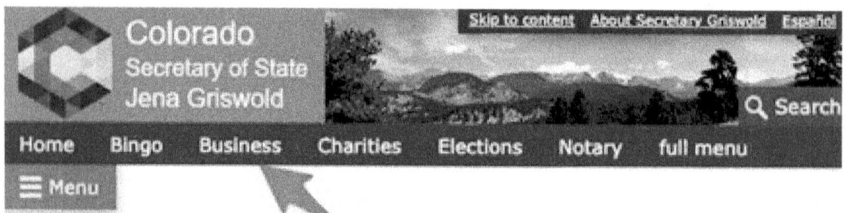

Colorado Secretary of State

Search & file

- Search business database
- Name availability search
- File a business document
- Periodic report filing
- Trade name renewal
- Forms list
- Oaths of office (PDF)
- Facsimile signatures (PDF)
- Personal identifying information removal (PDF)

Once that is done, select "File a Business Document" and from there, "File a form to create a NEW record."

File a Business Document

- File a form to create a NEW record

  Examples are:

    - a new LLC, corporation, trade name or trademark
    - refiling a trade name that has expired
    - a new foreign (outside of Colorado) entity

The screen to file a new record allows you to file all sorts of entities; LLCs, partnerships, and even socially conscious enterprises like cooperatives and public benefit corporations.

For this section, we will need an LLC. Note that you must include "LLC" or some version of that phrase in your actual business name in Colorado. Type the business name and click next.

That brings up the main form to fill out to register the LLC. In Colorado, the fee is $50.

Start with your physical business address and mailing address.

Next, fill in the information for your registered agent. A registered agent is a person who is served with papers if you get sued. Business owners often hire somebody to be their registered agent, but you can do it yourself.

The registered agent name and registered agent address of the entity's registered agent are

Name *   Last Name   First Name   Middle Name   Suffix
(If an
individual)

------ OR ------

(If an entity)

(Caution: Do not provide both an individual and an entity name.)

Next, verify that the registered agent has consented to be appointed as your registered agent.

For the next step, fill out the information for the person **forming the LLC.** It's not totally clear by the language, but a reasonable interpretation is that it is the business owner. If you're a single-member LLC, for example, you'd put in your own name and address.

If you are a multi-member LLC, you can add additional members by putting their names and address in a document and attaching it to your form (which comes on the next page).

Now you must identify the management type. There are two types of management for an LLC: **member-managed or manager-managed.** A member-managed LLC means that the member(s) of the LLC manage the company. Manager-managed means that you are hiring somebody else who is not a member to manage the company.

You can now attach additional information, such as a detailed operating agreement or a list of the other LLC members. You can also delay the effective date of your registration,.

For the penultimate step, put in your email address so that you can receive notifications when it's time to update your business information.

Then finally, put in the name and mailing address of the individual, **causing this document to be delivered for filing.**

Then you click submit! After you click submit, you will need to enter your payment information to cover the fees associated with registering. Fees vary from state to state, but they are generally reasonable. The process is straightforward enough, but if you are uncomfortable with these steps, it is best to hire a lawyer.

Next up on the agenda is selecting your tax treatment.

9. Select your tax treatment

After registering with your state, it is time to select your federal tax treatment. This is similar to choosing your type of entity, however, it is important to know that the IRS treats your entity differently from how the state does.

For example, the IRS does not recognize an LLC concept; a limited liability company is a state law concept. That means that the IRS does not have a designated way to tax LLCs. So, if you register as an LLC with your state, you will have to decide how you want the IRS to tax your company.

Tax Treatments for Corporations
You will also need to decide if you are a corporation. The primary options are to be taxed as a C corporation, or as an S corporation. We talked about the differences in Step #7: Select Your Entity Type. Basically, C corps have double taxation, while S corps do not.

That's selecting your tax treatment covered. Once again, this is a separate concept from selecting your entity type because the IRS does not recognize LLCs.

Next up, we will talk about obtaining your EIN or employer identification number from the IRS.

10. Obtain your EIN from the IRS

An EIN is your Employer Identification Number, and it's also commonly known as a tax ID. Your EIN is like the social security number for your business. All it is, is a unique identifying number. If you plan to have employees, you will need an EIN. You also need an EIN to open a separate bank account for your business, which we will cover in the next section.

We want to emphasize in this section that obtaining your EIN from the IRS is quite easy. Depending on your comfort level, you may be able to do it yourself without the help of a CPA or attorney. As always, make sure to do your homework and assess your level of comfort.

In this section, we will show you the process of obtaining your EIN from the IRS.

If you Google "IRS EIN," you will notice tons of sites with .com, .us, or .org URLs. You do not want to go to one of those sites. Make sure you are on the official government website (denoted by the .gov URL).

First off, to apply for your EIN, your principal business must be located in the United States or U.S. Territories, and you must have a valid Taxpayer Identification Number (SSN, ITIN, EIN). If you have those things, head to this page to begin the application process.

This first section of the application is to select your entity type (which is discussed in Step #7).

After completing the information about employees, you will have to answer more questions about your business type. All of the selections are very straightforward. Check "Other" if none of the business types match your line of work, like if you offer a service not listed.

You're almost done! After confirming information about your product/service, you can select to receive your EIN online. If you choose this method, you will receive a PDF immediately with your new EIN.

Congratulations! Now that you have your EIN, you can move onto the next step of the Legal Checklist for Start-ups: Open a Separate Bank Account for your Business.

11. Create a separate bank account

Now that you have obtained your EIN from the IRS, you can set up a separate bank account for your business.

It is essential to have your business and personal finances separate.

If a lawsuit is ever brought against your business, you may need to present your financial records. If your finances are mixed, you run the risk of airing your personal financial information in open court. An opposing lawyer could potentially come after your personal assets in a lawsuit.

You can reduce the risk of losing your personal assets in a lawsuit by keeping all personal and business transactions separate.

Having a separate bank account for your business is also helpful when you want to show your financials to someone. It is not uncommon for investors, and even landlords to want to look at your finances. It is also important for accounting. Everything is much simpler when they are separate.

For liability, privacy, ease of use, and accounting reasons, you should set up a bank account for your business.

If you have already started your business and have not created a separate account yet, it's not too late. Set up a new account as soon as possible and only use that account moving forward.

How about selecting a bank? Here are a few things to consider. First off, look for free checking. Free is always better but be aware of hidden fees.

Also, be mindful of your bank's location. Local banks generally offer better customer service, but national banks will be more accessible if you travel.

One option that you should strongly consider is a credit union. Credit unions often support your local community while providing low fees and excellent customer service.

That's step #11 in the Legal Checklist for Start-ups. Next up, we'll talk about determining your industry-specific regulations.

12. Determine your industry-specific regulations

The next step in the Legal Checklist for Start-ups is to determine your industry-specific regulations.

This is a complex issue, and we would not even be able to scratch the surface of all of the potential regulations for your business. Every business is different, and every location is different, so this step is here to flag the issue for you.

In prior sections, such as Obtaining Your EIN or Registering With Your State, we talked about some things that you might be able to do without an attorney's help. But determining your industry-specific regulations is often too complex to do on your own. For this reason, we highly suggest that you consult an attorney with industry-specific experience.

It is essential to ask if they are familiar with your particular line of work because industries can vary wildly in terms of the laws and regulations that govern their conduct. Not only do you have to adhere to state and federal laws, but many industries are also regulated at the county level.

Since we can't mention any specific regulations, let's look at some common things to look out for. First, does your line of work require special licenses? And does your line of work require specific permits?

Some particular industries that are heavily regulated are:
- Restaurants (anything that involves that sale of food)

- Liquor Sales (restaurants, events, venues, liquor stores, breweries, etc.)
- Transportation (the movement of goods or people)

Many industries may have regulations that you would never think about. For example, if you want to cut hair, your state might require a special license.

It is not only essential to think about the rules and regulations in your location, but you should also consider the rules and regulations in your customers' locations. If your business involves interstate commerce (the movement of goods or services across state lines), this is something to watch out for.

As you can see, the number of potential regulations is endless. That is why you should consider talking with a licensed professional in your state who has industry-relevant experience.

If you have questions about the regulations that govern businesses in the state of Colorado, send us a message, and we can help.

13. Determine your liabilities and insurance needs

Now that you have figured out what rules, regulations and licenses are specific to your line of work, it's time to determine your potential liabilities and insurance needs.

This is similar to Step #12 because potential liabilities also vary from industry to industry. When we say "potential liabilities," we are talking about potential risks.

A liability is a risk that you can be held legally responsible for.

For example, if you have a storefront or an office and your customers or clients visit you in that space, there is the potential that they could slip and fall. If a customer hurts themselves in your store, they could potentially sue your business. If they are successful, you could be held legally responsible and forced to cover the cost of the damages of that fall.

Determining Potential Liabilities

When determining your potential liabilities, you need to think about all of the things that could go wrong. It might not be a fun brainstorming exercise, but it is a necessary brainstorming exercise.

A few key groups to think about are our customers, employees, and competitors during this brainstorm. If you have a disgruntled employee, what actions could they take that could negatively impact your business?

You also need to consider the risks that are particular to your type of business. There are way more risks to consider if you work in a potentially dangerous industry, like construction or mining. Other industries, like anything to do with children, can also be considered very risky.

If you are unsure about identifying your potential liabilities, you should consult a flat-fee risk management consultant or an attorney.

Consulting with an experienced professional will help you pinpoint potential liabilities that you would never have thought to consider. In many instances, consulting with a professional can provide you with greater peace of mind. You might sleep better knowing that you've thought about everything that could go wrong with your business and that you've set up the proper protections.

Using Insurance to Protect Against Liabilities

One essential facet of being an entrepreneur is managing risk. We've already talked about selecting an entity type to manage your risk and limit your liability. Still, one of the other vital ways to limit your liability and manage your risk is to be adequately insured.

If your business has adequate insurance, you will be less impacted financially if you're found to be legally responsible in a lawsuit. Much like health insurance or car insurance, instead of paying "out of pocket," you can use your insurance to cover the damages.

There are many different types of insurance for business owners. Three common types of insurance policies for business owners are general commercial liability, umbrella, and professional liability.

Commercial General Liability
Commercial general liability policies are the most prevalent type of policy. This type of policy typically covers joint business liabilities as if your employee causes damage to property while on the job.

Many business owners make the mistake of assuming that commercial general liability insurance covers just about everything. That is why it is vital to make sure you read your insurance policy. Do your due diligence and make sure you understand what your policy covers and what your policy does not cover. You might be surprised by what it doesn't cover.

Umbrella
What if you identify liabilities that your commercial general liability policy doesn't cover? Or what if your other policy doesn't cover the full amount? If that happens, you can still get protection through an umbrella policy, which is a type of secondary insurance.

A secondary insurance policy only kicks in once you've exhausted the limits of your other insurance policies. Umbrella policies are usually cheaper because they are needed less often, but that doesn't mean you shouldn't consider purchasing one.

Professional Liability
Professional liability policies protect people in specific professions. The name varies depending on the profession, so you may have also heard professional liability insurance called omissions insurance or malpractice insurance. Professional liability insurance protects you from any lawsuits that seek damages.

Professional liability insurance is common among doctors, lawyers, accountants, and real estate agents. While it is not required to have professional liability insurance in all states, it can provide peace of mind for both you and your customers.

Buying Insurance

There is a massive misconception that insurance brokers out there are responsible for telling you what types of insurance you need and how much insurance you need. That is not the case.

An insurance broker's primary job is to sell insurance. They are typically paid by commission, meaning there is often the incentive to upsell. That creates a conflict of interest when it comes to suggesting how much insurance you need. The more insurance you buy, the more they get paid.

We're not saying that people who sell insurance are bad; we're just saying that it is not their job to tell you how much insurance you need. Your job as a business owner is to take a proactive stance on determining your liabilities and figuring out what type of insurance will protect you best against those liabilities.

14. Set up an accounting system

Step #14 in the Legal Checklist for Start-ups is to Set up an Accounting System for Your Business

Setting up an accounting system is another way to manage your risk as a business owner because. Sloppy finances can sink your business.

There are two main ways to set up an accounting system:
• Do it yourself.
• Hire someone.
There are pros and cons to both.
If you want to do it yourself, your best bet is to use a QuickBooks or Xero program. While these programs streamline the process, it's still a time consuming and confusing task that can take significant time away from your business.

The benefit of doing your own accounting is you are more informed of your actual financial position.

Since accounting is necessary to manage your day-to-day affairs and manage your risk as a business, it is a worthwhile expense to have somebody do it for you. That way you can invest more time on building your business.

That leads us to our second option - hiring somebody to handle your finances for you. As you can imagine, there is no shortage of bookkeepers and accountants who you can pay to look after your accounts.

The worry of hiring another person to handle your books is that you could become disconnected from your business's finances. You never want to let that happen. Losing track of your business's financials is a sure-fire way to sink a new business.

If you choose to hire someone to do your bookkeeping for you (which is generally an excellent idea), you still need to exercise adequate oversight of that person.

You must hire somebody who can give you to-the-minute access to your financials. Programs like QuickBooks Online make this relatively easy.

It is important that you hire a Certified Public Accountant (CPA) to manage your finances. CPAs must pass a certification test which ensures they have the necessary skills to adequately manage accounts.

To give you a fundamental overview of what an accounting system does, it breaks your money down into various categories. The essential categories for business owners include accounts receivable and accounts payable.

Accounts receivable are funds that you have earned but have not yet been paid on. In short, it is money that you are owed. If you've shipped your goods or performed your service and not yet been paid, that money is kept track of in accounts receivable.

Accounts payable is just the opposite - money you owe others (vendors, service providers, etc.). These are essentially unpaid bills.

Accounting systems also provide profit and loss statements and balance sheets. These two documents can give you a snapshot of your business's financial health. They are also important because many lenders and investors will want to see a balance sheet before lending money or investing in your company.

15. Set up your basic contracts

Now that you've laid down the necessary foundation for your business and reviewed your needs, it's time to put your plan into motion. But before you go out and start setting up relationships with clients, vendors, and employees, you need to complete the necessary contracts.

What is a Contract?
A contract is just an exchange of promises between two parties.

If you're not sure if you need a contract, think about whether you are exchanging promises. Are you promising to provide them with service, and are they promising payment in return? If so, you should have a contract.

Why are contracts important?
Contracts are important because they reduce the risk of miscommunication. In most states, oral contracts are binding. However, anytime you are exchanging promises with another party in your business, it is prudent to get it in writing. Contracts should create clear outlines of what is expected from both parties.

In addition to miscommunication, people sometimes don't deliver on their promises. Contracts give you a way to enforce a broken promise. For instance, if you provide a service and your client doesn't pay you, you can pursue legal actions to collect on that payment. Having a contract in place will make the legal process much more straightforward.

Types of Contracts for Small Businesses

Now that you understand what a contract is and why they are essential, let's talk about the basic types of contracts your business might need.

To figure out what types of contracts you need, we suggest you go back and review the section on Defining Your "Who."

In that section, we spend a lot of time discussing business partners. If you are going into business with a partner, you need a contract. Many partnerships exist with unspoken agreements or handshake agreements; get those agreements in writing to make them more enforceable.

In the section on Defining Your "Who," we also talked about who will work for your business. In some instances, it might make sense to have contracts with your employers. It's also important to have contracts with your independent contractors. Other parties that work for your business include vendors. When working with established vendors, they usually have standard contracts for all their partners.

As we mentioned earlier, when talking about providing a service for your clients, you may also need contracts with your customers. Another prevalent type of contract is an insurance policy. An insurance policy is a contract between you and the insurance company. You are promising to pay your premium, and the insurance company is promising to pay out on a claim.

The last prevalent type of contract that we will highlight for you is a lease. Commercial leases can be complicated, and they are often written by the landlord, not the tenant. Since the landlord usually drafts them, they usually heavily favor the landlord rather than the tenant.

How to Set up Your Basic Contracts

In many cases, the other party will provide contracts and ask you to agree to the terms outlined. Such is the case with vendors, landlords, and insurance companies. If you are presented with a contract, it is your responsibility to review it, understand it, and negotiate it.

In other cases, you will have to provide the contract. This is common if you are hiring independent contracts or bringing on clients.

How do you draft your contracts?

There are some online resources, like LegalZoom and Rocket Lawyer, to download basic boilerplate contracts. That is usually the cheapest way to create a contract without having to do it yourself. The problem with online boilerplate contracts is they are not specific. We've talked about this a lot in this checklist, but to reiterate: every business is different. That means the needs of every business are different. A boilerplate contract might not cover everything you need, leaving you legally exposed. At Lexyom, we are trying to automate Legal services and provide a seamless experience to start-ups, SMEs and Entrepreneurs.

You can also hire an attorney to draft your contracts for you. This can get expensive, so I recommend that you discuss your budget before starting with your attorney.

Reviewing Your Contract

If you already have a contract, whether you downloaded it from a legal website, wrote it yourself, or was presented to you by a landlord or a vendor, you can ask an attorney to review it.

One important thing to note, even if you have a lawyer write or review your contracts, it's still your responsibility to read and understand what's in the contract. The lawyer can highlight legal issues for you, but a contract is ultimately a business decision. You, as the business owner, are the ones exchanging promises in the contract. So, you need to make sure that you are okay with all of the promises exchanged in that contract.

16. Keep it simple

You've made it to the final step! Step #16 in the Legal Checklist for Start-ups is to Keep it Simple.

I appreciate some irony in saying "keep it simple" at the end of a long series, telling you all the steps you need to take (just from the legal perspective) to start your business. However, it is essential to keep it simple.

Once you've taken the necessary steps to set up your business, and after you've sufficiently protected yourself from a legal standpoint, it's essential to focus on your actual business.
Consulting with an attorney can be a great way to help you figure out whether you are correctly managing your potential risks so that you can focus on the actual substance of your business.

Legal Routine

In the book The Lean Start-up, author Eric Ries makes a great analogy about simplicity in business. He says that when on your daily commute to work, you make a thousand little decisions. You decide where to turn, when to slow down at a stoplight, whether to speed or take your time. But you make those decisions as you go. You don't plan out every single decision in advance. That's one end of the spectrum.

The other end of the spectrum is launching a rocket ship. Rocket scientists have to plan every single contingency and every single step in the launch of a rocket-ship.

It's the equivalent of trying to make every decision for the morning commute before you even get in the car. Here, the difficult part is that there are so many variables, and you don't know what will happen once you're behind the wheel. Rocket scientists have to account for every single variable beforehand and determine ways to navigate every single obstacle before the rocket takes off.

Eric Ries says that starting a business is, and should be, more like your daily commute. Too many business owners treat starting a business like launching a rocket. But the fact is, you don't know what's going to happen. You will need to navigate obstacles as they come up, and that's okay.

Make the minimum number of decisions that you can now, think through your end goal and the potential contingencies in all of that. **But don't let**

planning get in the way of actually starting.

Once you have gone through this checklist, consulted a licensed professional in your state, and set up your basic legal protections, don't add unnecessary complexity.

I still remember the day we graduated from UK Lebanon Tech Hub. We had all our legal framework in order and were heading in a new direction, on a new path. We were one of eight start-ups who launched that autumn day in a warehouse in the Beirut's suburbs. My parents were supposed to attend, but did not. The crowd was silent, the lights were dimmed, and my 3 minutes started. It was the first official pitch for Lexyom. We were on the road to a journey full of challenges, excitements, bumps, and thrills. I came back home that day full of dreams; little did I know how difficult it would be, with that many hurdles and obstacles. I woke up the next day at 6:03 AM, and the train was on the move again.

5. Start Today

Always looked at businesses and guessed whether their business is prone to succeed or not; whether it had potential or not; and whether it could survive or not. I have an eye for people, deals, and businesses, which is truly a blessing. On several occasions, I had

meetings with founders, and as soon as I sat with them, I picked up cues from their looks, movements, words, and small micro gestures. There is a series called "Lie to Me" which gives you huge knowledge in micro expression and universal reactions.

I like to look at starting a business as creating a piece of art. All the aspects have to match so it can impress and live through time. It would be best if you had many factors to make a venture succeed. I always inform the founders I mentor and assist that they need to look at the bigger picture but also work on the little parts of it to succeed. I once had to tell a founder to close shop after years of working because he was not fit for it. Yes, you may not be fit to be a founder and that is okay. Moreover, when people discover what a founder's life really is, they lose the hype and excitement surrounding it.

All my businesses have fantastic names, competent teams, and an excellent product destined for people who need it. I make sure that I have fun selling the products while simultaneously making profit. I started many E-commerce shops, drop-shipping businesses, retail businesses, events, and service companies. I am always on the lookout for new opportunities, and deals I can close fast to make as much money as possible in the shortest amount of time.

In this chapter, I want to share with you the five main steps you need to start your business today and succeed.

1. Find the problem or need you are solving

It all starts with a niche. Yes, it all starts with a niche. I WILL repeat this forever until everyone who is reading my writing or listening to me understands that nothing can work if it is not solving a problem or attaining a need.

If you want to build a huge business, you have to solve a huge problem. Luckily, there are hundreds of emerging areas that contain both big problems and ample opportunities. Some of them are already pressing issues, while others are just appearing on the horizon. These issues need courageous and inspired business leaders to build scalable solutions that can impact billions of people. A few areas that contain big opportunities over the next twenty years include clean energy, battery storage, clean water access, graphene desalination, global healthcare, telemedicine, cloud education, AI, robotics, quantum computing, synthetic biology, NUI software, clean transportation, anti-corruption tracking, cybersecurity, and private space exploration.

Of course, there are many more than just these. Challenge yourself to think bigger and push yourself to build a company that solves major human problems. That's how you become a billionaire while making a significant impact.

Before you begin a new business or find a new problem to solve, take the time to write down your life purpose. Think about the change you seek to create globally and then start a company to make that change real.

Ask yourself three simple questions: What are the big problems I see in the world? Which one am I most passionate about solving? How can I create a business that solves that problem, create value that people are willing to pay for, and makes the world better? Don't make the mistake of building a company if you're not deeply passionate about the problem you are trying to solve. Too many start-ups try to solve problems they're not passionate about and burn out because they don't have the inspiration and energy to carry them through the tough times.

Knowing that your business mission is aligned with your personal life mission can help immeasurably keep you on course and give you the resilience to weather the storms that are sure to come. Once you know who you want to become, you can direct your life rather than letting outside factors control you.

My life purpose is to build and invest in companies that use design and technology to solve significant humanitarian challenges. Finding this core motivation at age 18 has been critical to getting me through the difficult and challenging times. It's helped me to find the strength from within to persevere in the face of seemingly insurmountable odds.

In line with my life mission, I'm now building a company called Lexyom to make it easier for people to communicate with each other around the world. We hope to become the leader in Legal Technology, but we know we have a lot of hard work ahead. I am building all my other businesses based on Design and Technology, which is my core target.

Finally, if the scale of problems out there intimidates you, start smaller.

If you can start with a small problem aligned with your greater mission, it can act as a confidence-builder and a stepping stone to the more significant problems you care about solving. Let who you are and what you believe in come out in all that you create.

I like to apply the five point rule every time. I usually advise you to choose 3 External Life goals you want to achieve + 1 Internal Goal + 1 Social Goal.

2. Find the right name for your business

Here are some basic tips on how to name your start-up:
Avoid Hard to spell names.

1.   Don't pick a name that could limit the business as it grows.
2.   Conduct a thorough Internet search on a name.
3.   Get a ".com" domain name (not a ".net" or other variants).

4. Conduct a thorough trademark search.
5. Make sure you / your employees will be happy saying the name. Come up with five names you like and test market the name with prospective employees, partners, investors, and customers.

3. Build/source the best product/service

When starting out, your product or service has to be at least good, if not great. It must be differentiated in some meaningful and important way from the offerings of your competition. Everything else follows this fundamental principle. Don't drag your feet on getting your product out to market since early customer feedback is one of the best ways to improve your product. Of course, you want a "minimum viable product" (MVP) to begin with, but even that product should be good and stand out from the competition. Having a "beta" test product works for many start-ups as they work the bugs out from user reactions. As Sheryl Sandberg, COO of Facebook has said, "Done is better than perfect." There are many ways to build and source amazing products or even services. Ideally, you would want to find the best craftsman in the field you are producing in and try to have the best deal to make sure you are very competitive on the profit margin level. I always try to find the best craftsmen and producers when I go into specific products or items. I have been all the way across the globe to meet with people from China, Vietnam, Ohio, and Como. All for neckties.

4.Build an amazing team

We have discussed repeatedly the concept of building an amazing team. We are constantly working hard to liaise with people, work in specific environments, and make sure we are always on the lookout for the best people to join our team. We are always looking to win and make sense of what is and what is not. We will discuss the different facets of building a team as we go. We are no longer working or succeeding alone in 2021 and onwards. We are the consequence of our relationships and our teams.

5.Build an amazing website/platform to sell

You should devote time and effort to building an excellent website for your business. Prospective investors, customers, and partners will check out your site, and you want to impress them with a professional product. Here are some tips for building a great company website:

1. Check out competitor sites.
2. Start by sketching out a template for your site.
3. Come up with five or six sites you can share with your website developer to convey what you like.
4. Be sure the site is search engine optimized (and thus more likely to show up early on Google search results).
5. Produce high-quality original content.
6. Make sure your site is optimized for mobile devices.
7. Make sure the site loads quickly.
8. Keep it clean, simple; visual clutter will drive visitors away.
9. Ensure you have a Terms of Use Agreement and Privacy Policy (and comply with the European GDPR rules).
10. Make the navigation bars prominent.
11. Obtain and use a memorable ".com" domain name.
12. Make the site visually attractive.
13. Make sure it's easy for site visitors to contact you or buy your product.
14. Make sure to go back to Chapter 2 to read about strategies to build an amazing website and online selling platform.

6. Start selling, selling, selling

The most important thing you could do in business life is to start selling. You should start selling as soon as possible and make sure you are selling from day one. I believe in learning the art of selling from a very young age, which my parents taught me. See, I was brought up with a constant need to convince, and my parents would always ask me to convince them about things, argue my points, and that the sky is the limit with them as long as I find valid arguments. I always looked for arguments to convince and pushed myself to the limit to get what I wanted. As I grew up, I continued learning the art of sales and took several jobs selling products like PlayStation, mobile phones, clothing, and healthcare products. Add to that the fact that I already looked different from my surroundings, which pushed me to promote myself and work on my strengths and added values.

When I wanted to source fabric for Remy Remez, I went on many websites, spent days searching for contact information. I contacted most of them, checked their vibe on the phone because I genuinely believe in the vibe you get from discussing with someone. It does say a lot about who they are and what they are offering.

I then screened a few and booked my ticket, accommodation, and car rental. I went to visit them, to touch the fabric, and get a feel for their business vibe. This is how I was going to make sure that the quality was up to the standard. When I met Gio in his small factory in Como, a small one-floor factory filled with beautiful fabric, I went into his office. He offered me a Nespresso and initiated the conversation before moving to the actual floor where the machines are. As we were walking he put his hand on my shoulder and started telling me the factory's story and how his grandfather had started it all from scratch. Usually, when someone tells you things like these, unconsciously, you start relating to them and start feeling a sense of belonging and loyalty. This is typically an initiator to smoothness in the negotiations and makes discussing terms friendlier by all standards. You can use this strategy when selling to customers online and offline, mostly when selling luxury items and products with a high price tag. I left the factory with

20,000 USD worth of fabric in Neckties, and that was the start of Remy Remez, which is today an amazing Creative Fashion House with sales in Paris, New York, Tokyo, and Dubai.

So here are a few tools I found during my search:

Drop-Shipping Apps
Drop-shipping apps for sourcing products on Shopify and others:

1.Oberlo
Oberlo is an official Shopify app built that makes it easy to find products via third-party drop-shippers, add them to your Shopify store, and ship them directly to your customers.

You can choose from millions of products across almost any niche you can think of, curating them into a branded online store to serve a specific audience, like pet accessories for pet owners or smartphone photography gear for travelers.

You can source Bags, Sunglasses, Watches, Apparel, Electronics, Phone accessories. The possibilities really are endless.

2. Printify
If you're looking for a way to inject some of your creativity into what you sell, print-on-demand products are a popular choice. With Printify, you can choose from a large catalog of products to customize with your designs.

While Printify is free to use (you pay for the products on a pre-order basis), you can also upgrade to a paid plan for $29/month, when you're ready to scale, to improve your profit margins with a 20% discount on all products.

You can source: T-shirts, Hoodies, Tote Bags, Coffee mugs, Wall Decals, Posters, Beach towels, Dog Beds, etc.

3. Dropshipper: $25 a month
Do you consider yourself a coffee connoisseur, but are worried about

selling a defective product? Dropshipper, a coffee dropshipping app, might be for you. Whole beans are shipped on the same day they're roasted. That's as fresh as can be.

Upload your logo, choose the kind of coffee you want to offer, and customize your labels to sell white-label coffee under your brand directly to your customers. You can even offer a coffee subscription, so customers can get a fresh bag delivered as their previous supply runs dry.

The types of coffee products you can sell include:

Single-origin coffee (Laos, Papa New Guinea, Columbia, etc.)
12/60 pack of single-serve coffee capsules
Decaf coffee
Custom coffee product (select origin, roast, size, bag, etc.)

4. Spocket
Price : Free plan available

Spocket is another product sourcing app that lets you add products from drop-ship suppliers in the US and EU. It offers an extensive catalog of quality products and branded invoicing, plus fast shipping.

Through wholesale pricing, the service promises a 30-60% discount on all products' retail prices, enabling significant profit margins for you to get creative with discounts.

The products you can source through Spocket include:

Apparel
Apparel
Sports and outdoor equipment Footwear Bath and beauty items And more

5. Syncee

Price: Free for 14 days (first 30 products)
From inventory to reliability to delivery times, there are many factors to consider when sourcing a supplier.

With Syncee, you can browse a catalog of trustworthy suppliers worldwide and easily import products into your store to start selling.

Products you can import include:
• Baby products
• Watches
• Fashion
• Toys
• Fishing accessories
• Perfume

6. Creative Hub
This platform helps you sell art made by contemporary artists.

Price: Free to Install
With Creative Hub, you don't need to be an artist to sell art online.

This UK-based marketplace gives you access to premium art by contemporary artists to trade in your store. For each piece, you're given the retail price (the minimum price you can sell it at) and your share as a vendor (how much you stand to make at the retail price). Some prints are even limited edition, commanding a higher price tag. There is a £6 fixed international shipping, which keeps shipping simple and lets you sell to anyone worldwide. It's important to note that frames are not included (though you might be able to source them and offer them through one of the other apps on this list).

7. My Online Fashion Store

Price: $29/month

My Online Fashion Store is a US-based drop-shipper with a large inventory of stylish apparel for women. From tops to bottoms, jewelry to shoes, there's a large number of items, each with a suggested selling price. What's more, is that they offer free returns and great shipping rates; however, they can only serve customers in the United States at the moment, which limits your market. The products you can sell include:

- Scarves And more
- Tank tops
- Lingerie
- Sunglasses
- Handbags
- Hats
- Belts

8. Lulu Xpress

Price: Free to install

Lulu Xpress exclusively focuses on books and calendars, letting you use print-on-demand fulfilment to launch your book product. You can pick the book's format and size, whether you want a hardcover or softcover, color, black and white ink, and the quality of the paper you want to use for the interior pages.   Have an idea for a best-selling coffee book? Lulu Xpress is a low-risk way to try out your idea and prove it out before investing heavily in it.

The types of books you could create include:

Hardcover photo   Poetry books   Calendars Novels   Journals and Comic books notebooks
Workbooks

9. Shapeways

Price: Free to install

Shapeways is a 3D pricing and fulfilment service that lets you upload your own 3D models and bring them to life as physical products.

While this may be one of the most expensive apps to use on the list (considering the upfront costs of 3D modeling), you can use it to create genuinely unique, high-quality products to sell on-demand or for rapid prototyping.

The available 3D printing materials include

- Plastic And more
- Steel
- Gold
- Aluminium
- Sandstone
- Carbon

10. Modalyst

Price: Free plan available (5% transaction fee on sales) Modalyst is a supplier network that gives you access to drop shippers based in the US with relatively fast shipping times. You can find independent brands, trendy products, and low-cost goods to sell in your own store.

Many of their independent brands include other Shopify merchants who meet strict requirements and are open to forming drop-shipping partnerships.

Products you can find on Modalyst include
- Backpacks
- Swimwear
- Formalwear
- Jewelry
- T-shirts
- Electronics
- Footwear
- And more

11. MXED
Price: Free to install

Selling officially licensed pop culture merchandise often requires you to negotiate directly with the licensor. MXED offers an easier way to sell licensed merchandise legitimately from some of the most familiar brands around. Best of all, MXED offers fast 3-day shipping, letting you serve up an excellent customer experience that lives up to the premium products you'll be selling.

The pop culture products available through MXED includes backpacks, t-shirts, wallets, and other merchandise from iconic universes like:

- Assassin's Creed   My Hero Academia
- Street Fighter   Looney Tunes
- Overwatch   DC Comics
- Sonic the Hedgehog   Marvel Comics
- Star Wars   Naruto

13. Ali Express

Ali Express has everything. They also have customizable items.

You can literally find anything on www.aliexpress.com. Make sure you vet the suppliers, see if they have any reviews and comments on their pages, research them on google, and vet them with a brief conversation before moving forward.
Lastly, Order Samples.

For Wholesalers, there are also these options to check:
Alibaba:
Search millions of products available through import suppliers

ThomasNet:
Search thousands of domestic and international wholesalers and manufacturers

Wholesale Central:
A huge directory that matches millions of small eCommerce sellers with products

FG Market:
Search for thousands of gifts, home decor, boutiques, and personal care product suppliers.

Etsy Wholesale:
Find wholesale pricing on handmade and specialty goods.

proven sales strategies

1.Lead with what's in it for your prospect
Many salespeople, entrepreneurs, and even freelancers employ a sales strategy that ignores what they set out to sell to their prospects - solutions. When you are selling, you should sell by urgently diving straight into the different packages, price points, and special promotions your prospect can take advantage of by signing up during the day or week, or month.

Your sales strategy needs to lead with a clear articulation of the challenge you can help your prospect solve. Here's why: During the beginning of a sales conversation, your prospect likely doesn't fully understand the benefits of what you are selling. The last thing you want to do is immediately treat your product or service like a commodity rather than a valuable solution to a need they have. Do your best to research their needs upfront and start your outreach conversation by explaining what your prospect will get from your product.

2.Clearly articulate end results
People purchase results, not just products or services. Once you have captured your prospect's attention with what they will be able to achieve using your solution, it's your job to clearly explain how they will benefit after signing up. Suppose you are selling a premium CRM system to SMB's

that have never used one before. In that case, you will need to educate them about how the platform will work, how much of a time investment they should expect to make in managing it moving forward, and the types of ongoing support they will have access to.

This sales strategy is particularly relevant if you're selling a product or service that comes with an upfront fee, requires a complex rollout, time intensive integrations, or ongoing collaboration with your customers after closing a deal. Your prospect needs to know precisely what they are going to get as far as deliverables when milestones are met, and the downstream impact they're expected to have on their business.

3.Start with small niche markets

You can dramatically increase your cold outreach's effectiveness by targeting specific niche markets of people that share common pain. Rather than reaching out to businesses of all different sizes, industries, and offerings, focus on a narrow grouping of companies to pitch.

For example, if you are selling inventory management software, choosing a small niche market could mean starting with pitching only to businesses that manufacture construction equipment. You could narrow your beginning niche by focusing solely on these types of companies located in the western United States and have 100 to 250 employees. By working your sales strategy only with this homogenous group of companies, you will be able to perfect your pitch for this space much quicker than if you were mixing in businesses of all shapes and sizes.

Don't worry about the fact that choosing a small niche could limit your options either. Selecting a niche is a long-term decision, but it's not a long-term loss if it's the wrong one. You may fail, but as long as you learn, it's time well invested."

Choosing a small niche, in the beginning, allows you to specialize. It is great to think big and shoot for the stars, but you can get more results faster by thinking specific when it comes to niche selection. Start by picking a market that interests you. The competition doesn't matter at this point—just pick something you like.

The same principle applies to your decision to invest in starting a blog for your business—pick a niche to own and become the ultimate resource for your readers.

Here's another example—let's take a look at the email marketing software company, ConvertKit. They self-identify as "email marketing for professional bloggers." In the highly competitive landscape of email marketing providers like MailChimp, Constant Contact, and Active Campaign, this small company has carved out a curated niche market of customers to go after—professional bloggers. ConvertKit has gained invaluable brand advocates & affiliates to spread their message as a significant component of their sales strategy by forging creative partnerships with big-name bloggers and brands that reach an audience.

4. Be Flexible

During your sales conversations, you are naturally going to encounter new challenges and unique demands from your prospects. This makes sense as each company you work with is structured differently and has a distinct set of internal processes and objectives. Since saying "you can't," "won't," "that's impossible," and other variations of no to your prospect is not an option, your sales strategy needs to be flexible enough to adapt in the face of new challenges on the go.

As bestselling author and sales strategy coach Grant Cardone shares, "In selling, you are seeking an agreement. Your customer is almost always distrustful and uncertain, not about you, but themselves. Most

salespeople think selling is about gaining trust, but in reality, selling is about getting the customer to trust themselves enough to take action and close—which often takes flexibility. Learn to close the sale, not just make a sale."

It's that simple. You can't afford to say no. When you do, you lose your perception as a problem-solver and instantly close the door to a world full of possibilities. Instead of disagreeing with or flat out turning down a request from your prospect, use a response like, "I'd love to make that happen for you," which will allow you to check with the rest of your team and see if there is any possibility to accommodate the request. Even if that means coming back to the negotiation table with a minimum order quantity or project spend that'll justify the out-of-the-box solution, you'll keep the deal alive.

5. Use leads scoring to prioritize your prospects

If you are dealing with a large volume of leads, incorporating lead scoring into your sales strategy is necessary. Assessing the customers profile, the needs of customers, the decision-making process they must go through, and lastly, the competition.

1. Customer profile

How well do they match your ideal customer Profile [ICP]? How big is the company? What industry are they in? Where are your ideal customers located? What is the ideal use case? Which tools have they used in the past? What kind of ecosystem are they playing in?

How do you identify the ideal customer profile? Your Ideal Customer Profile is a living, breathing "definition" that you'll come back to – and modify – often. It would help if you thought of your Ideal Customer as to the customer type that – over a clearly - defined time frame – you will dedicate Sales and Marketing Resources to acquire. Your Ideal Customer is particular for:

The situation you are solving for
Your goal
Your capabilities
Before determining your ideal Customer Profile, make sure to remove any FOMO Effect. I always advise start-ups and entrepreneurs to do so. When I was launching Lexyom, which is technically a virtual law firm, I was clear on being very radical in my choices. I wanted to target Entrepreneurs "ONLY," and although any law firm starts rapidly getting requests from corporate clients, I directly rejected all these offers and focused on start-ups. It was challenging at the time to lose money and keep focus when just one corporate client's money would have helped. I remember one night,

as I was sleeping in my office on the air mattress looking at the sky from the office window (We had only one window), I looked high and started thinking, what if I take that one client just temporarily to cover some losses. I picked up the phone and texted him for a meeting. The next day I went to visit him at his office. It was entirely glass, with screens all over; I sat there suited up to fit in with the corporate environment I found myself surrounded by. As we were discussing, I felt sick to my stomach that I was going against my vision, just to make some extra money. I ended up not taking on the client, and honestly feel like if I had, Lexyom would not be what it is today.

Determining your Ideal Customer is not about choosing the only type of customer you will ever do business with. No, it is about finding the Ideal Customer for a particular situation. That should ease the FOMO pain a small bit.

The situation definition has three inputs:
A. The Timeframe

Use whatever timeframe makes sense, but 3 to 6 months is generally a reasonable amount of time for adequate testing. Less than that is likely not enough time, and more than that is, you guessed it, probably too much. But if you have a valid reason for the time frame you've chosen – a mandate from investors, a gut-level feeling, etc. – then go for it.

The key is to be specific with the overall timeframe and identify milestones along the way. Check-in to see if this hypothesis is proving true or false. If a 90-day hypothesis is proving false after 45 days, you can either adjust your tactics or make the call and pivot to a different ICP [Ideal Customer Profile].

B. The Goal
Just as you need to be specific with the timeframe for this situation, you need to be specific with the goal you wish to achieve in that time frame.

- X amount of additional revenue

- Y new customers

- Z customer advocates

You will notice that the goal isn't only revenue or new customers but could be customer advocates (those customers willing to help you land other customers). The goal can be anything you want, and it is this goal that will dictate how heavily we weigh the different inputs into the Ideal Customer Profile.

That said, it should be clear that once you define the timeframe and the goal, your customer becomes very important.

Reaching that specific goal in the specified timeframe without being too deliberate in your customer acquisition efforts is essentially a nonstarter. You will also need to be clear on where you are starting from (baseline) and what metrics you'll use to measure progress for this situation (and ensure you're keeping track of those)

C. Your Current Capabilities
This final point is critical; regardless of your goals, you must be realistic about what you can do for your customers. Sure, to grow and expand, you sometimes need to take on customers that require you to extend your capabilities. But you have to be realistic about the amount of responsibility you can handle.
Some things to consider:
- The maturity of your product (API only vs. MVP vs. Feature Parity with Market Leader, etc.)
- Your ability to serve customers (onboarding, training, customization, customer support, etc.)
- Technology or other dependencies (these will figure heavily into the Success Potential input.)

Strive to look beyond just a "recommendation" that can conveniently be solved by purchasing your solution; people who have been in business long enough will see straight through that tactic. When your sales strategy includes reaching out to your prospect to let them know about the cool thing you just did for them, rather than jumping straight into selling your solution, your chance of building a meaningful rapport increases tenfold. Keep in touch, continue providing value over the coming days or weeks.

Will you close a sale from that new relationship the day you reach out with this sales strategy? Probably not, but if your product or service has a long sales cycle with a hefty price tag, building meaningful relationships and listening to your prospect's unique needs will ultimately lead to your long-term success.

7. Perfect your sales pitch (Make it exciting!)

Once you are confident that you have connected with the right point of contact, you need to have an effective sales pitch. One that captures the attention of your prospect and keeps the conversation moving in the right direction. Spend too much time talking about your company, the clients you've worked with and why your prospect should sign up today will risk ruining the relationship before it begins.

Robert Herjavec, entrepreneur, investor, and co-star of ABC's Shark Tank has heard an elevator pitch (or two) in his day. When it comes to delivering an effective pitch, he says it is more about showing your expertise—not just rattling off numbers and clients you've worked with.

Herjavec shares, "You have 90 seconds if you're lucky. If you can't make your point persuasively in that time, you've lost the chance for impact. Facts and figures are important, but it's not the only criteria; you must present in a manner that generates expertise and confidence. If you're not prepared for it, you may just miss your next big opportunity."

How do you demonstrate your expertise within your elevator pitch? Lean heavily upon showing your prospect that you have already developed an understanding of the challenges they're facing related to the area of the business your solution will help with. Do the research up-front and use your knowledge about your prospect's business. This helps you take control of the conversation in your sales pitch by finetuning your message and not being afraid to share controversial views if they're ultimately in the best interest of your new customer.

I realized how complicated the time before pitching was, so I developed a process to determine the best pitch practice. Make it as easy as if you are talking about what you have eaten for lunch to a nine-year-old. Include small details without complicating. For Lexyom, I remember that this was the before and the after:

Before: An online platform that provides automated, personalized, and international legal services using artificial intelligence, machine learning, and blockchain.

After: A digital law firm providing personalized legal services using AI.

8. Use storytelling
Incorporating storytelling into your sales strategy can help captivate your prospects on a deeper level beyond just selling them strictly on the benefits, thus getting you more customers over time. Storytelling works well because our brains are wired to absorb information much better when we encounter it through stories.

As Stanford Graduate School of Business professor Jennifer Aaker explains, "Research shows our brains are not hard-wired to understand logic or retain facts for very long. Our brains are wired to understand and retain stories. A story is a journey that moves the listener, and when the listener goes on that journey, they feel different. The result is persuasion and sometimes action."

You can use storytelling at every stage of your sales process, even during the early formation. Explain product features by highlighting real-life problems a particular feature solved for your customers.

An example of this is the **story of a luxury furniture retailer helping high-profile clients like Floyd Mayweather, Jamie Foxx, and Robert Duvall with their interior design needs.** Their sales approach combined both highly targeted outreach and handling a high volume of inbound inquiries, often triggered when an Instagram influencer gave the company a shout-out from their Instagram account. Frequently, hundreds of questions about a particular piece of furniture would flood into sales reps' inboxes.

This presented its own unique set of challenges: How to move sales conversations forward with high-profile clients while also responding promptly to a large influx of questions that come in through social channels.

Close's Inbox and Smart View feature enabled the furniture retailer's reps to personalize their responses at scale while ensuring that no lead fell through the cracks. The result? An almost immediate 10% increase in revenue.

Handle objections by building trust and walking through a case study of how other customers moved past these same objections and now get positive results. Answer questions, negotiate and strive to use a diverse sampling of stories about your company, customers, product, and yourself to keep them captivated along the sales process. Keep in mind that storytelling can be applied to more passive forms of selling by incorporating a captivating story into your Ecommerce Website's sales pages.

9. Listen to what your prospects are telling you

Do you frequently get pushback from prospects on just one area of your pricing structure? How about requests for the same new features repeatedly that prospects cite as a top reason why they are not interested in signing up for your product yet? Are there specific competitor solutions that tend to be easier to win over new customers?

By building your sales strategy around listening carefully to (and recording) the most common objections, feature requests, competitor software in use, and other critical bits of information, you'll be able to perfect your approach and increase your close rate.

One of the most critical aspects of selling or even going into business for yourself is being flexible and listening to feedback from your prospects, watching the data, and making changes as needed. Sometimes having a rigid plan can limit you.

More than just listening, how are you sharing this feedback with the rest of your team? It's important to communicate the feedback to the other team members who make product decisions, as it could increase your product's effectiveness. Since side comments are often forgotten, use these strategies for sharing meaningful customer feedback with your team.

--- Create an internal Trello board
Keep a series of ongoing Google Docs

Host a public feature request page with voting options like Asana does.

Granted, you will need to decide if the prospect who's giving you the feedback or making a feature request is a good fit for becoming a customer of your product before rushing to make accommodations. Many start-ups make a common mistake in their sales strategy to make big decisions based on the sheer number of prospects requesting a specific function, even if they're not an ideal customer. And if you are using one of the CRM to track these requests, it can be tempting to make decisions based on the sheer number of feature requests—rather than spending the time to determine whether it's actually the best strategic move for your business in the long run.

Then, be sure to schedule a recurring review meeting with your partners and other key stakeholders at least once a month to compile and productively share this feedback.

10. Give your undivided attention to sales calls

Whether you're making a cold call or following back up with one of your sales leads, it's essential to treat the call at hand as the most important thing you could be doing. If you're not engaging with your prospect, expressing interest while they are talking, or asking them questions that show your understanding, they'll be able to see through your lack of attention.

Giving undivided attention to your calls, especially if your sales strategy relies heavily upon following a script. That requires removing yourself from distracting environments. If you typically make sales calls from a loud office space, try moving into an open conference room for your next set of calls and see if that gives you more focus. If you get sleepy at your desk, try standing up, walking around, or making your next sales call from a quiet outdoor location

11.Negotiate for a win-win

The real purpose of negotiating for a win-win with your prospects is to demonstrate respect and the intention to work with them again in the future. It is valuing long-term relationships over insignificant details.

You do need to know your walk-away number, the bottom-line price you're able to accept in a negotiation. If necessary, having this foundational number in mind and being willing to share it with your prospect near the end of your negotiation will give you clear guidelines by which to strike a win-win scenario. Providing additional value rather than axing your pricing structure is a must.

Prepare yourself ahead of time with a list of additional features, bonus add-ons, and special offers you can potentially throw in to sweeten the negotiation if necessary. Keep in mind, the higher the value of the solution you're pitching, the more important it'll be to remain flexible.

12.Follow up until you get a definitive answer

Following up is the necessary backbone of any good sales strategy. Having a couple of good sales calls with your prospect, only to let them silently drop off the face of the planet will lead you to fail. I follow up as many times as necessary until I get a response. I don't care what the response is as long as I get one. If someone tells me they need another 14 days to get back to me, I will put that in my calendar and ring them again in 14 days. If they tell me that they are busy and don't have time right now, I will ask when do have time.

The key here is to keep following up. If someone tells me they are not interested, I leave them alone. However, if they do not respond at all, I will keep contacting them until they do. And trust me, they always do.

The point of following up until you get a definitive answer is that you're never leaving a maybe on the table. In the world of start-ups, it could kill your business. You need to strive for extremely clear outcomes with every prospect you speak to. Get the definitive answer —no matter how long it takes or how many follow-ups you need to send.

Tip: Whenever a prospect gives you a follow-up date, make sure you follow up.

13. Highlight risks and opportunities

Many salespeople tend to focus most of their conversations on highlighting all of the potentially amazing benefits, and quick results their solution will give the prospect. Rather than presenting your answer as the sole solution to your prospect's problem, be honest with them about any risks associated with making the switch to your platform or venturing into this new strategy. There is no opportunity without a measure of risk in business, so why try and paint a reality that isn't true for your prospects? That's just setting yourself, and them up for failure.

Instead, focus your sales strategy around proactively identifying the potential risks associated with using your solution.

For example, suppose you are selling marketing software that includes a CMS platform for blogging, and the prospects you are pitching to don't currently have a blog. In that case, they need to be informed that blogging is a long-term investment that typically does not generate revenue overnight. To use your software, they will need to make a calculated risk of investing resources into people who can manage this new responsibility. If you close a client that isn't fully aware of the potential risks associated with what you've sold them, there's a good chance that they may close their account early or request a refund after running into their first speed bump.

Also, take the time to use research, share your own experiences and develop case studies with other customers to meet those risks head-on.

14. Sell yourself

Even if you have a great product that practically moves, if your sales strategy focuses solely on the product, you're missing most of the equation that can turn doubt into trust. Your prospects are buying more than just a product—they are expressing trust in you and investing in that relationship. They are also voting with their wallets and expecting your company to be around long enough for them to benefit from your solution.

Since most of the people you're selling to likely don't possess a strong understanding of how your product works from a technical standpoint, your sales strategy needs to get them to trust you—and your company. Build that trust by being completely honest. Share both the good and bad, stick to your commitments, and show them that you will be an advocate for them long after closing the sale.

15. Develop the right mindset

If you are going to be spending a lot of time picking up the phone, knocking on doors, or otherwise reaching out to prospects over the coming months, you need to prepare yourself for what's coming your way.

- You're going to hear no (A LOT).

- You'll experience that rejection multiple times every day.

That is the reality of being a salesperson or even an entrepreneur focused on selling. What you are selling isn't going to be perfect for everyone—regardless of what you may think. Sure, it will take a degree of product or market education to close most of your prospects. Still, all the education or sales strategies in the world won't turn some skeptics into paying customers. Therefore, you need to develop a mindset of resilience. You need thick enough skin not to take the inevitable dismissals personally, an attitude that allows you to dust yourself off and pick the phone right back up after hearing a hard no. The most painful mistake I see in entrepreneurs is thinking that just having a good plan or a great product is enough to guarantee success. It's not.

——————•●•——————

"Business success is 80% psychology and 20% mechanics. And, frankly, most people's psychology is not meant for building a business."

The biggest thing that will hold you back is your own nature. Few people are emotionally ready for the challenges of building a business.

16. Be helpful

At the end of the day, if your sales strategy isn't built around being genuinely helpful to your prospects, you'll leave many deals on the table. Being helpful throughout your sales process, whether through education, researching your prospect's challenges ahead of time, or coming up with creative solutions to present rather than simply pitching your product, is how you'll win their trust.

The best salespeople have always been helpful. As humans, one of the most genuine things we can do is to help each other. When you are selling a

The 3 Levels Of Trust

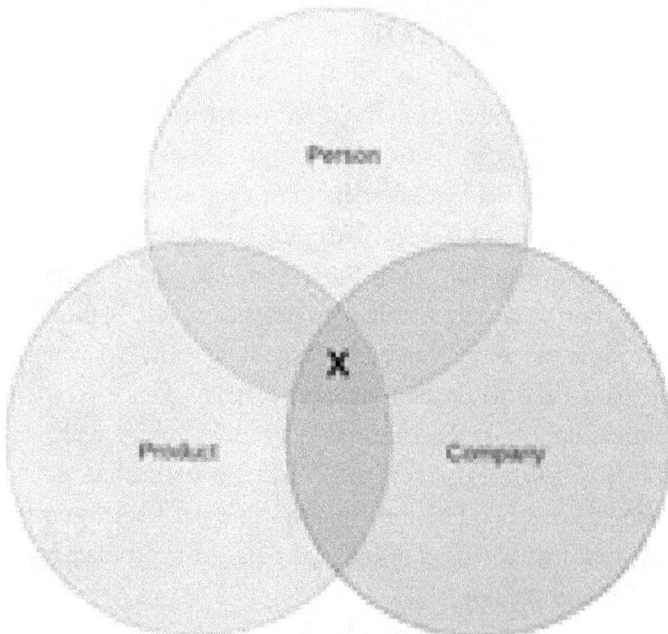

product or service, it's hard to go wrong if you're genuinely looking to help the customer. That's when selling becomes more than just sales. It becomes all about building a genuine, meaningful relationship instead of just selling what you have to someone.

By thinking of yourself as a proactive problem-solver for each prospect you engage with—especially if it's primarily over the phone—you can shift your perception of the role you're playing in the sales process. You don't want to forget your sales goals, benchmarks, and quotas, but if your primary objective is helping your prospects, you'll naturally be leading them to the best solution for their business. If your product isn't the best fit for their unique needs, be honest and point them in the direction of a more suitable solution. That's how you create the foundation for relationships that have the opportunity to continue onward.

A good sales strategy is that in the long-term, there's no substitute for making a positive lasting impression. Don't miss out on a future potential sale because you weren't helpful.

17. Ask for specific referrals
We've all gotten the casual ask for referrals, whether via a LinkedIn message or over coffee with friends, asking you for introductions to anyone that "might be a good fit" for the product they're selling. How often does that translate into new accounts? Not very.

In 99% of these scenarios, the person you ask for a broad referral from will tell you they need to think about it and get back to you—which rarely happens. Not because they don't want to help, but because they're probably busy doing their own job. Unlike when you've got the backing of franchise business to help with marketing and driving foot traffic to your business, if your sales strategy instead requires tapping into your existing network or leveraging current customers to get in touch with new leads, you can get more high-quality referrals by identifying prospects in advance. Check out their list of LinkedIn connections and look through previous companies they've worked with to create a shortlist of strong potential referrals you can ask for.

Eliminate even more friction by giving your connection a quick and easy referral email template, like the one below that they can use to make the introduction right away.

HELLO [FIRST NAME],
I wanted to connect you with Steli, their company does XYZ. I think this could be really interesting for you, and a conversation would be mutually beneficial.

I'll let you guys take it from here,
[your name]

This direct approach of giving your connection to a specific referral candidate and arming them with the tools they need to send that email right away makes it easier for them to take immediate action. You will be well on your way to getting more referrals with this sales strategy.

18. Give short product demos
Giving a product demo that sells isn't just about knowing your product inside and out.

As quickly as possible, get to 'here's what you told me your goal is, here are the challenges you told me about, and here's what it will look like when our product takes down those challenges.

By showcasing upfront how your product will specifically address your prospect's challenges, you're leaving no room for ambiguity. Focus on showing the solution your prospect is most interested in rather than running through a laundry list of product features.

Rather than showing up to your next product demo meeting with the standard prevention you use for everyone, craft your product demo to suit each prospect's needs. This will translate into more closed sales. Personalization is what matters the most. When you're demoing a product, you always want to demonstrate value, not features or functionalities. Nobody cares about your software's features—the only thing they care about is what it'll do for them.

19. Reach out to SQL's within 24hrs of sign up

Once you've qualified a sales lead, engaging them in direct conversation within their first day of signup is very important for keeping the momentum moving in the right direction.

Assume your prospect is also comparing competitor products, doing research, and coming to their own conclusions—based on what they can see about your product from reviews, videos, and screenshots—about whether or not you'll be the right solution.

By employing a sales strategy that allows you to stay on top of your qualified leads and get in touch with them as quickly as possible, you'll be able to answer questions, meet objections and help walk them through the different ways your product will help achieve their goals.

Depending upon the amount of information you have about the qualified prospect and how much interaction they've had with your company, it's usually best to keep your initial outreach email short. Engage them by asking if they have the time to speak on the phone today or tomorrow about a few ways you think you can help them—make it easy to accept by giving a few options for specific times you're able to connect.

Tip: Automate a "hot list" for fresh leads that are shared with your team. Our team does this using Smart Views in Close to make sure that inbound leads get contacted quickly.

20.Address uncertainty when you see it

Let's say you're in the middle of a product demo, and there's been some head nodding so far, but not too many questions from your prospects. You're starting to feel that there's a little uncertainty about whether or not this is right for them, but you're not exactly sure why.

Instead of pushing through your presentation for the sake of finishing up quickly, pause, and use this as an opportunity to address the uncertainty you're feeling in the room. The deal isn't lost yet and demonstrating how your product does what they need can help you recover in this situation. Refrain from asking things like, "Are you getting this?" or "Did that make sense?". Most prospects are not likely to give you an honest answer from fear of judgement from their peers.

Instead, when you're sensing that uncertainty, call it out. If you notice a questionable reaction to something in particular that you just said, acknowledge it by saying, "I feel that might not have come across 100% clear. Would you like me to explain that more?" If your prospects sound relieved to hear a better explanation of how a feature will help them achieve a specific goal, take note and consider these potential changes to your sales strategy moving forward.

21. Use the PAS Framework

According to behavioral psychologist, Adam Ferrier's, humans are ultimately motivated to act by pleasure or pain. The PAS [Problem - Agitate - Solution] framework should be at the core of your sales strategy regardless of what type of product you're selling.

P-A-S stands for problem-agitate-solution. This sales strategy is defined by shaping all interactions with your prospect around the context of identifying their most significant problems and positioning your product as the best possible solution to them—if indeed that is true. Here are the three stages of the PAS framework in action.

- **Problem**: Identify and clearly state the #1 problem your product solves for prospects.
- **Agitate**: Highlight how dangerous the problem is and remind prospects about all the negative implications it can have.
- **Solution**: Position your product as the solution to their specific problem.

It is important to note that the PAS framework isn't about generating false problems or convincing people to buy into your business idea out of misplaced fear. The goal of this sales strategy is to help your prospect identify their problems and make their challenges clearer. This allows you to agitate the problem and explain how the situation can worsen, and what would be different for their business if they could solve it.

If your product can genuinely help your prospect solve the problem at hand, positioning it as the only solution is the natural last step in this sales strategy.

22. Create Urgency

Most people don't buy until the last possible moment—until they absolutely need your product. This makes sense. We have been indoctrinated with mottos like, "If it ain't broke, don't fix it," despite this line of thinking being an excuse for inaction more than anything else. However, creating a real sense of urgency for your prospect is built around the sales strategy to realize why they need your solution right now. If your prospects aren't sold on why your product is vital for them to take action immediately, they'll push it off until the next quarter. Creating urgency is about helping your prospects acknowledge that they need to act now and do something about the area of their business or life that your product can have a positive impact on. This sales strategy is about showing them the understanding you have for their challenges, respecting their needs, and getting them excited to take the leap - today.

Once your prospect is entirely on board with why they need your solution, here are three foundational strategies for creating even more urgency with sales:

- **Limited enrolment:** If your product is new or you are rolling out additional features, frame your urgency around an offer to get them into your limited.
- **Upcoming price increases:** If you're adding more to your product over time, it'll increase the amount of value your customers get. Be sure to announce price increases in advance to existing customers & prospects to encourage quick buying decisions.
- **Custom offers:** Consider offering prospects on the verge of making a purchase an exceptional service, consultation, training sessions, plan upgrades, or short-term discounts in exchange for deciding today.

At the end of the day, there's no better sales strategy than guiding your prospects to a deeper understanding of your product's place can help them, showing them a clear path to that destination. Feeding your prospects words of encouragement and motivational quotes alone just won't cut it. You will need to create urgency without the need for employing flash sales, 24-hour discounts, and other tactics that won't work forever.

23. Sell more to your existing customers

Studies have shown that it's about 5 times more expensive to acquire new customers on average than to retain and continue providing value to your existing ones.

Of course, gaining new customers is an essential part of growing your business. Still, when you're considering piloting new features, expanding into new related markets, or thinking about potential shifts in company strategy, it's easy to overlook the value of selling first to your existing customers. For one, you already have an established relationship that's been built upon mutual trust and value.

Beyond new feature testing, if your existing pool of customers benefits from your product, what are some additional ways you can provide even more value to them? If it looks like they are frequently maxing out on their plan limitations each month, reach out to determine whether or not you can strike a mutually beneficial deal for an upgrade.

If there is a plan with features, you know an existing customer would get a lot of use from, invite them to test it out for a limited time, give them the resources and training they need to experience real results, and help them through the upgrade if it works out.

24. Intelligently use free trials

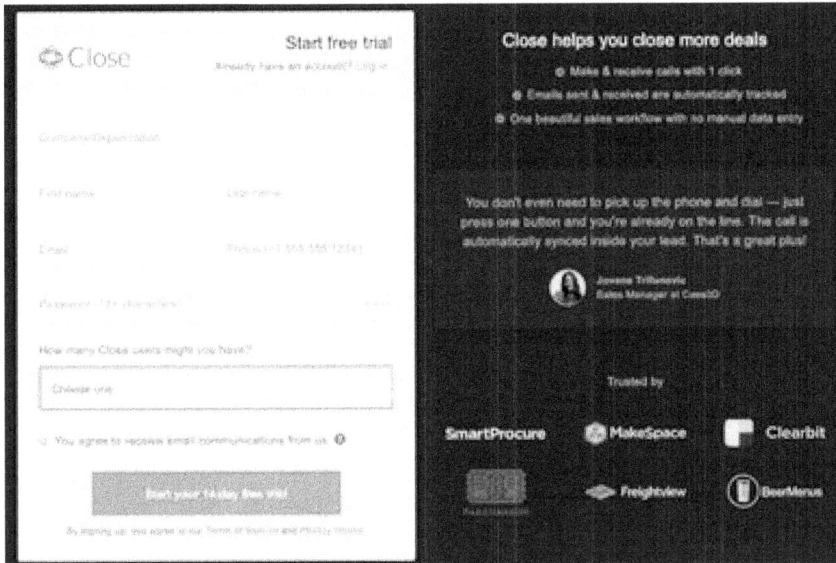

Incorporating a free trial into your company's sales strategy can lead to massive gains in paid signups—if you do it right.

What constitutes a smart free trial? A short one.
The real purpose of giving your prospects a free trial should be to help the right people commit quickly to signing up while allowing others to verify whether your product is right for them.

It's a tool that needs to be used sparingly, which for 99% of start-ups means no more than 14 days in length since usage statistics for most free trials show that only a small minority of people use products for more than three days in a row during trials. By keeping your free trial short (remembering that your goal is to learn more from offering the trial in the first place), you increase the likelihood of prospects taking it seriously and genuinely spending time evaluating your product.

Additionally, instead of just handing over the reins and letting your trial customers poke around entirely on their own (which isn't much of a sales strategy), invest in onboarding. Be sure to create the onboarding flow with a clear, simple goal in mind that will help your prospects get to their first small win using your product. If you can get them to experience real results and begin to invest in your product, their likelihood of conversion will significantly increase.

25. Employ email automation

Email automation will become an increasingly important component of your overall sales strategy as your organization grows. In the very beginning, manual outreach will suffice, but that won't last for long.

From delivering a timed sequence of educational content like free sales courses that introduce your product to new email subscribers to activity-based emails that get triggered when your prospects take a certain action, email automation is ultimately designed to create (or reinforce) the right behaviour for encouraging conversion to paid accounts.

To get started with email automation, think carefully about your customer's journey from first discovering your website to eventually paying for your solution (important: a slow website can lead to frustration early on in the sales cycle with your prospects, so if your site is hosted on a CMS like WordPress, be sure to set yourself up with a high-quality provider of a managed WordPress hosting plan that will guarantee fast page loading and no downtime).

Interview your existing customers to get a consensus on what was most convincing for them to sign up—then construct a series of automated emails designed to get your newest readers and subscribers to experience that same positive effect or result.

At the same time, it's also essential to humanize your automated emails. Your subscribers want to know that there are real people behind your emails and that when they hit reply to ask a question, they'll get an answer. Make your automated emails appear to be coming from a real person's email account on your team and write in a conversational tone representing who you are as a company.

What's your most effective sales strategy?

Whether you are running a start-up of your own, trying to increase your organization's sales effectiveness, or just become a better salesperson yourself, these time-tested sales strategies will help you hit the ground running.

At the end of the day, you can try all the world's sales strategies, but the best way to improve your close rate is through real experience. There is no substitute for emailing your leads, picking up the phone, and having conversations with your prospects. Learn what you can from every interaction and develop an understanding of what motivates your customers to buy or not buy.

Have amazing Customer Support

Customer support is one of the most crucial and pivotal parts of any start-up, E-Commerce, or even dropshipping business. There are so many pressures on new start-ups, from the finances (and seeking third party investment), through product development and delivery, to marketing and sales. Then there's customer support as they come on board with your company and its product(s). Your customer service setup must reflect your company's brand and culture and deliver a great customer experience – so what can you do? And what can you do quickly?

Please Don't Do These!

I always focus on learning from other people's mistakes. It just saves time, effort, and of course, money. Your initial customer service setup is potentially just as important as your product and marketing.

Your customer service will potentially make or break deals and strongly influence the "buzz" created around your company and its product(s). So, please avoid these five potential start-up mistakes:

Simply forgetting about the need for customer service (until it is too late). It is way too easy for start-ups to focus on product creation and then on its marketing obsessively. After all, start-up founders are often "product people."

Under appreciating the value of customer service and great customer experience. Good customer service can often go unnoticed—great customer service, perhaps (but hopefully not). Simultaneously, poor customer service will badly represent your business to your customers, and with social media platforms these days, you want to avoid making your start-up life more difficult than it has to be.

Under-investing time and resources in customer service. It doesn't matter how great your customer focus and customer-service policies are if you don't have the right people and suitable technological assistance to deliver against them.

Assuming that product-focused staff will be able to support customers. This is either that they have the time or have the right set of skills (or both). In many ways, it's the organic result of bullet 1, where customer queries and issues default to product staff who will probably struggle to deal with them effectively.

Thinking that customer service and customer experience are limited to customer support. This is not appreciating that many customers touchpoints impact customer experience – from the customer's initial search for a solution to their need, through marketing/sales and post-sales support, to the customer relationship's cessation.

There are probably many other "easy mistakes" that could be mentioned here, but it's more important to cover the keyways to ensure that your start-up customer service setup is right.

The Importance of Great Customer Service

The quality of customer support and the overall customer experience can make or break any company, let alone a start-up. And for new companies the stories told, and the recommendations offered from early-adopter customers form a big part of the initial marketing efforts.

Thus, neglecting your customer service setup (in terms of customer support personnel and fit-for-purpose help desk software) and providing anything less than a great customer experience from the get-go will have a detrimental effect on your start-up's brand and, ultimately, its future sales and growth. Ideally, your start-up's customer service will help to sell its product(s).

Hopefully, the five potential start-up mistakes mentioned above have you thinking about how easy it is to neglect customer service (as a start-up), as well as the broader scope of delivering a great customer experience. Ultimately, the important thing to remember is that legacy competitor companies will most likely already be employing customer acquisition and retention strategies based on customer experience. A customer will have expectations of support and customer service that go way beyond the product itself.

With experience building tens of businesses and helping hundreds, I have come up with out 10 Tips for Start-up Customer Service and a Great Customer Experience. In addition to avoiding the above mistakes, it is important to proactively address the inevitable need for customer service and a great customer experience.

Ensure that every team member understands the importance of customer service and experience. While your new customer service team might be the very visible face of your start-up's support capability, everyone has a part to play in delivering a great customer experience.

Decide whether to make a deliberate customer experience play. If your start-up understands and values the importance of customer service and delivering a great customer experience, then make it part of the company's DNA and market it.

Ensure that your customer service setup reflects your start-up's brand and culture. It's essential to decide how your customer service setup will operate in terms of customer perceptions. For example, you might want to appear "professional" but not "large-corporation professional." So, understand, design, and deliver the "messages" you want your customer service set up to provide to customers.

Recognize that customer experience isn't just about the right people,

technology, or processes. Instead, getting your customer service setup right and delivering a great customer experience is about creating the right combination of all three. If your start-up needs to move quickly, then the speed of getting started with new help desk technology needs to be factored in too.

Choose your customer support channels wisely. Don't limit the customer-service access and communication channels. These will include telephone, email, self-service/help, chat, and newer channels such as chatbots. Pay attention to, and invest further in, the ones your target customers prefer.

Realize that customer service/support is also a great feedback mechanism. As a start-up, you want to get as much customer feedback as possible. Your customer service setup should be designed to facilitate this.

Don't scrimp on customer service setup costs. Budgets can be tight for start-ups, but if you intend to deliver a great customer experience, it is important to employ suitably skilled and experienced customer service personnel and investing in a help desk that will augment and enhance their capabilities.

Set customer service and experience targets and meet them. Saying that you want to deliver a great customer experience is one thing; consistently doing so is another. This requires a suitable investment in people, processes, technology, and a mechanism to monitor, report, and improve customer service and experience. Then there is the question of where to set those targets – it's ultimately a case of managing customer expectations, so quickly find out what's expected of you!

Plan for future scale. While its crucial not to overspend as a start-up or delay the introduction of customer service capabilities, it's also essential to avoid investments that need to be "thrown away" as your business grows. Thus, while your customer service setup might start small, ensure that it can be scaled as your business thrives.

Take an 80:20 approach. The "Pareto principle" states that: "for many events, roughly 80% of the effects come from 20% of the causes." The important thing is to understand what will make the most difference to the customer experience in your start-up's target customers' eyes.

Choose metrics: As a founder, you instinctively trust the numbers and raw statistical data. To better understand in which direction your business is going, it's crucial to determine correct metrics. You won't have enough time to keep an eye on every metric possible. Choose only the most important ones for your business. Your business needs to review your customer support team's performance occasionally. For this purpose, there were various metrics created that make the process easier. Let's go through the most popular ones:

- **First response time** – the time between a customer submitting a case and a customer support agent replying to it.
- **First contact resolution rate** – the percentage of cases resolved after the first client's contact with your customer support representative.
- **Interactions-to-resolution** – the average number of interactions to resolve a case.
- **Escalation rate** – the percentage of customers that demanded to talk to a higher rank representative.
- **CSAT (Customer Satisfaction)** – indicates your customers' satisfaction, usually on a scale of 1 to 10. You'll need to set up an automatic survey to measure this metric.

Whatever I shared, I tried. This has been my motto for most of my life, especially in entrepreneurship, nothing no ultimate secret recipe. Those who tell you there is a rule are trying to put a frame on the un-framable. Entrepreneurship is an art in the sense that you do not and will not know when and why your amazing idea, concept, or trick will come to you. It is a mixture of so many factors, consequences, and interactions.

Lexyom kickstarted and picked up some steam following our first incubation with the UK Lebanon Tech Hub. That October was pretty rushed with activities, organizing, and working on our products and packages. We were focused on moving to an office, selling retainers to start-ups. I would come down to the office and adapt the lawyer's attitude in everything I do without feeling it. It was a dilemma, a struggle to understand and grasp change, even to the avid innovator I am. 6:00 AM, I open my eyes to a mirror on the roof (I always add mirrors above the bed, it is the best feeling ever). I head from my bed to the kitchen for coffee and the window for 10 to 15-minutes of thoughtfulness. I check my tasks for the day and head to the office. I rarely exercised during that time for no valid reason. However, I still think that with all the adversity involved in launching your business, you tend to get away from exercising the body as the brain moves at a pace that dilapidates all the nutrients and energy you have in stock.

If I were to change one thing, it would be to implement more exercise into my life. My house was around 20 minutes away from the office, and I enjoyed these 20 minutes so much, driving my old black Porsche 96. I would get in, smell the leather, turn the engine on and hear it roaring in the back. The feeling of driving a Porsche is one of the most exciting feelings you could have as a car enthusiast. It is not about the speed, or any other metric. It is about the experience, the smell, the touch, the fear of something going wrong. I drive to the office, get there, and open my laptop to start the hustle.

This lifestyle went on for about 4 to 5 months, and that is also a beautiful thing in entrepreneurship. Your life is constantly changing and evolving. One day you are the office guy, then the travelor, the exhibitor or the depressed founder trying to understand what went wrong in the last week. February came, and with it, the amazing trip to San Francisco and 500 Start-up's batch 23, which would be the turning point in building the Lexyom Team.

6. The Art Of Attracting People & Building A Team

ne of the most important and undervalued aspect of any start-up is talent. Launching a business is not easy; it requires funding, patience, and many other aspects to succeed. Most of the time, when you are looking at a project you want to launch, you are so excited and in such a hurry that you do not assess important features. When I started Lexyom, the first thing I did was meet with several people to discuss it. One day I was talking with R.D, an amazing entrepreneur and mentor, and I realized that the whole conversation revolved around the quality of the product I would be offering.

With quality comes a cost to produce, and in Legal, it requires smart people who are on board to produce and help build the best contracts. After that meeting, I placed a call to my cofounders and shared my vision and dream for a company that would become one of the biggest start-ups in Legal Tech. I also made sure to be very giving when it comes to remuneration and shares. Remember that your cofounders are your family, they are your backbones, and all of you will either make it or break it. I constantly look at cofounders when I am trying to help or mentor start-ups. I make sure to state it if I see that there is no synergy, no chemistry, and no alignment between them.

I remember having a start-up I was guiding for a meeting. They came into my office and started asking me questions regarding their start-up, and I listened. After a few minutes, one of them held his phone and started typing, so I stopped. He turned to me, and I told him, "If you want to look at your phone, please do outside; I am not giving my time and effort for you to be looking at your phone." He stood up and left, feeling offended. This move was part of his start-up's demise, which would fail epically instead of making millions of dollars. The ego can be a destroyer and a blinding aspect of any human behavior.

The most important thing is to surround yourself with loyal, talented, and honest. Trust the people who deeply selflessly love you as they will give you the best advice, the best tips, the best recommendations. Sitting on his death bed, machines sounding in the background in a dull hospital room, a white light hits your brain with rays of blackness making you feel empty and vulnerable. A voice suddenly whispers trying to get a message across, few words that would end up turning my life around, shape the future of my life and the changes I want to implement. The Small whisper turned out to be: "Habibe, khalleh Nadine 7addak" [Habibi Keep Nadine next to you]. The sound of an adoptive Grandfather, René, talking to his grandson during death, muskiness, and the sounds of silence.

This tells you that talent is acquired over time, and the people in your entourage can prove to be crucial to your future.

"Most people doubt their judgment because of time.
They think that if things did not happen the way they
saw them within a timeframe, then they are wrong.
What they fail to reconsider is not the opinion but
the timeframe."

In retrospect, most of your predictions when you are honest and direct to yourself concretize. I saw so many start-ups and influencers and founders fail epically and fall out of the surface of the earth when

I had predicted their demise. When a founder is not always learning, always hustling, being honest, harsh, straightforward, friendly, talkative, wise, result-oriented, charming, flexible, lean, and empathetic as needed, they will not succeed. They will not make the start-up and team succeed. I believe in communicating with others and vetting founders accurately. Also, it would be best if you had a particular "Baggage" to be able to assess founders, i.e., a level of experience, mindset, focus on getting you to the result, and have your brain compute all the information without you knowing about it.

1. Culture is key.

One of the most important factors for attracting talent is cultivating an atmosphere that makes your employees happy to come to work. Look first at what you have to offer a prospective employee. Have you created a fun, engaging work environment? Do you offer challenging work? Do people see a chance for growth and upward movement in your organization? Those are the things that matter to tech talent today.

Build a culture from day 1. Create office norms that make employees feel comfortable. Gusto has a no-shoes office policy inspired by its founding roots in an apartment - making everyone feel more home.

2. Build your employer brand.

If you have a good employer brand, you might not even need to post job openings -- top talent will come to you. What is involved in an "employer brand"? It is simple: having a reputation as a good place to work and providing value to your employees, rather than only asking for value from them.

COPPER COW COFFEE

Oscar Ko

Lillian Meyer

Waleed Mohsen

Eric La

LOOM

Alan Yu

Anatoly Yakovenko

Raj Gokal

Lexyom.

GO

el Alame

Magda-Christina Farhat

Samantha Tran

Jeremy Huff

Talent usually gravitates towards bigger names, so the more you can do to build your brand, the more that talent will come your way organically. Ensure you have a strong presence on LinkedIn, get integrated with your local community, host networking events, etc.

Not sure where to start? There are companies out there that can help you create more excitement and awareness of your brand. Stop being a 'best-hidden secret' and get yourself noticed.

3.Find small ways to stand out from the rest.
"As a start-up, you're competing for amazing talent against larger companies with well-known brands and more resources," says Amanda Bell, Director of Recruiting for Lever. "To stand a chance, show candidates the unique elements of your team they won't find elsewhere."**Partner with**

There are a couple of ways to showcase what makes you unique: maintain a blog with regular update posts about your team, office, company events, etc. This humanizes yourself to potential future employees. When you do job postings, include a blurb about the company, what you care about, and why candidates should want to work there. Emphasize the things that set you apart.

Partner with universities.
Fresh college graduates can be a great addition to a start-up because their skills are current. To get access, set up relationships with top universities and continue to recruit yearly from the same places, both for internships and regular employment. In this way, you build a brand on campus. Creating this pipeline requires focused short-term investment, but you get a long-term payoff.

One of our best tactics is to attack career fairs at universities side-by-side with our legal team members at Lexyom. This was of course before Covid and, now as Covid is ending we plan to restart this. Bringing technical talent allows prospective engineers to ask technical questions and gives them the chance to get to know the people that they may ultimately end up working with. We also typically invite candidates to join us for dinner at these events to get to know them as people and in a more relaxed environment.

4.Emphasize the product itself.
Most people love to work for a company with a useful, exciting product they honestly believe in. You start first with an amazing product and an incredible challenge. The best lawyers want to work on solving the thorniest and most challenging problems.

5.Great talent attracts great talent.
Work culture is not ultimately defined by a blurb about your company's mission - the people define it. Focus on really finding the right fits for your company rather than just accepting the first person who interviews. Evaluate potential candidates for shared values and aligned motivations.
People join us because we have a great culture and because we have exceptional, world-class tech talent. When a prospective employee meets

some of the talented folks we already have on board, they are more eager to join. Great talent attracts great talent, and it's a virtuous cycle.

6.Use the right technology.

When people choose to work in tech, they are usually excited about technology. When attracting valuable tech talent, it is important for the start-up to have technology that stands out to those who will be working with it.

Erin Flynn, Chief People Officer at Optimizely, says that using leading technology brings in top talent. "We've brought in certain technology that only top development talent would know about. Using these technologies in our tech stack has helped us to attract the right talent. For example, we are early adopters of Spinnaker, an open source contiunuous delivery tool, which has been a great incentive for many developers."

7.Show the candidate how they will make an impact.

Start-ups are perfect for mission-driven employees. Here they can make a much greater contribution to the company and customers compared to a larger company. In job postings and interviews, make sure to highlight how their specific role will make a difference.

We show candidates that the problems they solve at Lexyom make a real and lasting impact on people's lives and grow very quickly.

8.Utilize current employees for referrals.

Word of mouth is a great tool, and you'll have the benefit of the candidate being referred by someone you already work with and trust. Do what you can to foster positive word-of-mouth about your company and team. Build a robust referral program that excites your employees and will drive the referral pipeline. I remember several times team members leaving Lexyom and shortly after reaching out to refer someone to join the team.

Picture. My partner, Sister, and Amazing Lawyer @Nadine Imad.

9.Realize that all good things take time.

Hiring tech talent is a lot like dating: there is a rhythm and cadence to the process, and it doesn't happen overnight. It requires both parties to take the time to get to know each other and build excitement and connection.

Once you have made those first hires, lay the groundwork for future success by focusing on having a great workplace instead of just looking like one. Build your employer brand, and loyalty will follow. Remember that attracting talent takes thinking outside the box.

Tools to find talent

There are many tools to find talent and to reach out to them. But what is the best way to get talent? Think about it - talent is found where talent is appreciated, especially in our era. Hidden gems are much harder to find because they have much more exposure simply. The main tools to attract talent are actually branding and vision, from which derives culture & passion. Working on your branding, your start-up's image, the concept of the culture you want to have in your company, and how you structure yourself, will be the best way to attract effective talent.

This said, you would only be able to attract certain personalities at certain stages of your start-up growth. These personalities will differ and evolve as your start-up grows, diverging from day 1 to day 10 to day 100, and so on. When you start your you will logically attract people who trust you, and risk-taking people. You will attract the people who will jump on a train, unsure of its destination. You will attract people who are risk-takers and, therefore, have strong personalities. To add to that if we want to analyze the behavior of these people, we would find that these people tend to be less patient, a bit more independent, and most importantly, are looking for a sense of satisfaction that comes from growing on a personal level. Consider these traits carefully and grasp who you are dealing. Relationships in start-ups are similar to a poker, if you do not understand the people you are playing with within the first 15 minutes, you have already lost the game.

The younger your start-up is, the more you will attract risk takers, more courage oriented, more independent individuals. As you grow and show credibility, more technical, risk-adverse individuals will start to come. This is not to say that the rule will apply to every start-up, but this is usually the direction these things go.

The tools used to attract talent have nothing to do with the software or websites, etc. You want to choose people who can synchronize and work together, people you can trust, people who can relate to you and trust in your vision. Most importantly, who converge on ideas without being the same, because diversity helps a lot. When I started Lexyom, I wanted to build the biggest Legal Tech start-up in the world. Who can I do it with?

I started building the puzzle in the following order chronologically:

Idea —> market —> hq —> team —> budget —> time

These components are mutually correlated, and even though there was a specific order in the way I processed them, this order was not 100% segregated. Every time I focused on one component, my brain would be processing the other components in parallel at different percentage and performance levels. Think of it as different apps operating in parallel and delivering results that would ultimately converge to a result that would build up the idea and the vision you are trying to achieve.

Also, attracting talent requires a lot of effort in conversing with people and building rapport to lead to an actual relationship. The more you build relationships, the more

- Risk takers
- Independence

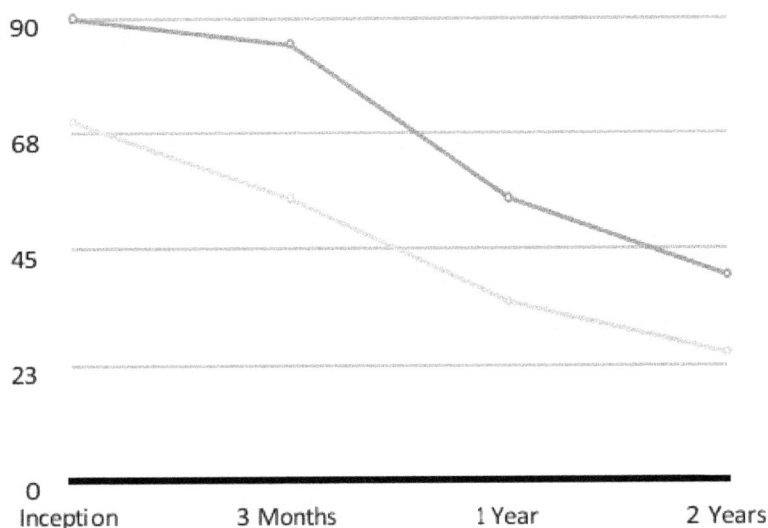

likely you are to surround yourself with amazing people. They in turn, can attract other amazing people and talent to you. The process of attracting talent would go as follows:

- Understanding the kind of people, you want at your side. Creating the exact role with all the boring tasks included.
- Understanding what traits and character is needed for your collaboration to succeed.
- Building a strong culture and vision to attract people to your business.
- Building strong relationships with key people to attract talent.
- Keep building a system to constantly integrate your team

I remember our first hire, G.M. She was an intern lawyer, and she had this amazing aura and enthusiasm to learn. I still remember her texting me over WhatsApp at 11:30 PM on the same day about work-related stuff while she had no idea about the effective work and the tasks. Five years down the road, she is a pillar at Lexyom, and we would not be here had it not been for her involvement. From day one, I wanted to share. I did not care about the money, percentage, or any material thing – just the success. I only wanted Lexyom to succeed, which is why I always remained credible. I care about the success of Lexyom far more than anything else and would prioritize

Lexyom's interest above my own, every day of the week.

My last piece of advice to you in this section is to play the long game. Create and surround yourself with a vibe - a dynamic aesthetic that will lead you to success. Most importantly, use money as a measuring unit, not as a target.

7. How To Take Advantage Of The Startup/E-Commerce Boom To Control Your First Market

We are living in amazing times where the start-up ecosystem, e-commerce stores, and the digitalization of business combined with the transformation of the way we communicate is reshaping the whole business world. You could have a talented stranger set up shop in your market and easily outgrow you with the right resources, team, and strategy. Don't let yourself get too comfortable making a few bucks, be it $10,000 or even $100,000. It could all vanish if you let your guard down. You only stop when you sell your business or delegate a competent team to run it.

When we started with Lexyom, we ran directly after the money and the support. On the one hand, we ran after the money, the funding, and the cash to kickstart our business. We understood quite well the ecosystem of getting funding for the company as we did not want to use our personal finances. We went after grants, competitions, events, and soon enough, we had raised around 100,000 in equity-free funding to help Lexyom grow. Yes, 100,000 USD in equity-free funding.

We then participated in different competitions. With competitions, there are specific strategies and tricks you need to implement. First, you need to try and connect with the organizers in any way possible to either get a discount or a particular spot to promote your start-up or project. The way you go about this is convincing them your project is already the next big thing. This will mostly depend on your character and personality rather than your company. Your attitude will shape the project's image as they are directly and intrinsically related. Think of it as faking it until you make it. At events, I remember going to every booth and listening to pitches, stories, and just getting their vibes to understand the dynamics. It's true when they say dynamics and vibes are the essential things in every environment as they transform into the cumulative addition of all other factors, whether direct or indirect.

The best strategy to adopt is a swift attack into a market that has space for a newcomer.

———————●◉●———————

"Get your idea clear, prepare your marketing in the dark, connect to as many people in your community, and swiftly launch your startup to create this hype that will elevate your marketing heavily increasing your marketing, pr, and brand reach."

There are many things to prepare before going live, however you don't have to finish everything before you launch. Preparation has to be rigorous and coupled with action and determination to be as programmatic and practical as possible. When you want to benefit from the ecosystem boom and the way start-ups and E-commerce are launched, do the following steps in the first week:

- Prepare a one-pager explaining your idea and dream [Vision] to yourself. [FREE]
- Go on any website that sells a domain and search for the name you want - Make sure to pronounce it in all languages you can and see how easy it is to pronounce. Buy the Domain even if you might change it later. [$20]
- Prepare a logo using www.canva.com, www.brandmark.io, or any other website you might know for branding. Buy the logo even if you will change it later. [$50]
- Go on all social media platforms, take all the accounts that match your brand name, and add a profile picture and a description. [FREE]
- Get G Suite or any other email service to have your Email with your domain name. [$5]
- -Buy a Video / Photo editor app subscription [$15]

- -Go back and write your business plan.

You will have started your business in one day with under $100 investment. This will create a brand identity and exposure for your product/service and help you sell to your surroundings, friends, network, and overall connections.

Then, your moves have to be swift. You need to reach out to your entire network, ask them to do a shoutouts, create collaborations and work with as many people as possible. Still, there are also a few techniques we will be covering in the digital marketing section next. Coming back to how to hack your way past your first market, the best advice I can give you is to hit a niche, a trend, a vibe that is going on around you, and move fast. Do not be afraid to jump on social media, in events, get out of your cocoon. About myself, I was a very silent person on Instagram and social media overall. I had created this attitude of a person working hard and not playing around or enjoying stuff. But the opposite is what is needed; the exact opposite is what is required to succeed; What got to me was a very nice challenge that an Instagrammer was doing asking all owners of luxury & exotic cars what they do for a living. The answers were quite enlightening. Most of them were Youtubers, bloggers, Entrepreneurs, E-commerce Owners, Insurance brokers & Lawyers. The competition was done in Los Angeles, so you draw your conclusions.

In summary, the most important thing is to be swift, and network your way to as much as an audience as possible.

My Brother, my inspiration, the most genuine and honest person I have met. The one I learn from in Marketing, Entrepreneur & life, Jad Fakhani, @Wolfofbey

8. Growth Hacking Digital Marketing

This is one of the most important chapters in this book, and you can read it as a standalone section.

My first interaction with digital marketing came in early 2013 when I discovered Facebook marketing's potential and how you could reach thousands of people with only a few dollars. When I was running an election campaign for my father at the Bar Association and had created a Facebook page to promote his achievements, I got an email from Facebook saying I could promote on their site, so I did. It was a revelation because $5 and two days later, my father was getting ads on Facebook like crazy, and at the time, the competition was scarce, so $5 went a long way.

This election was the start of my focus and passion for marketing strategies and technics. The election was happening at the Bar Association. Lawyers would come to the huge central room at the bar, write the name on a piece of paper, and vote. There were 32 boxes divided by age, tranche, and seniority levels for lawyers. Box number 1 was for the oldest, and box 32 was for the youngest. What did you do to make your candidate win, noting that he was 645 years old and was quite charismatic?

Add the fact that based on research, I found out that the ratio of male to female ascending the election was around 70% to 30%.

I did not give you other variables like the age average, confessional aspect, and other factors.

But take some time to think about how would you solve this matter? What I did was

• Brought 50 Hostesses, all wearing a white dress holding brochures with his pictures on the front page.

- 1 Hostess on each Electoral Pole, and nine on each entry point (There are two entries).
- I printed different lists, papers, and distributed pens.

- We have made sure to target young people since we were weakest with the young electorate.

I will not detail further, but we ended up winning by a landslide.

Stop everything and focus

Marketing is the process of getting people interested in your company's product or service. This happens through market research, analysis, and understanding your ideal customer's interests. Marketing pertains to all aspects of a business, including product development, distribution methods, sales, and advertising

Marketing is the process of getting people interested in your company's product or service. This includes market research, analysis of your customer, and understanding your target market effectively to know where, how and to whom you would sell your product/service. But what is advertising then? Advertising attempts to influence customers' or clients' buying behavior with a persuasive selling message about products and services. In business, advertising aims to attract new customers by defining the target market and reaching out to them with an effective ad campaign.

So now we understand that marketing is your selling strategy, and advertising is trying to influence the customer's behavior through ads.

So, what are the main strategies for marketing success? This is a straightforward and broad question. It all comes down to 1 thing:

———————•●•———————

Thinking outside the box

You must understand your product in order to sell it to your customer. I remember back in the days when I used to take litigation cases as a lawyer, and I used to really go in depth into understanding everything about the case, including the character and personality of the person I was defending. I gathered much information and would put myself in the person's shoes and try to understand the underlying motives that influenced the persons behavior.

There was a famous lawyer called "Jacque Verges," who inspired me by his ways and his style. He would defend terrorists like Carlos, Klaus Barbie [NOT THAT I APPROVE DEFENDING THESE CRIMINALS], but he would find arguments to ensure them the "right of defense," which is sacred for any human being. So put yourself on both sides of the coin. This is crucial to understand the real value of your product and what you can get from it. Start by doing the following exercise:

I am selling _____ [ex: Lights, legal services, T shirts ....] for _____ [ex: young married couples, young professionals, entrepreneurs], aged _____ [ex: 15 to 18, or 32 to 39....], living in _____ [City NOT Country], who are buying my product now because:

1. Time wise [ex: People tend to buy legal services at the beginning of every business quarter [January, April, September and less in summer, for example].
2. What is the urge they are fulfilling? Is it a need like coats at the beginning of winter or rather a trend?
3. Why from you? What makes you special for them to buy from you? Is it the brand, the celebrities, or influencers you are working with?

Your quality, mainly if it is handmade or not? Proximity? Giveaways?
Once this exercise is done, we will move to the second exercise, which is drawing your business personae. What does your customer look like? If

you are selling to both genders, then consider drawing a male and a female version. Start by drawing them on a paper and add the following to the table:

Question	Answers		
Where are they	City [Beirut]	Neighborhood	Location [Office,
Home, Car,			
Garden]			
Time	Which Month	Which days	Which Hours do you think they would want to see your product/service
What do they eat	Type of Food	Restaurants or	
Chains they visit	Supermarkets or online Grocery they use		
What do they wear	Type of		
Clothing	Shops / E-Shops they visit	Fashion brands they follow	
What activities they like?	Sports?		
Music? Art?	Celebrities?	Famous Places? Attractions?	
How do they behave on social media	Likers? Silent Profiles?	Comment a lot or not?	Followers ranges?
Marital Status	Married?		

Divorced?	Children?	How many years since Married?	
Question	Answers		
Age	What are their ages?	What generations are they from? Generation X, Generation Z, etc.…	What age tranche do they interact with the most?
What are their beliefs?	Political?		
Economical?			
Social? Causes they defend?	Dietary? Vegan?	Celebrities they defend	
What colors do they like?	Colors? Patterns [You can make assumptions]	Designs? Trends in designs?	Artists?
Architecture? Etc.			
Education?	Which degrees?	Which Schools?	

Once you have done this exercise, it is time to set your strategy. What does a strategy revolve around? It revolves around what you want to achieve and ways to achieve it. Sometimes success is measured with time, and the exact campaign does not have to be a standalone success as per numbers, conversions, and/or impressions. Part of your strategy is to establish KPIs [Key Performance Indicators] and allocate the resources to reach them.

After we have identified our core customers and target market, we need to start analyzing our strategy. It all begins with psychology; Yes, it all begins with a psychological pinpoint strategy. All start-ups and great ideas started from a psychological point.

Look at Facebook, the psychological need was a mixture of Voyeurism, social integration, and the romantic side of discovering personal things about others. Yes, the main feature that shaped Facebook and took its huge step forward was one feature only. Can you guess what it is? I will answer later in the chapter on the one feature that changed Facebook.

Look at Instagram; the psychological need to be different, to create and share your messages, feeling special is the key behind the success of Instagram.

Look at Uber. Do you think it is the need for a cab that made it a success? No, it is the integration between the drivers and the passengers, the social belonging to a group of people using this particular solution called Uber [Branding]. Most importantly, the psychological feeling of freedom and control for the passenger to click for someone to come, and the driver to close and open the app whenever they feel like. However, they sometimes end up working even more than regular jobs.

Look at Google. Do you think it was the search engine? No. It is the psychological will to have access to things, data. It is not at all the actual need that is being fulfilled, and Google understood that incredibly early by creating a super simple user experience and an image of a fun and chill company. Did you know that Google used to pay 1,000,000 USD to eBay to be redirected from eBay to Google whenever they searched for something available on Google? And eBay was so confident that they did it, not knowing it would be a pavement to their demise.

We established that you need to think about a psychological need in your start-up, e-commerce, or any other project, but how do you practically do that?
Let's try it together.

------ If you are selling neckties, what would be the psychological pinpoint? If you are offering a marketplace for architects?

If you are offering a marketplace for tutors?

If you are providing auditing services? If you are selling jeans?

Take a few minutes before reading the answer and check the answer on the QR code.

We have now established:
1. Our brand, product, or service
2. Our Target Market
3. Our Customer Personae [The people we are selling for]
4. The Psychological Pinpoint

If you have not done so yet, go back and read the previous parts. So

After that, you must build your campaigns and marketing overall. To do that, you have to understand what channels and ways you have available to you. So here are the channels and ways you have to market your product. I will lay down the most important, and you can check for other channels that could be niche to your product or service. There are 12 main ways and/or channels to market yourself:

1. Self marketing

To me, this is the most critical part of marketing, and it is what shapes your future, the future of your brand, and your growth.

Self-Marketing is working on yourself to become a channel for your brand, starting with your personal social media, your personal profiles, which should be very, very up to date, and very easily reachable. Choose a unified structure for your social media so people can recognize you and recognize your social platforms and social appearance. Start by adding the same profile picture on all channels, add the same description, the same hashtags, the same categories, and the same profile components without using the same content for all platforms.

Choose a specific design for yourself and branding for what you do. Let us say you want to have this entrepreneurial look with a basic T-shirt, jeans, or pants, etc. If you want to be a stylish, elegant person, you must understand the feel you want to convey. Your talk should be in line with what you do, your looks, presence, the places you visit should be the places your customers are at, or where they want or aspire to create this successful image, they so eagerly desire.

I grew up different, special. I was born very blonde in a Middle Eastern country. This made me stand out at a young age, and at a very young age, you do not realize, you do not assess the depth of situations and integrations. You are facing situations without any background, so technically, you face a binary solution: Integration or marginalization. Getting stared at and being bulled on a daily basis is not easy to accept, so you face a choice to evade and pass or just do the opposite by being larger than life, loud, arrogant, and full of yourself. Think about it this way, when you see someone so arrogant, full of themselves, you are in a way skeptical as to why is this person so confident? Why is this person so full of himself? Your focus diverges towards these questions and a particular interest in this person and what they are doing. So suddenly, you deflect from criticizing, focusing on this person's physique or any weird aspect they have.

Another thing I did was surround myself with so-called "Cool" friends. This is another layer of building your social image, social involvement, and effort to integrate and socialize.

This resulted in the start of this concept of self-marketing, which I had to do and then enjoyed doing. This is the essential part of any human behavior, and I believe the more special and unique you are, the easier it is for you to self-market. Add to that, when you are special, as I said, you are keener on facing binary decisions rather than a multi-layered decision. When you are faced with binary decisions, it is much easier and simpler to pick a decision. Therefore, you are no longer under the burden of complexities when the outcome is either destruction or success in such a drastic way.

Look at CEOs who succeeded, from Steve Jobs to Elon Musk to Carlos Ghosn; they all share the same attributes from communication to an association to reporting to executing. In success, 20% is planning, and 80% is execution, so an average plan with an amazing execution will create great success.

2. Social media

Many social media channels are available for you.

- The Facebook Network:
Facebook, Instagram, Messenger, WhatsApp, and the Facebook Network [Websites dealing with Facebook].

The Facebook Group is a significant player in the social media industry. Using Facebook business manager for ads and the channels to market your product is essential in your business's success.

Facebook
As the movie name suggests, this is "the social network". When Mark Zuckerberg and his co-founders created the site in a Boston dorm room in 2004, it was only accessible by Harvard students. After expanding to Ivy

League colleges and a few others, they opened Facebook to everyone in 2006, and it exploded.

Today, it is the biggest social media platform out there. It offers marketers the most data and the most targeted ads. You can be as specific as defining your customer down to the socks they are wearing. With Facebook Ads, you can target management executives in the Bay area between 45 and 54 who play golf regularly and regularly spend money on equipment (thanks to credit card data).

Context: Facebook gives you a lot of freedom when it comes to content. Images, videos, and text posts all work. What matters though, is that you **integrate your content into the platform as much as possible.** For example, instead of just posting a link to a YouTube video, you can upload the video to Facebook's own platform. You can also go live, share stories, and even shop on Facebook Marketplace.

Try to keep your user on the platform for as long as possible. People trust Facebook, and they don't want to leave the comfort of "their homes."

Facebook Business Manager (Now Called Facebook Business Suite)
If you want to advertise on Facebook, you need to know about the Facebook Business Suite tool. You can think of this as a hub for managing your advertisements, pages, inboxes, and people. Go to the landing page for the Facebook Business Suite. Click "Create Account" in the top right-hand corner.

Enter your business name and click "Continue."
Then, enter your name and your business email, then click "Finish."

You will now see your Business Suite dashboard. Feel free to browse around to get a feel for its capabilities.

This tool is an absolute must for anyone serious about advertising and marketing on Facebook. It will give you a single place to worry about your marketing performance rather than having to jump from tab to tab.

Facebook Advertising Options

Perhaps the best part about Facebook is the specificity with which you can target your ideal customer.

You can choose to target people based on their demographic, device, age, interests, and a load of other characteristics. That's a wildly valuable benefit for any marketer.

After all, marketers take tons of time creating customer avatars and target market portfolios. Facebook allows you to put those things into action. The first thing you'll get to choose when creating a Facebook advertising campaign is the goal of your campaign.

Do you want to drive traffic to your website, drive conversions, promote your Facebook Page, get engagement on your post, or something else? Just select the one you want.

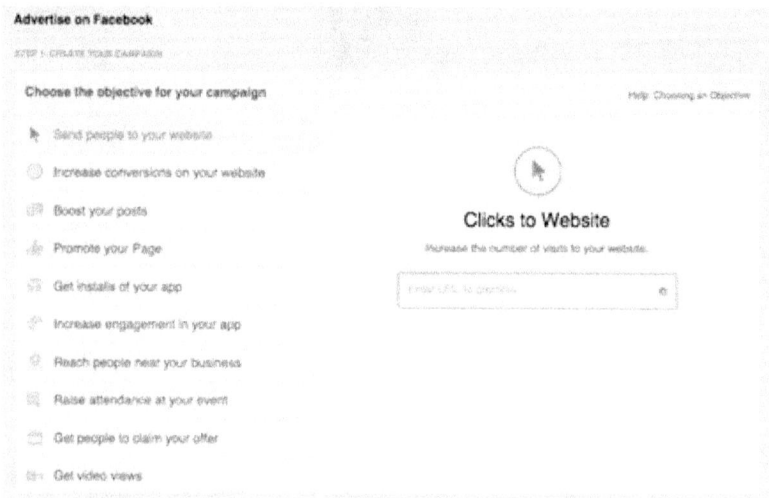

Then, you will also get to choose your audience based on their location, age, gender, language, interests, behaviors, and connections.

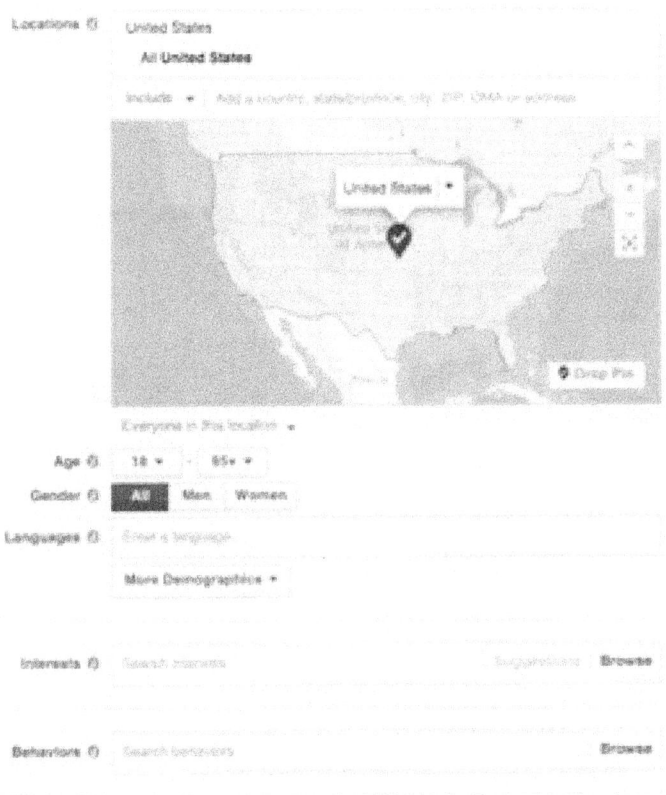

Finally, you will be able to select the devices you want to target and where you want your ads to show up.

Facebook recommends using auto ad placement, but if you disagree, you can just as easily decide where you want your ads to go and what device you want them to target.

Many social media platforms will make these decisions for you. But Facebook puts you in the driver's seat because they know you will likely do the best job of finding your ideal customers. You, after all, know your target market best.

Understanding Facebook's Lookalike Audiences

What happens when you find the perfect audience to target?

You are ranking in traffic and leads like never before. But does it have to end there? Finding your perfect advertising audience can take quite a bit of time, so naturally, you want to make the most of it.

Fortunately, when you find your perfect audience, you can leverage it. Facebook allows you to create lookalike audiences.

Create New   Use a Saved Audience ▼

Custom Audiences ⓘ   Add Custom Audiences or Lookalike Audiences
                      Exclude   Create New ▼

Locations ⓘ   Everyone in this location ▼

              United States

              ♀ **United States**

              ♀ Include ▼   Type to add more locations   Browse
              Add Locations in Bulk

Age ⓘ   18 ▼ - 65+ ▼

Gender ⓘ   **All**   Men   Women

Languages ⓘ   Enter a language...

These are audiences that mimic the characteristics of one of your current audiences. That means that if you have an audience that is performing remarkably, you can create a similar audience that should also perform well.

Advertisers everywhere run to this feature because it streamlines the process of finding and expanding your target market.

Instagram Integration
Did you know that when you create an ad on Facebook, you can also run

that ad on Instagram by clicking a single button?

That's right. It takes you no extra work.

You can simply click the Instagram ad placement button and select "Feed," "Stories," or both.

If your ad is highly visual and your target market includes younger people, you might want to consider using the automatic integration. It will expand your reach with no extra work.

Facebook Live

For a while, marketers have stood in awe of the power of video marketing. At least they did until the live video came on the scene. There is just something about live video that makes it more appealing. Maybe it is the chance that people will mess up. Perhaps it is the transparency, or it makes us feel more connected. Whatever the reason, the fact is the same.

People enjoy live videos far more than they do traditional videos. That's particularly true on Facebook.

Users spend three times longer watching live videos than they do pre-recorded videos.

In other words, a live video might be well worth your marketing time and money on Facebook. It quickly engages people, and they watch it for longer than alternative video content.

Instagram

History: These guys did everything right. They had the perfect app and released it at the ideal time. Within three months of releasing Instagram in the app store, it had reached 1 million users.

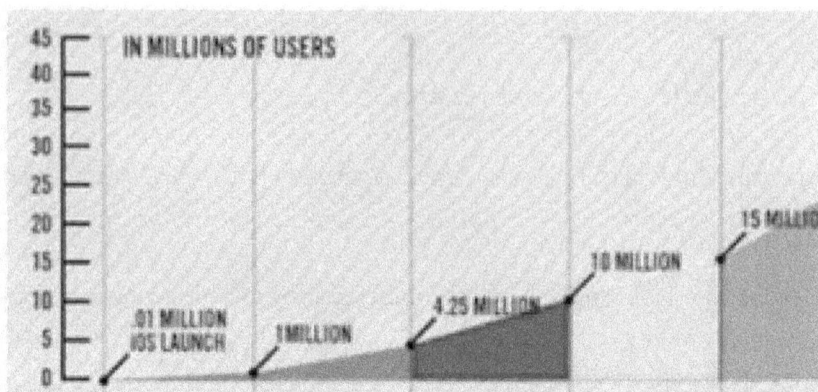

Their growth was entirely organic. The app was so good that it dominated the app store charts for months. And it still does. When the app came out, Apple had just unveiled the iPhone 4. That brought a major leap forward in the quality of pictures that users could take with their smartphones. Seven years and a billion users later, the way the app works is almost entirely the same. People post pictures, tag friends, insert hashtags, and double tap to show they like what others share.

It might seem like nothing has happened, but let's not forget the fact that Facebook acquired Instagram in 2012, only 24 months after they started, for a whopping $1 billion. In 2015, they rolled out the use of ads for everyone.

Context: Pictures and videos. Instagram is and always was about pictures — but videos are gaining ground. Out of all the big networks, Instagram has the highest engagement rate.

Since liking is so easy (you just double tap on a picture as you scroll through your feed), people tend to do it more on Instagram than on Twitter or Facebook.

However, posting a video on Instagram can certainly work, too. Ms. Dash, for example, has done well with videos on Instagram. Her videos routinely collect 3,000+ likes and hundreds of comments within a day of posting. She has amassed just under 300,000 followers because her videos are excellent. Each one shows you an entire recipe in 15 seconds.

Of course, make use of hashtags, give a call-to-action with each photo or video, and make sure that you're using your bio right (it's your only chance to link back to your site unless you have 10K plus followers.). But we will talk more about that below. You can also focus on Instagram influencer marketing.

Influencer Marketing on Instagram

If there is one social media platform that represents the pinnacle of influencer marketing, it is Instagram. The reason for that is difficult to understand. Perhaps it is because the platform is so visual. Or maybe it's because advertisement overloads haven't yet annoyed the user base. Or perhaps the influencers enjoy sporting their content more on Instagram than on Facebook, Twitter, or the like. Whatever the case, Instagram is winning big.

For micro-influencer marketing programs, which social platform do you feel is best for branded content?

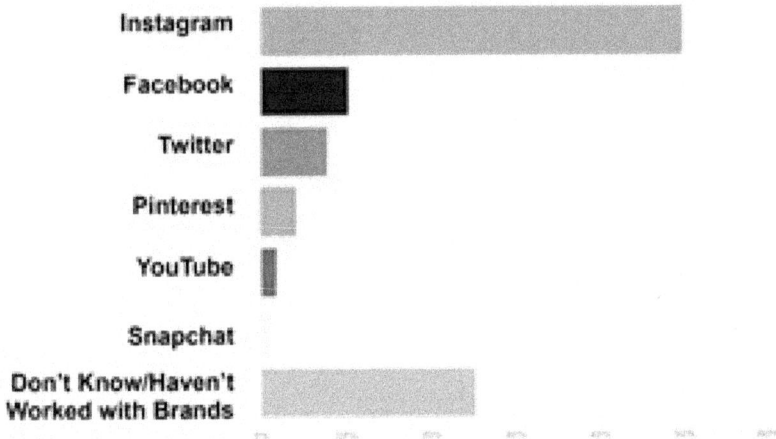

It's no surprise, then, that 65% of brands participate in influencer marketing and it's increasing.

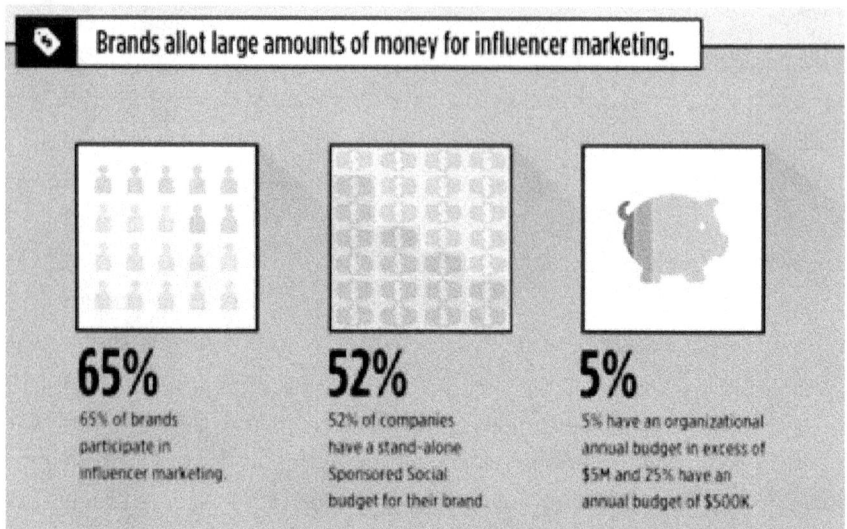

Brands allot large amounts of money for influencer marketing.

65%
65% of brands participate in influencer marketing.

52%
52% of companies have a stand-alone Sponsored Social budget for their brand.

5%
5% have an organizational annual budget in excess of $5M and 25% have an annual budget of $500K.

You might want to consider joining them, and it's not because you want to give in to the trends of today. It's because the influencer marketing trend on Instagram is a powerful one. It is one that you shouldn't easily ignore.

Instagram Stories and Reels
Instagram Stories is a feature that lets users create a coherent series of pictures, videos, or gifs. The feature exploded the moment that Instagram created it.

In fact, in 2017, the number of people using Instagram Stories flippantly passed the number of users on Snapchat, a similar platform. In other words, if you're going to use Instagram, then you should probably create a Story of your own.

Perhaps you should create a Story that shows users behind your business's scenes or offers special deals.

How Brands Are Using Instagram Today
Instagram is awesome and growing in power.

However, an important question is raised. How, exactly, are brands using Instagram? What do they use it for?

Well, the answer to that question is quite simple. They are using it for engagement. Instagram is the best social media platform for engagement. It beats Facebook and Twitter.

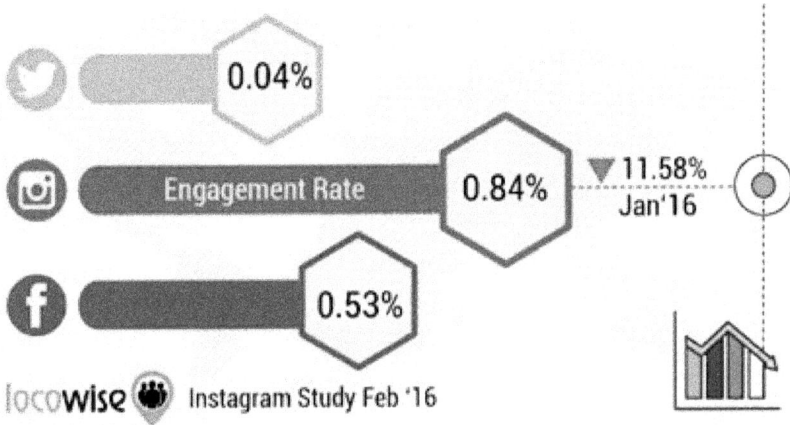

0.04%

Engagement Rate   0.84%   ▼ 11.58%
                              Jan'16

0.53%

locowise Instagram Study Feb '16

Of course, that doesn't mean that you can't sell on these platforms and market your products as well (Especially now that there are features like product tags and links in Stories.)

But trying to push for audience engagement is your best bet. Then, once people learn to love your brand, the will buy from you. On Instagram, though, engagement must come first.

Here are steps to take to get your followers to 10,000. These are recommendations, and do not guarantee results. I try to give you some insight, but I never claim these are the ultimate strategies because experiences differ.

Choose Instagram content that is right for you, for what your audience wants, and what you can deliver.
- Creating content that your audience will interact with, people like seeing other People —> Voyeurism.
- Create a Call to Action —> CTA.
- Develop a Story of Who you are and What you do.

- Choose a Theme for your Instagram.
- Create a community of people you interact with.
- Use Hashtags.
- Tag others, so they tag you. Communities and connections get you the most.
- Do videos, Lives and share your Username in all workshops and conferences you attend or give.
- Be Consistent.

LinkedIn

LinkedIn have been around for 18 years and have grown to over 706+ million members. The strategy that got them some traction was focusing on what worked well. For example, they gave a lot of attention to their homepage, which accounted for 40% of their sign-ups.

They quickly increased that number to 50% within four months (13,000 more people per month), while getting email invitations to increase from 4% to 7% (19,000 more people per month) took two years.

What they always had going for them was being profitable very early. Thanks to premium subscriptions, a paid job board, and a few other freemium options, they were making money after only three years of being in business.

They experienced several key turning points, such as allowing users to import contacts, focusing on the professional San Francisco tech scene, and acquiring and integrating great services like SlideShare and Pulse. These decisions helped them grow into a 7,600-person company that Microsoft bought for over $26 billion.

Context:

On LinkedIn, it is all about being professional. The casual writing style used to make some blogs, including my own, so popular, doesn't work as well on LinkedIn. People are there for one thing only: business.

They want to learn about what is new in their industries, who's hiring, who's firing, and how to optimize their performance at work.

A SlideShare about baking muffins won't do nearly as well as an in-depth company presentation from a tech conference.

If your content helps people expand their networks or conduct business in a better way, it has a place on LinkedIn. If not, you might want to focus on other channels first.

LinkedIn Groups

If you are familiar with Facebook Groups, then LinkedIn Groups shouldn't be hard to grasp. Just think of Facebook Groups but for businesspeople.

Basically, LinkedIn Groups are places for like-minded professionals to gather and discuss interest topics or establish their expertise.

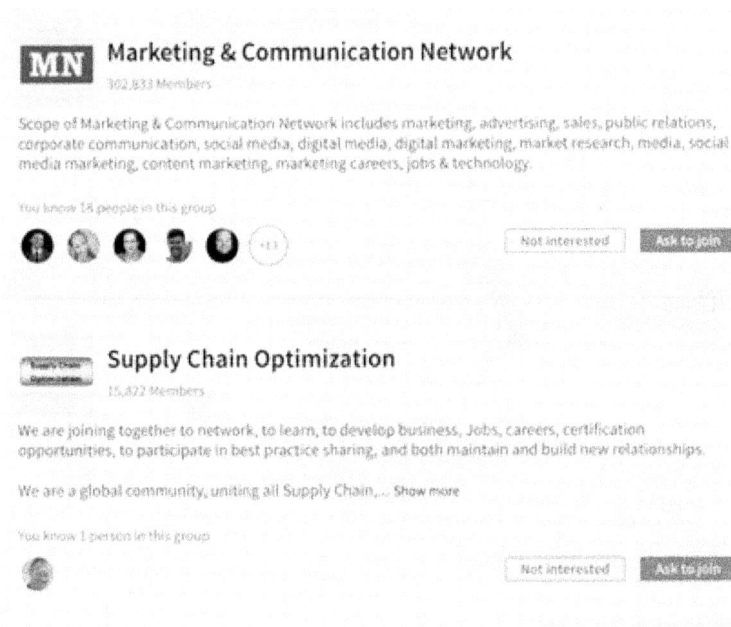

MN Marketing & Communication Network

302,833 Members

Scope of Marketing & Communication Network includes marketing, advertising, sales, public relations, corporate communication, social media, digital media, digital marketing, market research, media, social media marketing, content marketing, marketing careers, jobs & technology.

You know 18 people in this group

Not interested   Ask to join

Supply Chain Optimization

15,822 Members

We are joining together to network, to learn, to develop business, Jobs, careers, certification opportunities, to participate in best practice sharing, and both maintain and build new relationships.

We are a global community, uniting all Supply Chain,... Show more

You know 1 person in this group

Not interested   Ask to join

You might want to consider joining one to establish your business as an expert on specific topics.

After all, the more people that believe your business knows what it's talking about, the more people who will want to work with you in the future. It is an easy strategy for making connections and growing your content marketing audience.

LinkedIn Advertising

As with all social media platforms, you can also use LinkedIn to run your advertisements.

And if your business falls into the B2B category, LinkedIn might just be the best place for your advertisements.

Marketers rate LinkedIn as the most effective social media platform for B2B companies.

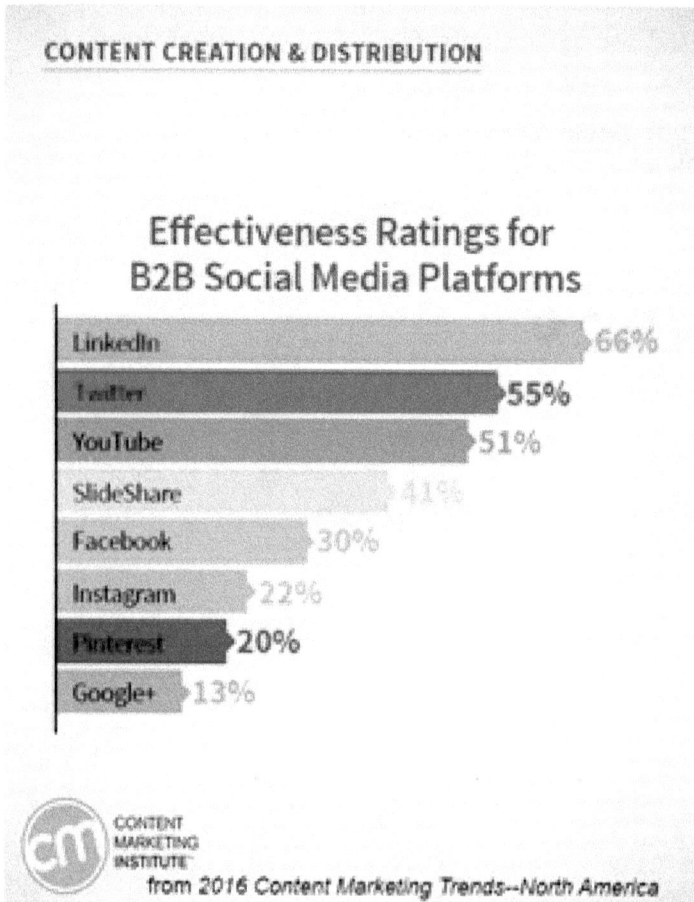

CONTENT CREATION & DISTRIBUTION

Effectiveness Ratings for B2B Social Media Platforms

Platform	Rating
LinkedIn	66%
Twitter	55%
YouTube	51%
SlideShare	41%
Facebook	30%
Instagram	22%
Pinterest	20%
Google+	13%

CONTENT MARKETING INSTITUTE

from 2016 Content Marketing Trends--North America

LinkedIn is also the top platform for lead generation by a long shot.

LinkedIn Leads the Pack

TOP IN LEAD GENERATION...BY A LONG SHOT'   #1 SOCIAL MEDIA CHANNEL'

LinkedIn **59%**

Twitter 28%

Facebook 24%

92%
of B2B Marketers
LEVERAGE LINKEDIN
over **ALL OTHER** social platforms

80%
of leads sourced

THROUGH SOCIAL MEDIA FOR B2B MARKETERS COME FROM
LINKEDIN.

Since people on LinkedIn are there to talk business, they also don't mind interacting with businesses.

That means that your business can get some serious attention on the platform if you play your cards right, and advertisements might just be the way you choose to do that.

REDDIT

Reddit is another college-originated social media site, and is a very special one at that. It focuses entirely on community benefit. In fact,

Reddit's users will ferociously attack you for spamming link bait or dumping promotional links on their boards (or subreddits).

But if Redditors like what they see, they can easily drive enough traffic to your site to crash it. You shouldn't take a Reddit traffic storm lightly. Two key factors that helped Reddit grow to such a massive platform are AMAs (Ask Me Anything) and their voting feature.

Users can upvote and downvote entries, links, and comments. The most popular and helpful submissions always show up on top.

Reddit rewards (or punishes) accounts with karma, which they display separately for links and text posts.

This way, users don't have to dig through tons of content before finding what's good. They can see what's popular at the first glimpse.

The platform took off when celebrities started doing AMAs. During AMAs, Celebrities hang around on the platform for a while and answer user questions live.

People who have done AMAs include Barack Obama, Arnold Schwarzenegger, Tim Ferriss, David Copperfield, and even Bill Gates

Bill Gates
@BillGates

Hi @reddit, I'm starting my #AMA now: b-gat.es/18v4lyl.

RETWEETS 1,338   LIKES 1,640

Reddit requires people to post proof that they are doing an AMA.

Context:

Reddit is tough to crack. You can't use it as another distribution channel and just submit a link every time you publish something on your blog.

You must be present, communicate, and provide value to fellow Redditors without asking for anything first.

Submit funny and helpful links for a while to build up your karma, and then refer back to your content. But only do so where appropriate. Be sure to make the links a side note rather than the entire content of the post.

For example, the e-commerce brand Findlay was able to generate $28,000 in sales using Reddit correctly.

Reddit Marketing Fails

Reddit mostly hates marketers. It's not necessarily the fault of marketers, though. Reddit is just a unique community.

They don't like people who are too blatant in their marketing, and they don't like businesses trying to be pushy. For that reason, even some of the top businesses have made massive mistakes on Reddit.

The CEO of a large outdoor gear retail chain started an AMA on Reddit, hoping to generate brand awareness. Here's what he got instead.

[-] Cnotabua 262 points 2 years ago

I'm sure you don't know this, but the snake bite kits that you sell actually have been proven to make the situation worse and cause more damage to the victim. I realize they may be a profitable item, but would you consider removing them from the shelves? It seems contrary to what REI feels like to have harmful snake oil for sale. Removing these could literally save lives.

The study I'm citing is by Dr. Sean Bush at Loma Linda, one of the leading experts in the world on North American viper treatment. These bite kits are also recommended against in any modern bite protocols, and advised against by the CDC.

http://www.doctorross.co.za/wp-content/uploads/2009/01/bush-sp-snakebite-suction-devices-suck-emerg-med-clin-n-am.pdf

Thank you for considering.

And look at this response.

Take some time to understand the audience before you start using the platform to advertise and market. Once you understand Redditors, though,

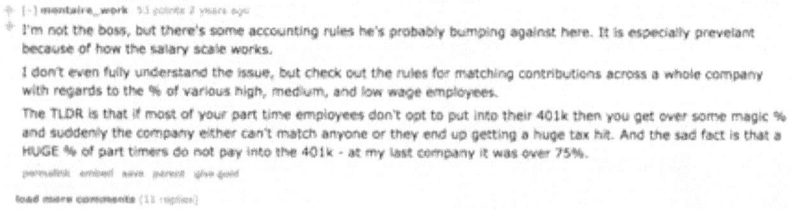

the platform represents a well of marketing potential you won't be able to pass up.

Reddit Ads

If you don't want to grow an organic following on Reddit, you can consider simply posting ads on the platform.

First, though, you will need to determine if Reddit is the right place for your advertisements. As we already discussed, advertising done wrong can hurt instead of helping your business. Make sure that you know what you're getting yourself into first. Here's some help in terms of demographics.

The platform consists primarily of males under the age of thirty. And users highly discourage content that is too salesy.

Is your business a fit for Reddit?
If so, then you can create an ad and see how it performs.

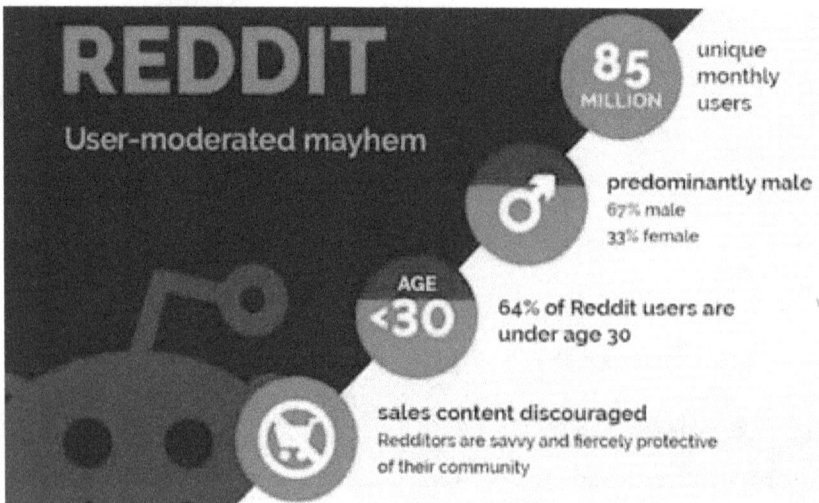

Is your business a fit for Reddit?
If so, then you can create an ad and see how it performs.

Watch it carefully, though, so that users don't bombard you with hateful comments and hurt your brand image before you're able to respond. If you are going to run ads on the platform, then be ready to respond to some serious heat. But if you live through the heat, you could harness some serious potential.

Snapchat
Snapchat has 238 million daily active users. While most of those are female (about 70%), the males who share on the platform have one thing in common: They're young.

71% of the users are under 34 years old. The hacks and spam and naked selfie scandals might easily distract the average adult because this is one serious platform for marketers.

Though the app has only been around for a few years (since September of 2011), it is worth around 1.7 billion dollars. (Though there is some disagreement amongst sources).

Context: If your products target 14-year-old girls and you are not on Snapchat, you are doing something wrong. However, even if you are on the platform, it's easy to do many wrongs.

Since all images and videos disappear after 10 seconds max, the context suggests that all content on the platform is fleeting and short-lived.

Naturally, it makes sense to provide content around that same theme. For example, you could give your audience access to a live event. If you're giving a talk at a conference, take a few snaps when you're on stage and share them with your followers.

Bill Russell & Finals MVP Kawhi!

Let them behind the scenes. Show them the happy hour on Friday at the office, the IPO party, and even how you act when you are alone at home. You could show them your practice run of the speech, how you screwed up your makeup, or what cool car picked you up from the airport.

Snapchat is all about sharing those precious moments that we all have so few of in life, so make sure that you use it for just that.

B2B Marketing on Snapchat
Can you market your B2B company on Snapchat? Some people think you can't.

After all, a large portion of the current Snapchat user base consists of teenagers or younger. But don't let that young audience deceive you. As the platform finds its footing in the digital world, older populations are flocking to Snapchat.

One entrepreneur uses the platform to offer regular advice to other entrepreneurs.

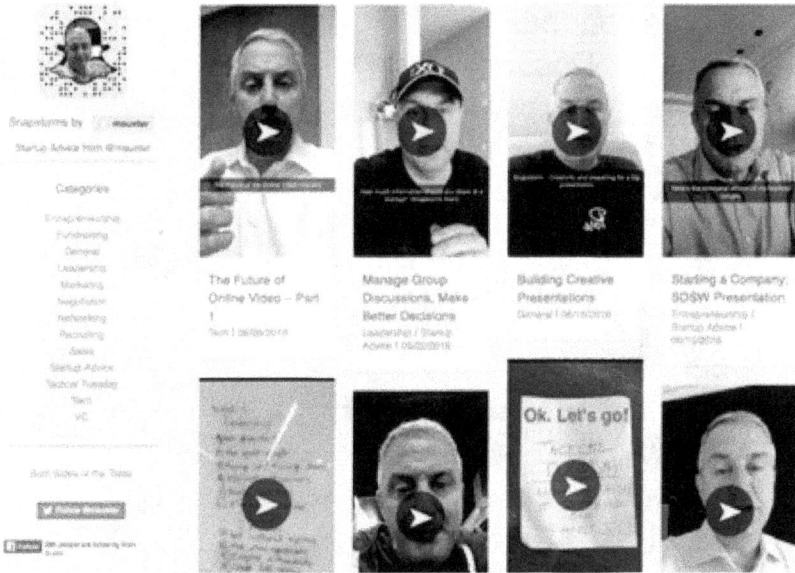

And HubSpot uses it to increase and establish its brand's personality.

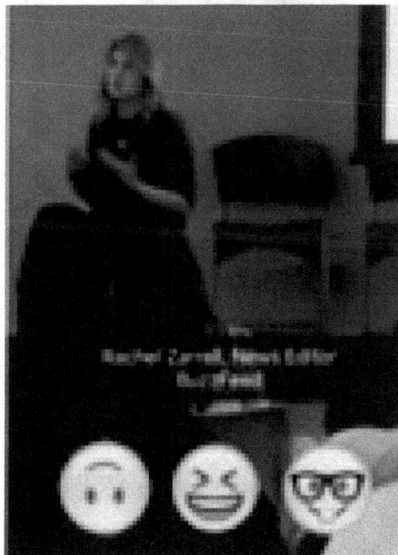

And DocuSign used it to interact with people during a conference.

So yes. You can use Snapchat to market your B2B company. Plenty of other businesses are doing it, and you can do it too. Of course, Snapchat requires a bit more creativity on your part than other platforms. Keep in mind that users can only view your images and videos once.

That should at least partly define the type of content you put out. Plus, that restriction can also work in your favor.

Since all your content is temporary, people might be more inclined to view your snaps while they can and fully take in the content.

Once they do, it goes away.

Pinterest
Between their closed launch in 2010 and 2012, you needed an invitation to get on the platform, so it's only been open to the public for five years. Nevertheless, the leads you acquire from Pinterest are high-quality.

And from funding round to round, they increased their valuation. Today, the social media app is publicly traded with a debut market cap of $12 billion.

Even though Pinterest doesn't yet make any serious money except for a few ads for famous brands, they are one of the **top ten most influential social platforms** right now.

That is one of the most popular boards on Pinterest.

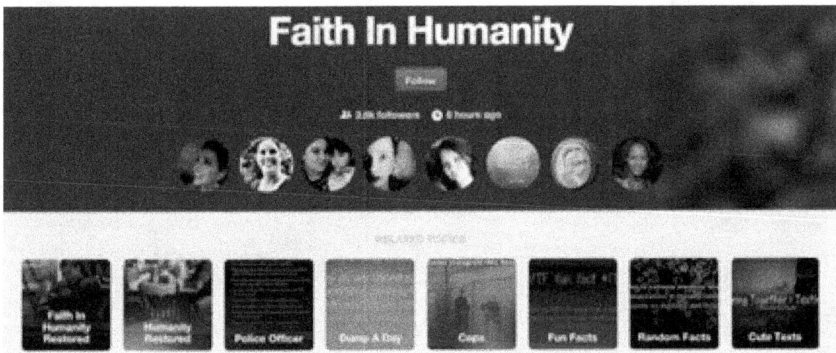

Context: Always, always, always remember that 71% of the audience consists of women. They collect, they curate, and they share. Topics like decorations, interior design, cooking, and clothing do extremely well. Pinterest is also one of the only platforms where images look best when you display them vertically due to the pinboards' nature. Keep in mind that your pics need special formatting to look good on Pinterest.

Influencer Marketing on Pinterest

If Instagram is the god of influencer marketing, then Pinterest is this god's son (or, more appropriately, his daughter).

Since Pinterest allows users to market within whatever niche they like, influencers flock to the platform like hotcakes at IHOP. But that is a good thing for your business.

Since you are a marketer within a specific niche, you can use those influencers for advertising your product to their existing audiences.

Growing your own audience takes a ton of time. And maybe you don't have a ton of time. In that case, influencer marketing is your answer. Here's a Pinterest account that puts out recipes, for instance, with almost four million followers.

And here's another influencer who posts about everything from recipes to decorations and fashion.

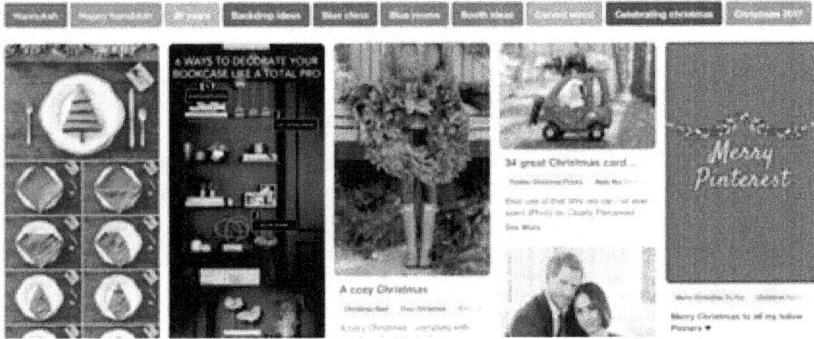

There's a niche for everything on Pinterest. That further means that there's an influencer for everything.

Pinterest Ads and Buyable Pins

Of course, not everyone will want to go through the hassle of finding, talking with, and hiring influencers.

Some of you will simply want to run advertisements on the platform and get on with your lives.

In that case, remember that the vast majority of people on Pinterest are women. For some of you, that is a good thing. For others of you, not so much.

However, despite that gender-leaning, Pinterest is a remarkable platform for getting people to buy your products.

93% of users use Pinterest to plan their purchases, and 96% use it to gather product information.

Pinterest Statistics

93% Pinners — Use Pinterest to plan purchases

96% Pinners — Use Pinterest to gather product information

87% Pinners — Have decided to purchase because of Pinterest

100 million
Average Monthly Active Users

...and growing.

—————— Pinterest drives **7.17%** of all social media referral traffic ——————

goecart

And the best part is that the ads fit right into the boards seamlessly. Here's an ad you probably wouldn't have noticed if I hadn't highlighted it. If you have a product for highly visual women and you don't want to deal with influencers, then Pinterest ads are your solution. Run them and see how it goes.

TikTok
TikTok, a Chinese video-sharing app, first launched in 2016. Unlike other social media apps with humble roots in basements or dorm rooms, the company results from two different apps merging. Today, the app has more than 800 million active users around the globe.

TikTok users share short video clips of themselves dancing, lip-syncing, or sharing thoughts about politics and social justice matters. The app stands out due to the number of interactive features, such as filters, music, and editing capabilities that allow users to be incredibly creative.

TikTok Controversy
The Chinese-owned app is viral in the US, particularly among Gen Z.

TikTok Marketing

Why consider marking on this highly popular video app? For starters, competition is low. Most businesses aren't bothering with it yet — and ads are still quite affordable.

The newish platform is also a great place to get creative and try out fun strategies that might not work on more elevated platforms, like LinkedIn. Are you considering diving into the world of marketing on TikTok? Here are a few ways to leverage the platform.

TikTok Marketing Videos

The most straightforward way to market on TikTok is by creating exciting content related to your brand.

For example, you could create short how-to videos about topics related to your brand. Use a keyword research tool like Uber, suggest to find topics your audience cares about, and then create short, snappy videos for TikTok.

You could also use the fun style of TikTok to introduce your team members, show off your headquarters, or highlight the features of a new product. Consider using the platform's interactive elements, such as polls.

Influencer Marketing

If you want to improve your engagement rates, consider working with established TikTok influencers in your market. The average US influencers on TikTok have a 17.99% engagement rate, making influencers a powerful tool for brands.

To find influencers, use the search feature to look for hashtags related to your industry and look for users posing high-engagement content.

You can also use the Influencer Marketing Hub's free influencer search tool. Just type in a topic of interest, and the tool will provide a list of up to 10 relevant influencers.

Free TikTok Influencer Search Tool

We can now offer you a simple way to find TikTok influencers in a niche. All you need do is enter your topic of interest, and possibly a location if that matters to you, and our tool will come up with a list of ten relevant TikTok influencers.

TikTok Ads

TikTok gives brands four different options for paid ads: brand takeovers, native ads, branded lenses, and hashtag challenges. Before diving into these, you will want to understand the differences:

- Brand takeovers: Exclusive category takeovers that show up in users' feed before any of the accounts they follow.
- Native ads: Similar to boosted posts on Instagram, these ads give your posts a wider reach.
- Branded lenses: Design and promote a filter related to your brand, similar to Snapchat's sponsored lenses.
- Hashtag challenges: TikTok is known for sending viral challenges. Hashtag challenges allow the brand to use banner ads to improve challenge visibility.

Why TikTok Marketing?

Many business owners haven't taken the time to figure out how TikTok can work as a marketing tool. Perhaps this is because they think the platform only has a "young" user base.

However, TikTok is now attracting a wide range of people. In fact, nearly 38% of TikTok's users within the US are above 30.

The low business competition presents a massive opportunity because you can reach many people at a relatively low cost.

But should you use it for your business?

How Does TikTok Work?
Before we talk about how you can use TikTok, let us quickly cover how the platform works. The platform is based around videos that max out at 15 seconds and can be combined for up to a total of 60 seconds. People interact with videos by scrolling through.

One of the cool things about TikTok is it allows people to add all sorts of editing effects and background music to their videos. This has resulted in lots of dance videos going viral on the platform.

When it comes to interacting with videos, people can "like," comment, or share the videos they like with other users through direct messages, SMS, and other apps.

Engagement figures are exceptionally high on the platform. According to one study by Influencer Marketing Hub, TikTok beats all other platforms for engagement levels across accounts of all sizes.
TikTok is also great at keeping people on the app, as users typically interact with it 45 minutes a day.

If you have a TikTok profile, people can follow your account and set up notifications, so they're alerted whenever you post a video.

The tricky part is working out how to create the kind of content that resonates with TikTok users. After all, the content and style of TikTok content are different from those on other social media platforms.

If you use the platform as an observer for a week or two, you'll be able to develop a feel for things. This may then make things much easier when you use the platform as a marketing channel.

Create TikTok Marketing Videos
The simplest way to create videos is by logging into the TikTok App and clicking on the "plus" sign shown in the image below.

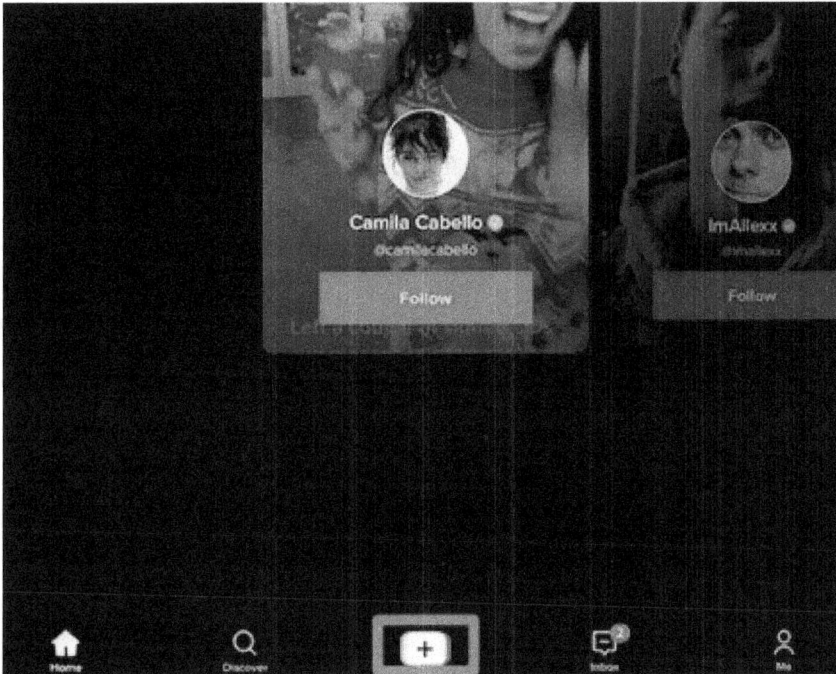

Once you do this, you will then see the screen that allows you to record videos. As mentioned earlier, you can record a short video or combine videos for a maximum of 60 seconds. If you look in the upper right corner, you find options to tinker with the recording settings. If you experiment with certain features, such as the "speed" option, you can make your videos even more unique.

As you might have guessed, the effects feature allows you to add cool animations to your videos.

There are lots of effects that use "augmented reality" technology. With these effects, you can make it seem as though you're interacting with virtual items, and you can also change your appearance.

Once you have recorded a video, you then have access to a "postproduction" area. You can add additional effects to your videos in this area, such as voice effects and filters.

At the bottom of this screen, you can customize your videos even more. Once you have completed this post-production phase, you can then go through the upload process.

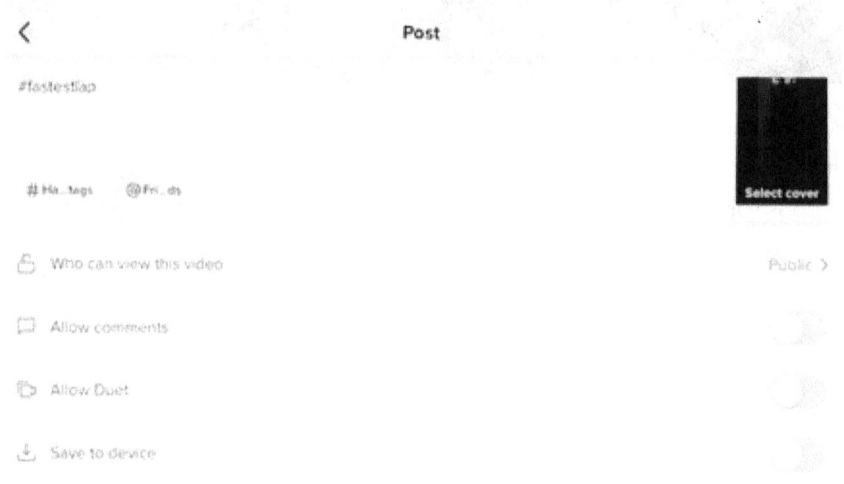

There is a section allowing you to add some hashtags to your video. You can also choose a "cover," which gives your viewers a preview of what they are about to see.

The hashtags you select can have a significant impact on the "discoverability" of your video. You should try to choose hashtags representing your video's theme or central ideas.

Additionally, the cover you choose can significantly impact the likelihood of someone viewing your video. You should select a cover image that represents one of the most visually striking moments in your clip. Once you are done with all of this, you can click on "Post," and the video will be added to your library.

You can also automatically share your video with other social media platforms.

You should enable this, so your existing social media followers are aware of your presence on TikTok. This is important, as these individuals may interact with your content directly on TikTok, which could result in the platform's algorithm recommending your video to others.

How to Create Interesting TikTok Marketing Content
Succeeding with TikTok comes down to creating exciting content. If you can do that, people are more likely to watch and engage with your videos, resulting in the algorithm putting your content in front of more people.

Perhaps the easiest way to create exciting business content for your TikTok profile is by adopting the same approach you would use when coming up with blog post ideas.

If you wanted to create engaging blog post content, you'd first need to think about some of the problems or topics that interest your target audience.

If you don't know how to identify problems or interests, ask! Your existing audience may be excited to share some of the issues they're struggling with or what they want to learn more about. Alternatively, you could look at some of the common questions your audience is asking on popular forums dedicated to your niche.

The "autosuggest" feature within Google Search is another way to develop good content ideas.

Suppose you know your audience wants to learn about Instagram marketing. If you Google "Instagram marketing tips," you'll see a list of search suggestions related to this topic.

You can use these suggestions as a source of inspiration when creating your TikTok videos. You can also search for ideas from your ideal keywords through an SEO tool like Ubersuggest.

All you need to do here is type in a broad keyword associated with your chosen topic.

Once you do this, you will see a Second that allows you to view content ideas.

If you use a few variations of a given keyword, you may come up with a vast number of ideas. Aside from informational content, you might want to create humorous content as well. This kind of content can work well on TikTok since most people use the platform to have fun.

An example of humorous content might be a joke about your industry that your target audience can relate to.
If you find it challenging to create humorous content, think about using lots of effects when recording your videos.

For instance, you could use certain filters or songs for nearly all your videos. In doing so, you may make your informational videos more engaging, even if the content itself is serious.

Use the Right Hashtags for TikTok SEO

If you want people to find your content on TikTok, you need to put some thought into TikTok SEO. TikTok SEO simply means you're optimizing your content, so people see it when they're using the search feature on the platform.

Perhaps the easiest way to go about this is by using relevant hashtags whenever you post a video.

If you don't know what hashtags you should use, type in a relevant, broad keyword within the search section on TikTok. When you do this, TikTok will suggest a range of hashtags associated with what you typed.

If you want to reach a broad audience, you might use relatively generic hashtags. A generic example of the hashtag shown above might be "#socialmediamarketing" or "#smallbusinesstips."

There isn't a limit to the number of hashtags you can use for a video. However, your hashtags will appear in your video's caption, and captions are limited to 100 characters.

Therefore, you might just want to focus on roughly two to three hashtags, as this will give you some space to write a description for your video.

Partner With Other Creators Through TikTok Marketing Campaigns
If you are struggling to build a following on TikTok, you might want to think about partnering with relevant creators on the platform.

For instance, if you are in the digital marketing niche, you may want to create videos with other people within this field that have more followers.

You can find these individuals by searching for relevant content on TikTok.

When you come across someone who looks as though they would be a good fit, send them a short, friendly message letting them know you are interested in partnering.

This can be a bit of a numbers game, so it might be a while before someone takes you up on your suggestion. That said, as your follower count begins to grow, you may find more people are willing to partner with you because the benefits of doing so are now greater.

TikTok Ads

TikTok ads are another great way to market your business on this platform. One of the TikTok ads' benefits is you don't have to spend a lot of time building an audience. You set up an ad campaign, and you'll be able to reach your target audience—often within 24 hours. TikTok offers five different kinds of ad products:

- In-feed ads
- Branded hashtags
- Top view ads
- Branded effects
- Brand takeover

Many small businesses find in-feed ads to get the best results. Plus, the other ad products are typically only open to companies that have sizable advertising budgets. If you want to set up in-feed ads, you first need to create a TikTok ad account. After doing so, click on "Create an Ad." At the end of the signup process, you don't end up with an ad account right away—you'll need to wait until TikTok reviews your application. Once it's reviewed, you should receive an email telling you whether you've been given access.

With in-feed ads, your videos typically have to follow the same rules as "normal" content, so the video can't be longer than a combined sixty seconds.

That said, TikTok recommends you make your ads run between nine and fifteen seconds in length.

Additionally, when setting up in-feed ads, you can select from several different advertising objectives.

You'll also have access to relevant features after you pick the appropriate advertising objective.

For instance, if you use the "App Installs" objective, you can provide people with a direct link to your app store page.

When it comes to targeting TikTok ads, you typically have two options:
- Interest targeting
- Behavioral targeting

Interest targeting works similarly to Facebook ads. If you're using this targeting method, you select an interest relevant to your target audience, and TikTok will show your ads to those people. Behavioral targeting allows you to target people based on their behavior on TikTok within the past seven or fifteen days.

With this method, you simply select a particular behavior and a video category this behavior applies to. By using this method, you can reach people who are actively engaging with the TikTok platform.

It's also worth noting TikTok offers "custom audience" and "look-a-like audience" targeting.

With custom audience targeting, you're able to target people who have already interacted with your brand. This can include interactions both on and outside of TikTok if you provide TikTok with a customer email address list.

The graphic below highlights some of the options you have if you want to use custom audience targeting.

Create a Custom Audience

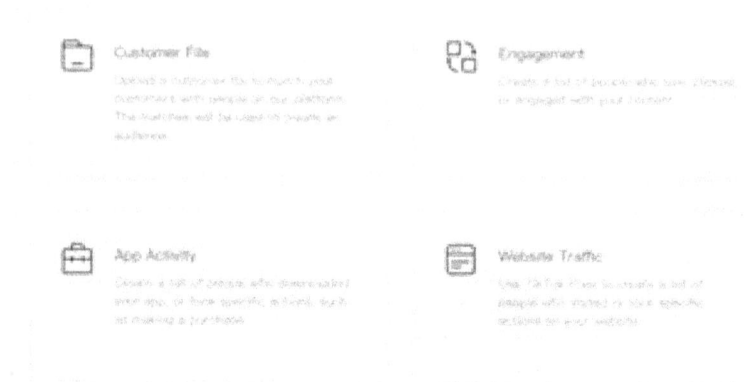

Customer File

App Activity

Engagement

Website Traffic

As mentioned, there is also something known as lookalike audiences. With this targeting method, you can reach people similar to an existing audience.

This targeting method works well if you find the other targeting methods are starting to deliver subpar results.
If you don't know how you should create your TikTok ads, consider visiting the "Inspiration" section on the TikTok website.

In that location, you'll be able to see examples of ads that have produced excellent results. If you click on one of these ad campaigns, you'll be able to see how the company went about creating a winning TikTok marketing campaign. You can then use this information to help you create a winning campaign of your own.

TikTok Influencer Marketing
According to recent stats, nearly 86% of marketers have used influencer marketing to generate sales or brand awareness.

Influencer marketing is popular because it can be one of the fastest ways to generate results on a social media platform. However, sifting through influencers can be difficult, and it's not easy to work out whether a particular influencer will deliver good results. To address these issues, TikTok has developed the "TikTok creator marketplace." If you join this marketplace, you will see the metrics associated with a given influencer.

Audience Demographics

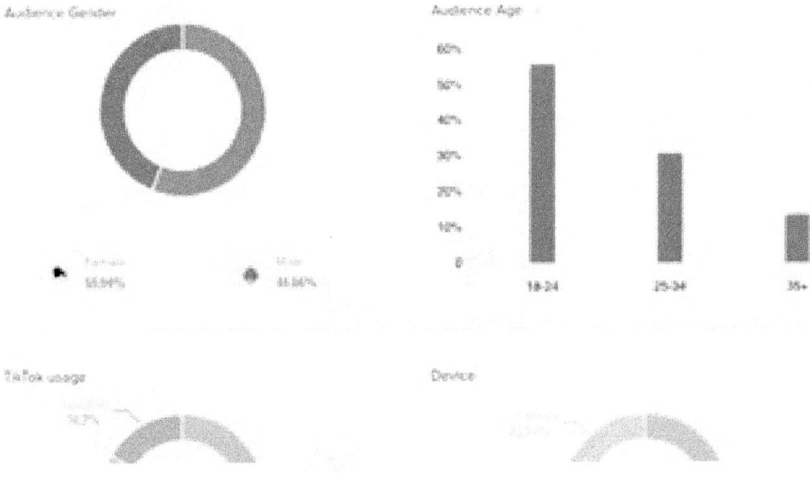

With this data's help, it may be a lot easier to determine if an influencer is right for your product/service. This may help ensure a good ROI if you embark on an influencer marketing campaign. If you want to join this program, you will need to go to the creator marketplace and sign up for an account. TikTok will then notify you if it accepts your application.

How to Get TikTok Marketing Analytics Data

Analytics can be a big help, no matter what platform you're using for digital marketing campaigns. In fact, two out of three marketers state their decisions based on data outperform their choices based on "gut feelings."

If you want to get detailed analytics data on your TikTok videos, you need to upgrade your TikTok account to a "pro" account. This doesn't cost anything.

All you have to do is go to the "Privacy and Settings" section on the app, click "Manage my account," and you should see an option allowing you to enable the "pro" upgrade.

Once you click on this option, select a "category" to gain access to an analytics dashboard like the one shown below.

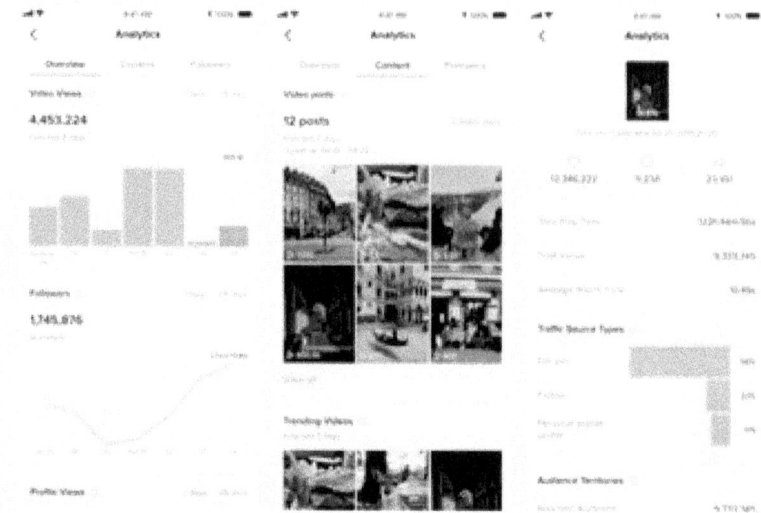

If you keep a close eye on this data, you should identify what is and isn't working in your content creation. You can use these insights to improve the way you create content in the future.

One of the interesting things about the analytics section is you can access something known as "Followers Analytics."

This section gives insight into your followers, such as what your audience is watching (aside from your content) and when they're most active. This information can also be used to inform your approach to content creation and the times you decide to post new videos.

If you are using TikTok Ads, you can use this information to help you do a better job targeting your ads.

TikTok Marketing Best Practices and Examples

Now let's talk about some best practices regarding TikTok marketing and some examples that show these practices in action. First, we're going to touch on the best time to post your content on TikTok.

The jury is still out on whether there is a specific time that works for everyone. Some experts feel you'll get the best results if you post between 10 AM and 6 PM. That said, this isn't universal.

Over a given week, post videos at varying times to see what works best. You can then review your engagement stats at the end of the week, and this could give you a sense of what works best.

It's also a good idea to create a detailed bio so people have some context on who you are.

You can use the bio to encourage a certain kind of action, such as joining your email list or following your account.

If you want to add a link to your website, you should use the dedicated website section in the "account preferences" area.

This will allow you to insert a clickable link right beneath your bio without sacrificing word count.

You should also link to your other social media profiles, as doing so might allow you to grow your followers on other platforms. Another TikTok best practice is to jump on trends.

Often, you'll find there's a specific hashtag trending on TikTok. If you make a video based on this hashtag, there is a better chance your video will reach a broader audience.

The easiest way to find trending hashtags is by going to the "search" section on TikTok, also known as the "discovery page."

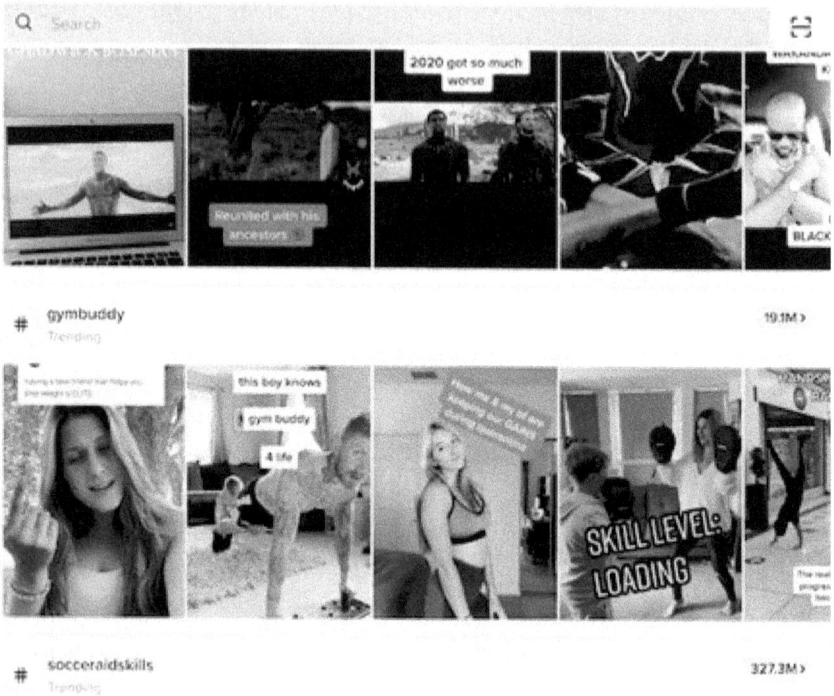

TikTok is an excellent method of earning user-generated content (UGC), which shares social proof while giving your customers a voice. Even better, it opens a channel of communication between a brand and a customer. Plus, free marketing content is nothing to snub. Several companies are crushing it at getting their fans involved.

Chipotle: Lid Flip

For example, #ChipotleLidFlip was trending. Participants had to show off their abilities to flip the lid onto their bowl without using their hands. The company launched this challenge as a way to promote their Cinco de Mayo deal – free delivery.

But aside from promoting the free delivery, it also created a space for their fans to purchase their product and play a game with it. Then share that content with their followers and gain views by using the hashtag.

GUESS: In My Denim

Another great example comes from the fashion world. GUESS partnered with the app to launch TikTok's first branded content in the U.S. to host the #InMyDenim challenge, where they enlisted the help of popular content creators to show off their new denim outfits.

These influencers are great for promoting the campaign. Users who are fans of these influencers will feel excited about recording their own denim transformations.

These examples are excellent demonstrations of how brands can get their target audience excited about the products or services while also sharing and advocating for the brand with their followers on social media networks.

Showcase Your Products or Services in a Fun Way.
While hashtag challenges are one way to get users to see what you're selling, there are several other ways you can present your products or services to the TikTok world.

Given that the app's primary audience is young, consider how to make your content engaging and fun. There is a light-hearted nature to most TikTok content.

NBA: Diversified Content
With over 6.5 million followers, the NBA does an excellent job of engaging its audience. They produce a wide range of content that celebrates their brand and the sport itself in fun, impactful ways. For example, they will share a highlight reel of mascots shooting trick shots and making big slam dunks, set to upbeat music. Or they'll post funny videos of halftime show antics. These are light-hearted and entertaining.

Some of their content aims at humanizing the athletes so fans feel a deeper connection to them. For example, they posted a video of RJ Barres reacting to getting drafted. This gives fans a great experience of following Barres's emotional journey to the pros.

Gymshark: Targeted Messaging
Rather than simply posing videos of people showing off their gym clothes,

Gymshark posts educational content, like workout videos.
This speaks directly to their target audience – fitness enthusiasts. Other TikToks include flexibility tests, boxing training, challenges, and inspirational stories. Naturally, their audience is interested in learning about new workouts and staying motivated through their fitness journey. This is a great method for indirectly promoting their gym gear. In short, if you want to succeed with TikTok marketing, you need to be creative.

Partner With Relevant Influencers.
As you saw with GUESS, promoting your content through influencers with massive followings can be incredibly lucrative. But you shouldn't just connect with any influencer.

You need to find the influencers who are right for your company and fit your budget and goals.

Crocs: Thousand Dollar Crocs
The famous footwear brand produces a diverse amount of content, including ads and challenges. One of the most notable examples is the #ThousandDollarCrocs challenge.

A Post Malone lyric inspired this campaign. This lead to a collaboration between the artist and the company, which sold out in no time.

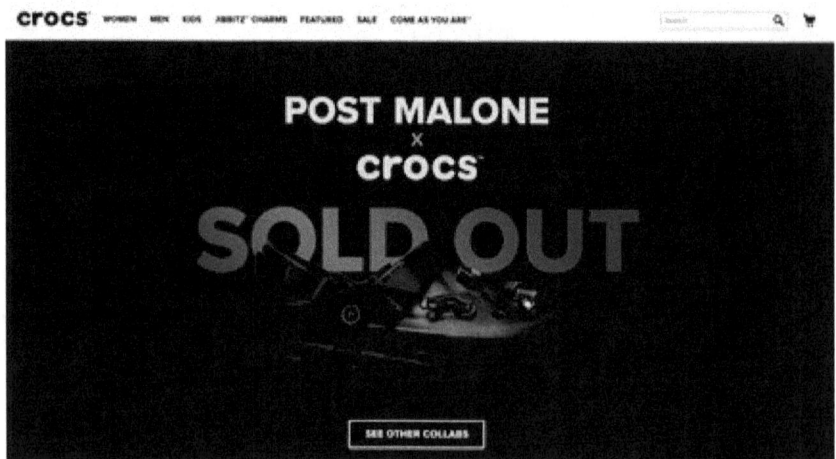

The hashtag challenges encouraged users to post what they think their

Crocs would look like if they were priced at $1,000—the results: an 18 percent boost in followers.

Calvin Klein: My Calvins

As part of their #MyCalvins campaign, the luxury fashion brand enlisted celebrities' help showcasing their favorite clothing items.

For example, musician Shawn Mendes, wearing a Calvin Klein outfit, talked about how he wished others could experience what it feels like to have large audiences sing back to you.

This campaign leveraged other celebrities that catered to the company's TikTok audience segment. Other influencers involved were A$AP Rocky and Kendall Jenner. They made the content appeal to the younger audience by choosing a suburban setting.

Medium

History: You would think by now that there are enough blogging platforms out there. But nope, apparently, there are not. Somehow, within five years, Medium grew into one of the largest blogging sites on the web with an Alexa ranking of 88.

A big reason for this success is its sleek and simple design. Ev Williams, one of the co-founders of Twitter, initially launched it in a 2012 closed beta before eventually opening it to the public.

Like some apps, such as Hemingway, the user interface is straightforward. The difference is that users can press publish directly instead of copying the content to their own blog.

Before Williams founded Medium, he also created Blogger, which he eventually sold to Google. He has a knack for blogging platforms.

Thanks to its numerous significant publications, Medium can be a way to build an entire audience without ever creating your own website.

Better Humans is another popular one.

The most popular topics are design, start-ups, marketing, and social or political matters.

Context: Since it's a blog platform, Medium naturally does well with long-form content. However, posts shouldn't be too long. Medium shows the estimated reading time for each post right at the top of them.

If people see that it'll take 20 minutes to read your post, you'll scare most of them away. Most users aren't willing to make such a big-time commitment. Seven-minute posts do best, so it makes sense to break up longer articles into a series of posts.

Ali Mese has done exceptionally well on Medium, creating a huge audience from scratch, thanks to several posts that have gone viral.

If you have a big following already, you can use it to **catapult your articles to the top** since the posts that users recommend the most land in the featured stories where most users will see them.

As few as 50-100 recommendations within an hour or two can drive your article right to the front page.

Big outlets like Huffington Post, Business Insider, and Entrepreneur often pick up content that has done well on Medium. That gets it additional exposure.

Medium Audience Demographic

In September of 2020, Medium received nearly 200 million visits. And most of the traffic to the site (nearly 26%) came from the United States. This offers you a lot of potential to get yourself and your business in front of new prospects. Also, keep in mind that most visitors to the site are men with an above average education.

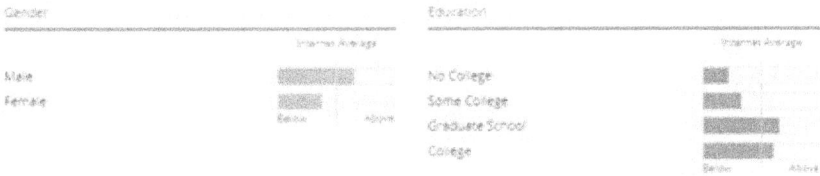

Gender			Education		
		Internet Average			Internet Average
Male			No College		
Female			Some College		
	Below	Above	Graduate School		
			College		
				Below	Above

What does this mean for you? Well, if your social media strategy revolves around posing cooking recipes or cat videos, then Medium may not be the right site for you.

Similar to LinkedIn, Medium is ideal for posing content that's more professional. For example, the most popular tag in 2016 was politics.

Now, that doesn't necessarily mean that you need to post political content. All I'm saying is that the gap between politics and business is a lot smaller than the gap between politics and DIY crafts.

Take, for instance, the Marketing and Entrepreneurship section on Medium. It has 146,000 followers. There's an audience for this sort of content.

Marketing and Entrepreneurship

Tips & News on Social Media Marketing, Online Advertising, Search Engine Optimization, Content Marketing, Growth Hacking, Branding, Start-Ups and more.

More information

FOLLOWERS
146K

In a more niche-specific session like this, you may not attract the attention of as many people as you could on Facebook or a larger social networking site.

But because the following is narrower, you will likely get a higher percentage of the right people to interact with you and your brand. So, what's the verdict: should you use Medium?

If your content is more light-hearted or is likely to appeal to a predominantly female audience, then consider a platform like Pinterest instead.

But if the topics you blog about relate to more serious matters, then you have nothing to lose, but much to gain by posting them on Medium.

Marketing Content on Medium

If your content is relevant for Medium users, then using the platform for marketing is a no-brainer.

Using the platform to benefit your business will require almost no additional effort.

All you must do is take blog posts that you've already written and repost them on Medium. Since you still own the rights to the content on Medium, you can do it as you like. And it's an easy way to get additional eyes on all your hard work. Dave Schools, for instance, experiences a lot of success on the blogging platform.

Help Scout also reposts their already-existing blog content.

Remote-First Companies Require Radical Commitment

One of the best decisions we've made at Help Scout is to build a remote-first company. While the benefits of a remote culture are tremendous, being successful requires radical commitment from leadership on your team.

Larry Kim does this as well.

Multitasking is Killing Your Brain

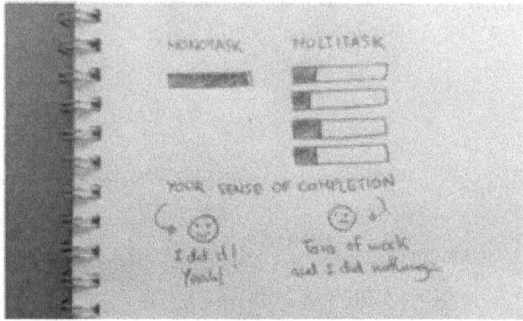

What do you have to lose?

You can use Medium to get your blog content in front of new eyes easily without any extra work. Just copy and paste content from your website and more people will see it.

QUORA

It turned out that they were right. With a comparatively low $80 million in funding, they built Quora up to over 190 million users in eight years. By 2020, Quora had 300 million monthly active users.

Users can **ask questions, and if they're popular, users can re-ask them.** Users can also upvote answers to make sure that quality answers show up first.

People have built entire platforms from Quora's questions, and some answers boast more than 1 million views.

Oliver's Answer

Wow!

Originally Answered: How do I get over my bad habit of procrastination?

I'll answer your question, but first I need to explain all of human civilisation in 2 minutes with the aid of a cartoon snake.

The start-up just implemented advertisements in the middle of 2016, drawing marketers' eyes all around the digital globe.

Context: This platform centers around one thing: questions. You can get the most out of it by providing quality answers to popular questions that users have repeatedly re-asked.

Thanks to the voting system, quality answers make it to the top. And they usually stay there for a long time.

Try to give answers that will still be valid in a year or two, even five. Some of the most popular Quora answers came from years ago.

You can **double your benefit from Quora** if you use it to come up with content. For example, you could write a blog post that gives an incredibly detailed answer to a popular question.

Not only will you have a great blog post then, but you will also be able to republish it as the answer to that question. This will also help you build a reputation as an expert on your topic. If someone likes an answer that they read from you, they'll often browse through the other answers you've given.

Quora and Content Marketing
Quora is an excellent place for establishing yourself as an expert on a specific topic. And that can happen in two different ways.

It can happen on or off Quora. Either way, the question-and-answer platform helps.

How does it help?

Well, first, you can answer your target market's questions. Imagine, for instance, that you are a digital marketer, and you want to start establishing yourself as an expert in the digital world. You can go to Quora and answer questions like these.

Quora   Ask or Search Quora   Ask Question

Quora (company)   Making Money Online   YouTube Videos   Videos   +2

How can I use Quora answers to create YouTube videos?

Guys as on Quora there are 1000's of different questions with great answers, which can be used to create YouTube Videos

Ex- Millionaire/billionaire came from nothing

Now this question will be having many answers with great explanations.

how can I use them in my video & make a ultimate compilation?

Edit Draft   Request ▾   Follow 5   Comment 1   Share   Downvote   ···

Then, if your answer is remarkable, people will upvote it, making it a winner in the Quora SEO system. In case that's not good enough, you can also use Quora to find topics for your own blog.

After all, your audience has a lot of questions. And finding out what those questions are can be seriously tedious. Fortunately, Quora makes it easy. Simply go to Quora and type in your Question. Browse through the questions people are asking.

All you have to do is take those same questions and create your own website content around them. It's an easy way to come up with content topics that your audience is interested in digesting.

Quora 🏠 Home   ✏️ Answer   🔔 Notifications   digital marketing

By Type

Results for **digital marketing**

All Types
Questions
Answers
Posts
Profiles
Topics
Blogs

What are good ways to learn to become the best digital marketer?
Answer 1 of 590 · View All
Gary Vaynerchuk, Family 1st then...Entrepreneur, Investor, Best-Selling Author,
Jets Fan, Speaker — Being the owner of an 800 person full service digital agency,
means that there are many ways I could answer this question... But the response I
always gravitate toward is pr... (more)

By Topics

All Topics
Topics You Follow
Select Topic

Which is the best digital marketing course?
Answer 1 of 429 · View All
Anindita Debnath, Digital Marketing Strategist — Instead of looking for a best
course, I would recommend that you focus on strengthening your basic
knowledge and understanding of Digital if you are planning to apply for
a... (more)

By Author

All People
People You Follow
Find People

What is digital marketing? What are the basics of Digital Marketing? What is
digital marketing strategy? Who needs digital marketing services?
Answer 1 of 447 · View All
Chris Hines, Founder CEO Vineclick — **Digital Marketing** is making use of
various types of digital technologies to promote yourself or your business. There
are many types of digital marketing. It is very importa... (more)

By Time

All Time
Past Hour
Past Day
Past Week

Which are the top Digital marketing agencies in India?
Answer 1 of 270 · View All
Angel Priy Tarzan, Co-founder at Sarvotarzan (2014-present) —
Disclaimer: I am the co-founder of Sarvotarzan.
Sarvotarzan comes in the the Top Digital Marketing Agencies in India.

3. Email marketing

Email marketing is the strategy of reaching out to potential lead customers through their emails. With GDPR and CCPA, you have to make sure they opt into your newsletter. They provide you the information knowingly to ensure you are not intruding on their privacy, rights under privacy regulations, and other laws. There are many ways to do email marketing and find strategies to reach the customer, leading them to sign up or purchase your product/service.

There are many email marketing tools such as Mailchimp, SendGrid, and many others. Many YouTube tutorials are available to check them out. Here is a Tutorial of Email Marketing.

Once you have watched this tutorial, let's go through some of the amazing examples of Email Marketing you can use.

Examples of Brilliant Email Marketing Campaigns

On any given day, most of our email inboxes are flooded with a barrage of automated email newsletters that do little else besides giving us more tasks to do on our commutes to work -- namely, marking them all as unread without reading or unsubscribing altogether. But now and then, we get a newsletter that's so good; not only do we read it, we share it, and recommend it to our friends.

Email marketing is the practice of sending various types of content to a list of subscribers via email. This content can serve to generate website traffic, leads, or even product signups. It's important that an email campaign's recipients have opted to receive this content and that each newsletter offers something valuable.

How to Create an Effective Email Marketing Campaign

Effective email marketing campaigns need to be cleverly written to attract attention in busy inboxes. Here are four steps you should follow to create an effective email campaign.

1. Use a comprehensive email builder.

The first step to creating an effective email marketing campaign is to use the best email builder.

Depending on your needs, there are several options, including HubSpot, MailChimp, Pabbly Email Marketing, and Constant Contact.

With a comprehensive email builder, you can create, optimize, and personalize your own email campaigns without needing technical or graphic design experience.

2. Include personalization elements in the copy and excellent imagery.

Marketing emails need to be personalized to the reader and filled with attractive graphics.

Few people want to read emails that are addressed "Dear Sir/Madam" -- instead of their name - and even fewer people want to read an email that simply gives them a wall of text. Visuals help your recipients quickly understand the point of the email.

3. Add an appropriate call-to-action.

Once you have included personalization elements and added your copy and images, it's time to add a call-to-action (CTA).

Above all, exceptional marketing emails must contain a meaningful CTA. After all, if brands are taking up subscribers' time and inbox space with another email, it must have a point to it. People get multiple emails every day. Why should they care about yours?

4. Make sure it is designed for all devices.

Effective email marketing campaigns are designed for all devices on which users can read their emails -- desktop, tablet, and mobile. Email campaigns that are designed for mobile devices are especially important -- a quality known as "responsive design." In fact, **73% of companies today prioritize mobile device optimization when creating email marketing campaigns.**

Email Marketing Examples

Charity: water: Donation Progress Update

Brooks Sports: Desiree Linden's Boston Marathon Victory
BuzzFeed: 'BuzzFeed Today' Newsletter
Uber: Calendar Integration
TheSkimm: Subscription Anniversary
Mom and Dad Money: Get to Know Your Subscribers
Poncho: Custom Weather Forecast
Birchbox: Co-marketing Promotion
Postmates: New Product
Dropbox: User Reengagement
InVision App: Weekly Blog Newsletter
Warby Parker: Product Renewal
Cook Smarts: Weekly Product Newsletter
HireVue: Customer Retention
Redbubble: Featured Artist

Paperless Post: Mother's Day Promotion
Stitcher: Recommended for You
RCN: Storm Update
Trulia: Moving Trends

1. Charity: water
Marketing Campaign: Donation Progress Update

When people talk about email marketing, lots of them forget to mention transactional emails. These are the automated emails you get in your inbox after taking specific action on a website. This could be anything from filling out a form to purchasing a product and updating you on your order's progress. Often, these are direct text emails that marketers set and forget. Charity: water took an alternate route. Once someone donates to a charity: water project, the money takes a long journey. Most charities don't tell you about that journey at all, charity: water uses automated emails to show donors how their money is making an impact over time.

2. Brooks Sports

Marketing Campaign: Desiree Linden's Boston Marathon Victory

When Desiree Linden won the 2018 Boston Marathon, she became the first American woman to win the race in more than 30 years. To her shoe and apparel sponsor, Brooks Sports, it was an opportunity to celebrate their long partnership together. The resulting email campaign focuses almost entirely on the Olympic marathoner's amazing accomplishment.

Email campaigns like this one allow companies to demonstrate their loyalties and add value to the products their best users have chosen. The blue CTA button at the bottom of the email reads, "See Desiree's go-to gear." What better products to call attention to than the stuff worn by America's latest legend?

After Desiree's victory, everyone knew her name. Brooks Sports struck while the iron was hot with a proud email that was sure to be opened and forwarded.

3. BuzzFeed
Marketing Campaign: 'BuzzFeed Today' Newsletter

I already have a soft spot for BuzzFeed content ("21 Puppies so Cute You Will Literally Gasp and Then Probably Cry," anyone?), but that isn't the only reason I fell in love with its emails.

First, BuzzFeed has awesome subject lines and preview text. They are always short and punchy, which fits in perfectly with the rest of its content. I especially love how the preview text will accompany the subject line. For example, if the subject line is a question, the preview text is the answer. Or if the subject line is a command (like the one below), the preview text seems like the next logical thought right after it:

Once you open an email from BuzzFeed, the copy is equally good. Just take a look at that glorious alt text action happening where the images should be. The email still conveys what it is supposed to convey and looks great whether you use an image or not. That is definitely something to admire.

Boston 2018 —
One for the History Books

Over three decades have passed since an American woman last won Boston, but today that all changed. Congratulations to Brooks Elite athlete Desiree Linden who finished first place. We're beyond proud.

Congratulations, Desiree Linden

See Desiree's go-to gear

Sorry, Wrong Number   🖨 📄

BuzzFeed <today@buzzfeed.com> Unsubscribe   Aug 17 (7 days ago)   ↩ ▾
to me ▾

BuzzFeed TODAY

32 Texts That Will Make You Laugh Way Harder Than You Should

There are some texts so strange, you just can't explain why they're funny. And that's certainly the case with these gems.

4. Uber
Marketing Campaign: Calendar Integration

The beauty of Uber's emails is in its simplicity. Email subscribers are alerted to deals and promotions with emails like the one you see below. I love how brief the initial description is, paired with an obvious CTA - perfect for subscribers who are quickly skimming.

For the people who want to learn more, these are followed by a more detailed (but still pleasingly simple) step-by-step explanation of how the deal works.

How consistent the design of Uber's emails is with its brand is another thing I admire. Like its app, website, social media photos, and other visual branding parts, the emails are represented by bright colors and geometric patterns. All communications and marketing assets tell the brand's story. Brand consistency is one tactic Uber's nailed in order to gain brand loyalty. Check out the clever copywriting and email design at work in this example:

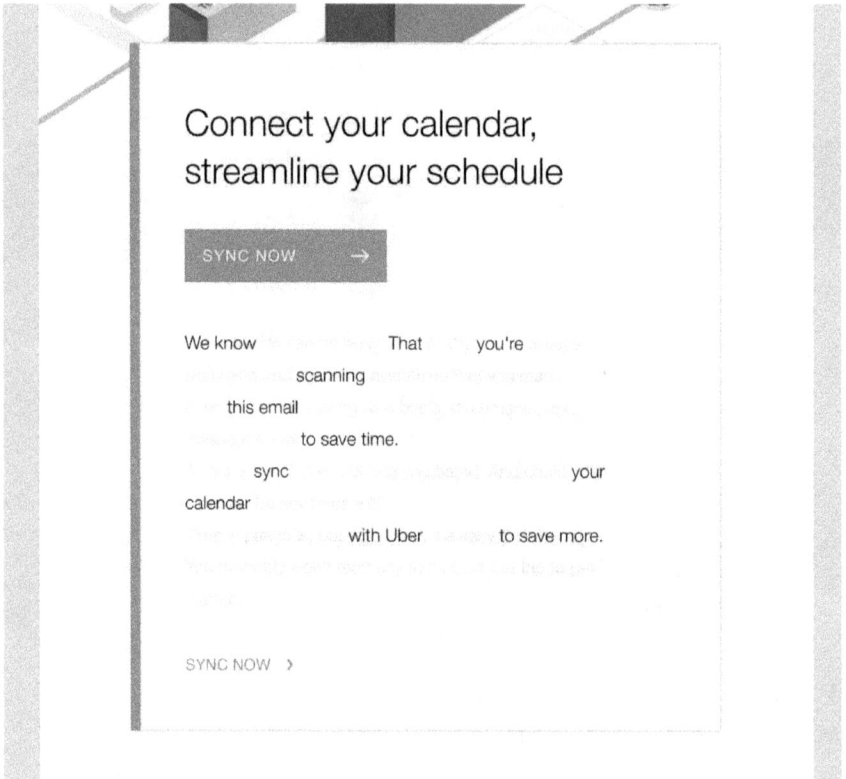

5. TheSkimm
Marketing Campaign: Subscription Anniversary

We love TheSkimm's daily newsletter, especially its clean design and its short, punchy paragraphs. But newsletters aren't TheSkimm's only strength when it comes to email. Check out its subscriber engagement email below, which rewarded fellow marketer Ginny Mineo for being subscribed for two years.

Emails triggered by milestones, like anniversaries and birthdays, are fun to get. Who doesn't like celebrating special occasions? The beauty of anniversary emails, in particular, is that they don't require subscribers to input any extra data, and they can work for a variety of senders. Plus, the timeframe can be modified based on the business model.

Here, the folks at TheSkimm took it a step further by asking Mineo if she'd like to earn the title of brand ambassador as a loyal subscriber, which would require her to share the link with ten friends, of course.

6. Mom and Dad Money
Marketing Campaign: Get to Know Your Subscribers

Do you think you know all about the people who are reading your marketing emails? How much of what you "know" about them is based on assumptions? The strongest buyer personas are based on insights you gather from your actual readership, through surveys, interviews, and so on - in addition to the market research.

That's precisely what Mas Becker of Mom and Dad Money does, and he does it very well.

Here's an example of an email I once received from this brand. Design wise, it's nothing special, but that's also the point. It reads just like an email from a friend or colleague asking for a quick favor.

Not only was this initial email great, but his response to my answers was even better. Within a few days of responding to the questionnaire, I received a long and detailed personal email from Mas thanking me for taking the time to fill the questionnaire out and offering a ton of helpful advice and links to resources specifically catered to my answers. I was extremely impressed by his business acumen, communication skills, and evident dedication to his readers.

7. Poncho
Marketing Campaign: Custom Weather Forecast

Some of the best emails out there, pair super simple designs with brief, clever copy. When it comes down to it, daily emails I get from Poncho, which sends me customizable weather forecasts each morning takes the cake.

Poncho's emails are colorful, have delightful images and GIFs, and are very easy to scan. The copy is brief but clever with some great puns, and it aligns perfectly with the brand. Check out the copy near the bottom asking to "hang out outside of email." Hats off to Poncho for using design to communicate its message in a more productive way.

8. Birchbox
Marketing Campaign: Co-marketing Promotion

The subject line of this email from the beauty product subscription service Birchbox got my colleague Pam Vaughan clicking. It read: "We Forgot Something in Your February Box!" Of course, if you read the email copy below, Birchbox didn't actually forget to put that discount code in her box, but it was undoubtedly a smart way to get her attention.

As it turned out, the discount code was a bonus promo for Rent the Runway, a dress rental company that likely fits the interest profile of most Birchbox customers -- which certainly did not disappoint. That's a great co-marketing partnership right there.

9. Postmates
Marketing Campaign: New Product

I have to say, I'm a sucker for GIFs. They're easy to consume, eye-catching, and have an emotional impact.

You, too, can use animated GIFs in your marketing to show a fun header, draw people's eyes to a specific part of the email, or display your products and services in action.

10. Dropbox
Marking Campaign: User Reengagement

You might think it would be hard to love an email from a company whose product you haven't been using. But Dropbox found a way to make its "come back to us!" email cute and funny, thanks to a pair of whimsical cartoons.

The email is short and sweet, which emphasizes the message that Dropbox isn't intrusive, it just wants to remind the recipient that the brand exists and why it could be helpful. When sending these types of emails, you might include an incentive for recipients to come back to using your service, like a limited-time coupon.

11. InVision App
Marking Campaign: Weekly Blog Newsletter

Every week, InVision sends a roundup of their best blog content, favorite design links from the week, and a new opportunity to win a free t-shirt. (They give away a new design every week.) They often have fun survey questions where they crowdsource for their blog. This week, for example, they asked subscribers what they would do if the internet didn't exist.

Not only is InVision's newsletter a great mix of content, I also love the balance between images and text, making it easy to read and mobile-friendly, which is especially important because its newsletters are quite long. (Below is just an excerpt, but you can read through the full email here.) We like the

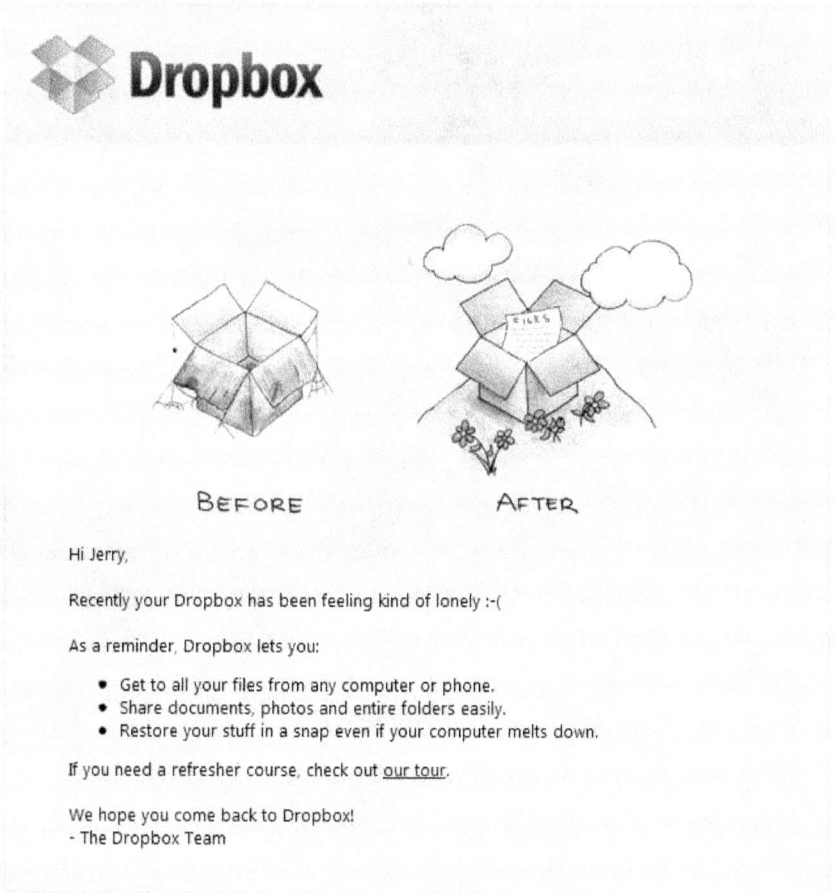

Dropbox

BEFORE   AFTER

Hi Jerry,

Recently your Dropbox has been feeling kind of lonely :-(

As a reminder, Dropbox lets you:

- Get to all your files from any computer or phone.
- Share documents, photos and entire folders easily.
- Restore your stuff in a snap even if your computer melts down.

If you need a refresher course, check out our tour.

We hope you come back to Dropbox!
- The Dropbox Team

clever copy on the call-to-action (CTA) buttons, too.

12. Warby Parker
Marketing Campaign: Product Renewal

What goes better with a new prescription than a new pair of glasses? The folks at Warby Parker made that connection very clear in their email to a friend of mine in 2014. It is an older email, but it's such an excellent example of personalized email marketing, that I had to include it here. The subject line was: "Uh-oh, your prescription is expiring." What a clever email trigger. Speaking of which, check out the clever co-marketing at the bottom of the email: If you don't know where to go to renew your subscription, the information for an optometrist is included in the email. Now there is no excuse not to shop for new glasses!

Take the email below from Paperless Post, for example. I love this email's header: It provides a clear CTA that includes a sense of urgency. Then, the sub-heading asks a question that forces recipients to think to themselves, "Wait, when is Mother's Day again? Did I buy Mom a card?" Below this copy, the simple grid design is both easy to scan and quite visually appealing. Each card picture is a CTA in and of itself. Click on any one of them, and you'll be taken to a purchase page.

16. Stitcher
Marketing Campaign: Recommended for You

As humans, we tend to crave personalized experiences. When emails appear to be created especially for you it implies, you're not just getting what everyone else is getting. You might even feel like the company sending you the email knows you somehow and that it cares about your preferences. That's why I love the on-demand podcast/radio show app Stitcher's "Recommended for You" emails. I tend to listen to episodes from the same podcast instead of branching out to new ones. But Stitcher wants me to discover (and subscribe to) all the other awesome content it has - and I probably wouldn't without this encouragement.

Their email also has quite a clever use of responsive design. The colors are bright, and it is not too hard to scroll and click. Notice the CTAs are large enough for me to hit with my thumbs. Also, the mobile email has features that make sense mobile devices. Check out the CTA at the bottom of the email - The "Open Stitcher Radio" button prompts the app to open on your phone.

STITCHER
DISCOVER NEW SHOWS
Recommended For You

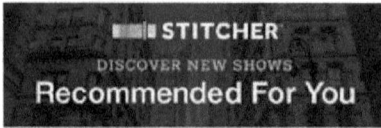

Hello, here are a few of the most popular trending shows on Stitcher right now that we thought you'd enjoy.

5 Seriously Stupid Movies That Will Be Studied By History
The Cracked Podcast
The most important movies in history don't always walk away with Academy Awards. In this podcast, you'll hear Jack O'Brien explain what Teen Wolf can tell us about the history of race relations in America - and much more!

▶ Listen

→ LISTEN LATER   < Share

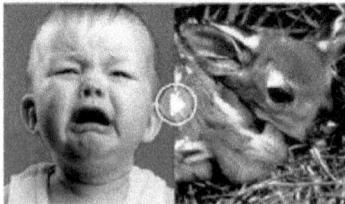

Where The Heck Are Our Robot Nannies?
NPR's Planet Money
More than half of all Japanese women quit their jobs after giving birth to their first child. That's more than double the rate in the U.S. Here's how Japanese working moms can survive - until the robots arrive.

▶ Listen

→ LISTEN LATER   < Share

Can You Tell Which Of These Baby Cries Is Human?
Quirks and Quarks from CBC
Infant cries seem to have a universal appeal, no matter what the species. White Tail Deer mothers respond to many infant distress calls, including those of human babies.

▶ Listen

→ LISTEN LATER   < Share

So, What Will The World Look Like In 2030?
The Brian Lehrer Show from WNYC
Author Matthew Burrows looks at the big changes that require attention - like a growing middle class, demands for self-determination, a shift in U.S. power, and climate change.

▶ Listen

→ LISTEN LATER   < Share

This Mayor Is Running His City As If He Were Its CEO
CityCast
LA Mayor Eric Garcetti says he governs like he is "the city's CEO," requiring department heads to reapply for their jobs and undergo data-driven performance reviews.

▶ Listen

→ LISTEN LATER   < Share

f Like us on Facebook

Open Stitcher Radio

Get the Stitcher App for you!
iPhone, iPad, Android Devices, Kindle, or Kindle Fire

Stitcher is here to help you discover new and interesting shows.
If you do not wish to receive emails from us,
please click here to safely unsubscribe.
Delivered by Stitcher Inc, 121 2nd St #6, San Francisco, CA 94105

17. RCN
Marketing Campaign: Storm Update

Internet providers and bad weather are natural enemies. You would think telecommunications companies wouldn't want to call attention to storm-induced power outages at it's one of things that sets off customers' impatience. Then, there's RCN.

RCN, a cable and wireless internet service, turned this email marketing campaign into a weather forecast just for its customers. This "storm update" got the company out ahead of an event that threatened its service while allowing its users to get the weather updates they needed right from the company they count on for Wi-Fi.

As you can see below, the email even advises personal safety - a nice touch of care to go with the promise of responsive service. At the bottom of the email, RCN also took the opportunity to highlight its social media channels, which the company appropriately uses to keep users informed of network outages.

RCN   STORM UPDATE

RCN IS PREPARED

Dear RCN Customer,

RCN is preparing for winter storm Quinn. The combination of heavy snow and strong winds may lead to additional tree damage and power outages. Due to winds and heavy snowfall, travel may be difficult.

Be assured that when major weather events threaten our area, we take appropriate measures to monitor and respond to the possible impact of the storm. Please be sure to follow travel advisories, take precautions, be aware of your surroundings and do not touch any downed lines and wires and, above all, stay safe. For ongoing news and updates, visit rcn.com/stormwatch.

WE'LL KEEP YOU POSTED:

Facebook

Like our page on **Facebook** to see storm alerts and relevant updates.

Twitter

Follow us on **Twitter** for the latest news and updates.

rcn.com

18. Trulia
Marketing Campaign: Moving Trends

I am a huge advocate of thought leadership. To me, some of the best companies gain customer loyalty by becoming the go-to source for expertise on a given topic. Trulia, a property search engine for buyers, sellers, and renters, are experts in the real estate biz. Just read their email below.

"Why aren't millennials moving?" This email campaign's subject line reads before citing interesting data about relocation trends in the U.S. Trulia doesn't benefit from people who choose not to move. Still, the company does benefit from having its fingers on the industry's pulse -- and showing it cares which way the real estate winds are blowing.

?trulia

Younger Americans Aren't Moving Like They Used To – What's Changed?

Americans are moving at historically low rates. In 2017, 34.9 million Americans changed residences, translating to a household mobility rate of 10.9%.

Find Out Now

Is Renting Or Buying Better For You?

Find Out Now ⊘

Will You Love a New Neighborhood?

Find Out More ⊘

19. RedBubble
Marketing Campaign: Featured Artist

This email marketing campaign crushes for so many reasons. Not only is the design below super eye-catching without looking clustered, but the artwork is also user-made. RedBubble sells merchandise featuring designs from artists all over the world. It presents a golden opportunity to feature popular submissions across the RedBubble community.

The example below showcases artwork from "Letter Shoppe," When that artist sees RedBubble featuring her content, she's more likely to forward it to friends and colleagues.

In addition to linking to Letter Shoppe's designs (available on merchandise that RedBubble ultimately sells), the email campaign includes an endearing quote by the featured artist: "Never compromise on your values, and only do work you want to get more of." RedBubble's customers are likely to

agree - and open other emails in this campaign for more inspiring quotes.

4. Search engine marketing

Search engine marketing is marketing a business using paid advertisements that appear on search engine results pages (SERPs). Advertisers bid on keywords that users of services such as Google and Bing might enter when looking for certain products or services. This gives the advertiser the opportunity for their ads to appear alongside results for those search queries.

These ads, often known by the term pay-per-click ads, come in a variety of formats. Some are small, text-based ads. Others, such as product listing ads (PLAs, also known as Shopping ads), are more visual, product-based advertisements that allow consumers to see important information at-a-glance, such as price and reviews.

Search engine marketing's greatest strength is **that it offers advertisers the opportunity to put their ads in front of motivated customers who are ready to buy.** No other advertising medium can do this, which is why search engine marketing is so effective and a compelling way to grow your business.

SEM versus SEO: What's the difference?

Generally, "search engine marketing" refers to paid search marketing, a system where businesses pay Google to show their ads in the search results. Search engine optimization, or SEO, is different as businesses don't pay Google for traffic and clicks. Instead, they earn a free spot in the search results by having the most relevant content for a given keyword search.

Both SEO and SEM should be fundamental parts of your online marketing strategy. SEO is a powerful way to drive evergreen traffic at the top of the funnel, while search engine advertisements are a highly cost-effective way to drive conversions at the bottom of the funnel.

Keywords: The Foundation of Search Engine Marketing

Keywords are the foundation of search engine marketing. As users enter keywords into search engines to find what they're looking for, it should come as little surprise that keywords form the basis of search engine marketing as an advertising strategy.

SEM Keyword Research

Before choosing which keywords to use in your search engine marketing campaigns, you need to conduct comprehensive research as part of your keyword management strategy.

First, you need to identify keywords that are relevant to your business and that prospective customers are likely to use when searching for your products and services. One way to accomplish this is by using a Free Keyword Tool. Simply enter a keyword that's relevant to your business or service and see related keyword suggestions that form the basis of various search engine marketing campaigns.

Keyword Suggestion Tool
You have 23 of 30 free searches remaining.

Results for: building materials / Showing top 100 of 6,438 keywords   RESET

Keywords	Relative Frequency	Google Search Volume	WS Search Volume	Competition	Remove from List
building materials					☒
building materials diy					☒
industrial building materials					☒
used building materials					☒
recycled building materials					☒
building materials construction					☒
green building materials					☒
sustainable building materials					☒
home hardware building materials					☒
hardware building materials					☒
building materials windows					☒

6,338 more keywords available   GET FULL KEYWORD LIST   1 2 3 4 5 ... >> See All

In addition to helping, you find keywords, thorough keyword research can also help you identify negative keywords, which are search terms you should exclude from your campaigns.

Negative keywords are not terms with negative connotations, but rather irrelevant terms that are unlikely to result in conversions. For example, if you sell ice cream, you might want to exclude the keyword "ice cream recipes," as users searching for ice cream recipes are unlikely to be in the market for your product.

This concept is known as search intent or the likelihood that a prospect will complete a purchase or other desired action after searching for a given term. Some keywords are considered to have high commercial intent or a strong indication that the searcher wants to buy something.
Examples of high commercial intent keywords include:

- Buy
- Discount(s)
- Deal(s)
- Coupon(s)
- Free shipping
Keywords and Account Structure
Another crucial aspect of keywords that is essential for the success of a search engine marketing campaign is account structure.

Logical keyword grouping and account structure can help you achieve higher click-through rates, lower costs-per-click and stronger overall performance. Keyword research can help you think about how to best setup your account.

AdWords and Bing Ads accounts should be structured in the following way for optimal results:

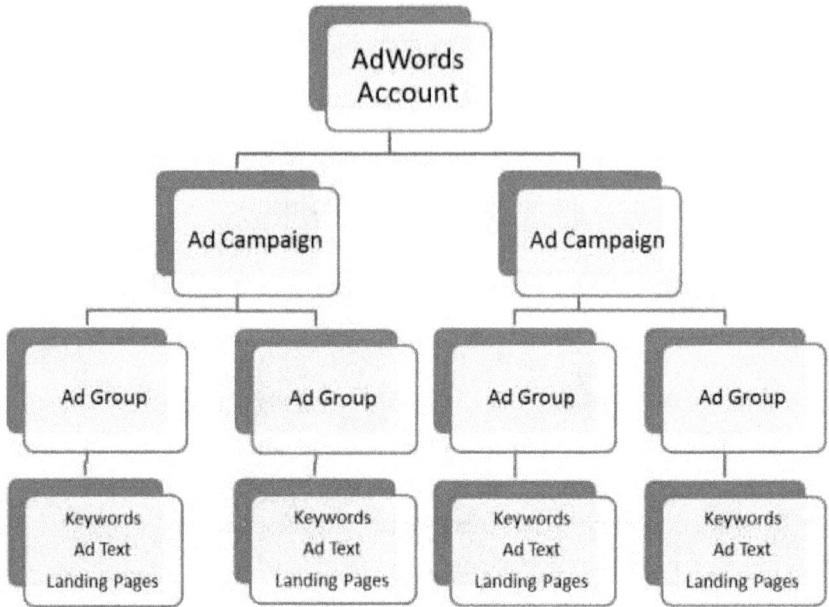

As you can see in the figure above, an optimally structured account is comprised of five distinct elements:

- Ad campaigns
- Ad groups
- Keywords
- Ad text
- Landing pages

Ad campaigns focus on similar products or services. For example, if you run a hardware store, one ad campaign could focus exclusively on autumnal products such as leaf blowers, rakes, and leaf bags, whereas another might focus on power tools.

Ad groups allow for each campaign to be further subcategorized for relevance. One ad group could be for different types of rakes or varying leaf blowers in our hardware store example. For the power tools campaign, one ad group might focus on power drills, while another could focus on circular saws. This organization's level might take slightly longer to set up initially, but the rewards - namely higher CTRs at lower cost, make this effort worthwhile.

The Search Engine Marketing Ad Auction

One of the most enduring misconceptions about search engine marketing is that those with the largest advertising budget wins. Although a larger advertising budget can certainly be advantageous, especially when targeting highly competitive keywords, it is far from a success requirement with search engine marketing. This is because all ads go through a process known as the ad auction before appearing alongside search results. For this explanation, we'll be focusing on the ad auction in Google AdWords.

How the Ad Auction Works

The ad auction process takes place every time someone enters a search query into Google. To be entered into the ad auction, advertisers identify keywords they want to bid on and state how much they are willing to spend (per click) to have their ads appear alongside results relating to those keywords. If Google determines that the keywords you have bid on are contained within a user's search query, your ads are entered into the ad auction.

How Ads 'Win' the Ad Auction

Not every ad will appear on every single search. This is because the ad auction takes various factors into account when determining the placement of ads on the SERP. Not every keyword has sufficient commercial intent to justify displaying ads next to results.

The two main factors that Google evaluates as part of the ad auction process are your maximum bid and your quality ad's score.
The maximum bid is the maximum amount you are willing to pay for a click. Quality Score is a metric based on the overall quality of your advertisement. Google calculates these metrics during the ad auction to determine the placement of advertisements. The result of this calculation is known as ad rank.

HOW DOES GOOGLE DETERMINE WHICH AD IS SHOWN WHERE?

Once you are entered into the auction, Google looks at two key factors to determine where your ad ranks: your **maximum bid** and your **quality score**.

$$\text{AD RANK} = \frac{\text{CPC}}{\text{BID}} \times \text{QUALITY SCORE}$$

The best combined
CPC Bid x Quality Score
gets the best position:

This is the maximum bid you specify for your keyword

This is a metric to determine how relevant and useful your ad is to the user (components are CTR, relevance, and landing page) The higher your quality score, the better.

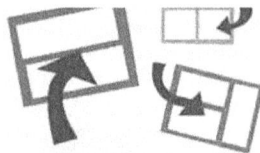

The Importance of Quality Score in SEM

Given that Google AdWords' Quality Score comprises half of the ad rank formula, it is one of the most crucial metrics search engine marketers can focus on. High-Quality Scores can help you achieve a better ad position at lower costs because Google favors ads that are highly relevant to user queries.

In the table below, you can see that although Advertiser 1 has the lowest maximum bid, they have the highest Quality Score, meaning their ads are given priority in terms of placement during the ad auction:

$$\text{YOUR PRICE} = \frac{\text{THE AD RANK OF THE PERSON BELOW YOU}}{\text{YOUR QUALITY SCORE}} + \$0.01$$

	MAX BID	QUALITY SCORE	AD RANK	ACTUAL CPC
ADVERTISER 1	$2.00	10	20	16/10 + $0.01= **$1.61**
ADVERTISER 2	$4.00	4	16	12/4 + $0.01= **$3.01**
ADVERTISER 3	$6.00	2	12	8/2 + $0.01= **$4.01**
ADVERTISER 4	$8.00	1	8	**HIGHEST CPC**

Quality Score is arguably the most important metric in search engine marketing.

Pay attention to your search engine marketing and, most importantly, work on your search engine optimization. You would want to focus heavily on increasing your search engines rank, which is done through simple steps. Understanding how search engines go on your website, take the data and analyze it is crucial to understand how you can increase your positioning. It is straightforward to imagine a box —> Inside this box is content —> This box is connected to other boxes —> People are looking at all the boxes.

- The fuller your box, the better. This means engaging content, meta tags, and adding relevant descriptions with keywords to everything on your website.
- The more the box is connected to other boxes, the better. Backlinks are essential, so being mentioned on other major websites, the more the search engine will rank you.
- The more the box is seen by people, the better. This means if you are attracting content through digital marketing, social media, organic reach, etc.
- The more the box is relevant to people, the better. The more interesting your website, the longer people stay on your website and search engines will rank you higher. The faster people leave your website, the more it will become irrelevant for search engines to rank you.

Check your seo score here and improve what needs improving

SCAN ME

5. Influencer marketing

How to create an influencer marketing strategy

Like any marketing tactic, an influencer program takes deliberate targeting and planning. You won't find strategic success just by sending free things out to everyone who asks or to your existing friends and acquaintances.

1. How to find influencers and what to pay them

Much like any strategy, research is the first step. Choose the network you want to focus on first. You can always expand to other networks later but stick with one to start. Ideally, your brand should already have a presence on this network or be looking to expand into it. Demographics vary on each network. If you are unsure where to begin, our article on social media demographics is a good starting point.

The industry you are in also matters when you're planning to implement an influencer marketing strategy. Beauty and fashion brands shine on Instagram and YouTube. The video game industry dominates on Twitch.

During your research phase, investigate the type of influencers you're interested in. Are you going for celebrities with massive followings? Or micro-influencers with less than 2000 followers? Perhaps something in between the 5–10k follower range is more your preference. Whatever you decide to focus on will determine your budget.

The compensation varies wildly, too, so be sure to look at standard rates for those influencer types. Micro-influencers tend to be focused on a few topics and accept products. Some micro-influencers work independently, while an agency or network may represent others. Larger accounts and celebrities will need compensation and might even go through a talent agency.

You will need to think about the expected ROI of your social influencer marketing campaign: how will you gauge the contributions of influencer posts to your overall marketing goals? One approach might be to compare your expectations for influencers to other firms. Look at how you might gauge the budget for a video production firm's work in creating an ad for you, versus an influencer creating a video. It may initially seem like judging influencers' value is unpredictable, but this type of approach will give you a familiar point of comparison and contrast.

In 2017, Influence co-published the results of their research into Instagram influencer payment. They looked at the average cost per Instagram post and found:

- The overall average price was $271 per post.
- The average price for micro-influencers with fewer than 1,000 followers was $83 per post.
- The average price for influencers with more than 100,000 followers was $763 per post.

2. Set a budget and management strategy

Now that you have some idea of what to pay influencers, you need to create your budget. Be sure to also factor in time for planning, executing, and reviewing your influencer program. Running a successful influencer marketing campaign is not a set-it-and-go type of strategy. It will involve careful monitoring and follow-up.

Unlike a more automated ad strategy, influencers are human and frequently balancing multiple partnerships. Some may fall behind in their commitments to post on time or make errors in your requested tags or calls to action. You will need to have the time to be more hands-on with these relationships to cultivate them and refine your approach through experience. If you have the time and money, consider setting up a formal ambassador program. Fujifilm utilizes its ambassadors in new product launches and in supplementing their content.

With various photographers and videographers at their disposal, the company can diversify its feed to showcase what its equipment can do.

For brands that need a wider pool of influencers, hiring an influencer marketing agency who will do the research and coordination for you is a good bet.

3. Decide on goals and message

The two most common reasons for using influencer marketing are to elevate brand awareness and increase sales. However, instead of setting these broad targets as your two goals, it will be more useful to kick off your strategy by honing your brand's needs. Perhaps you want to increase your customer base in a younger demographic. Or you want to expand into a new user group with a new product.

Influencers can reach specific audiences. Instead of relying on thousands of followers, influencers will help you ensure a very targeted audience who is likely to be interested in your product, reads, and engages with your content.

Your message is just as important as your goal. While you don't want to stifle an influencer's creativity and uniqueness, you also don't want them to post about something unrelated to your campaign. Determine how you want to structure your influencer marketing campaign and message so you can stick to it.

4. Influencer outreach:
How to contact influencers

Back to step one: research. With a plan set around your network, goals, and what types of influencers you want to target.

During this research, keep in mind the following:

- Does the influencer already post about things like your service? For example, if you're a restaurant and you want to promote a new menu you should be looking for influencers who regularly post about dining out and the food they eat.

- Are they legit? This means scrolling through their feed and clicking through posts. A low engagement ratio to follower count and spam-like comments are signs of a fraudulent account.

- Have they worked with similar brands before? Depending on what type of influencer you're looking for, a seasoned one will be able to show you a portfolio of their work. The more you invest in an influencer, the more you will want to vet them.

You can also use Twitter analytics tools to identify potential influencers that will fit your campaigns.

Next, determine how you will be reaching out to them. For micro influencers, you could reach out directly in a private message on the same platform. For more established ones, click around their profile, and they may list contact information for business inquiries in their bio. They may also link a website that denotes brand partnerships.

Make sure to offer them discounts, promo codes, and other discounts related to your product, and give them access to your branding insights to understand in depth what your brand is all about.

Keep adding, commenting, and interacting with people who have many followers as this will help you scale your reach and business.
Let's talk about YouTube. Chances are we have all went down a rabbit hole or spent hours watching silly cat videos.

YouTube has always been a source of entertaining content, but it's also staking its claim as an essential tool for marketers. In fact, nearly half of all marketers (48%) plan to add YouTube to their marketing strategy over the next 12 months.

You may be thinking: "That's great, but my audience isn't on YouTube." Well, think again.

One-third of the total time online is spent watching videos, and YouTube

has more than a billion active users. The platform is so extensive that it can be accessed in 76 different languages, accounting for 95% of the world's population. Still not convinced?
300 hours of video are uploaded every minute.

YouTube reaches more than 18 to 49-year-olds than any broadcast or cable network on mobile.

59% of executives prefer watching a video to reading text.
Not only is your audience on YouTube, but as the internet's second largest search engine, YouTube can help improve your SEO and overall brand presence. YouTube allows marketers to present unique content that is easy for viewers to consume and share.

YouTube marketing can be an intimidating tool for brands. That is why we have created this complete guide for YouTube pros and newcomers alike. Below we will walk through each step of marketing on YouTube — from creating a YouTube channel and video optimization for SEO, to running a YouTube advertising campaign and interpreting video analytics.

Read along, **email it to yourself**, bookmark it for later, or jump to the section that interests you most.

So, you've decided to create a **YouTube channel.** Great! I can't wait to see the amazing content you promote. Before we dive in, it is important to note that maintaining a YouTube channel takes a lot of time and planning. Are you ready for it?

Unlike other social networking platforms, YouTube exclusively hosts video content. You will need to set aside plenty of time to plan, film, edit, market, and consistently analyze your content. You will also need to define your brand's goals and plan for how video can specifically help you achieve these. If you can devote an appropriate amount of time and energy to the platform, you'll be able to create engaging, shareable content for your growing audience.

Creating a Google Account

Before you start filming video content, you will need to set up your YouTube channel. This can get a bit complicated. As you probably know, YouTube is owned by Google. As a result, when you sign up for a Gmail account, you automatically gain access to a YouTube account, a Google+ account, and much more.

Depending on your business, you may not want to tie your email to your business's YouTube channel — especially if you need to share access to the account with team members or an agency partner. We suggest that you create a common email account that multiple people can use. To get started, visit Google and click "Sign in" in the upper right-hand corner.

Click on "Create Account" at the bottom of the page.
You'll see an option pop up to create an account for yourself or to manage your business. Since your YouTube account will be for your business, choose "To manage my business."

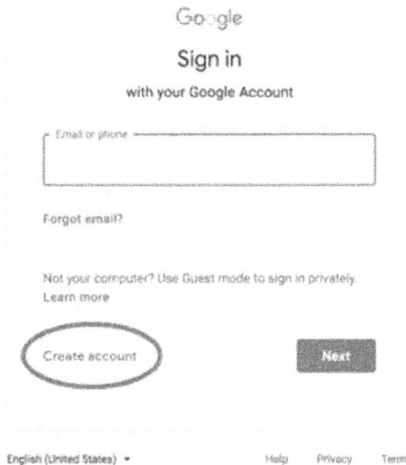

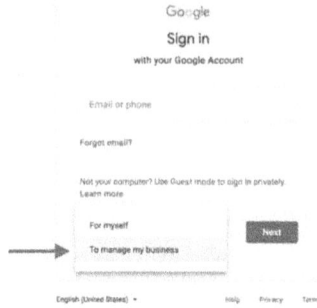

To officially create your Google account, enter your name, desired email and password before clicking "Next." Then, enter a recovery email and your birthday, gender, and phone number. Note: Google requires all users to be at least 13 years old.

To officially create your Google account, enter your name, desired email and password before clicking "Next." Then, enter a recovery email and your birthday, gender, and phone number. Note: Google requires all usersto be at least 13 years old.

Lastly, agree to Google's Privacy Policy and Terms of Service and verify your account with a code sent via text or phone call. Congratulations! You are now the proud owner of a Google account.

Creating a YouTube Brand Account

We're not done quite yet. You now need to set up a YouTube Brand Account. A brand account allows users to manage editing permissions and create a more holistic online presence.

To get started, visit YouTube. In the upper right-hand corner, note that you're probably already logged into your new Google account. (If you are not, click "Sign in" and enter your new Google account username and password.)

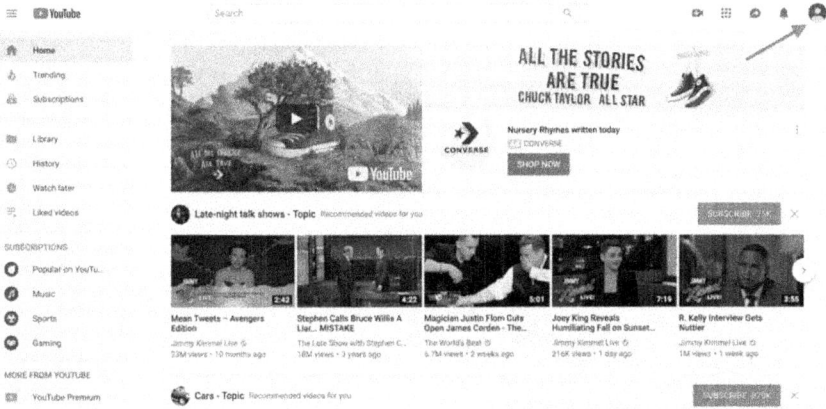

Once you have signed in, tap your account module, and click "My channel" in the drop-down menu.

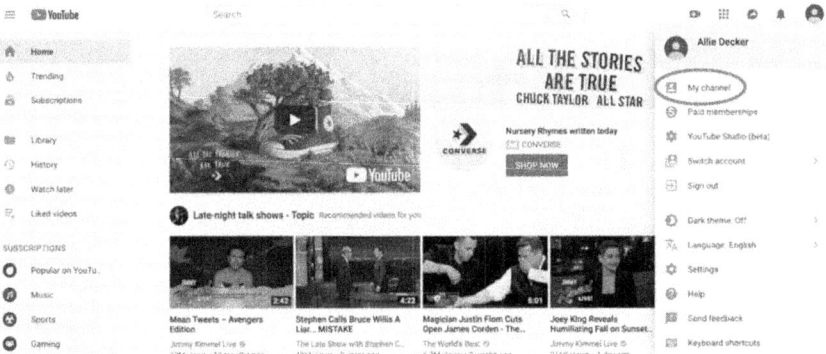

You will see the option to create a channel right away. Do **NOT** enter your name and click on "Create Channel." Instead, click on "Use a business or other name" at the bottom.

Now you should be prompted to create a brand account. Enter your brand account name and press "Create." **Note:** You can always update or change your channel name from your account settings, so don't worry if you aren't 100% sure about your selected label.

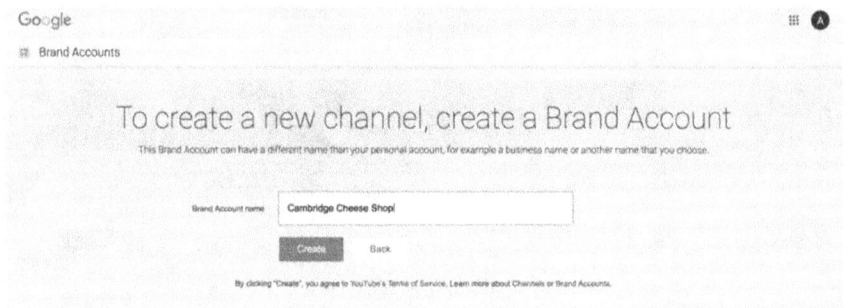

Customizing Your YouTube Brand Account
Now, let's customize your brand account. Click on "Customize Channel" to get started.

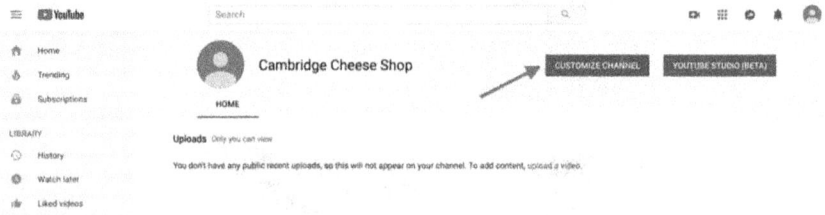

Start by adding a **channel icon** and **channel art.** These will be the first parts of your YouTube account that users see when visiting, so be sure to use easily recognizable images and consistent with your overall branding.

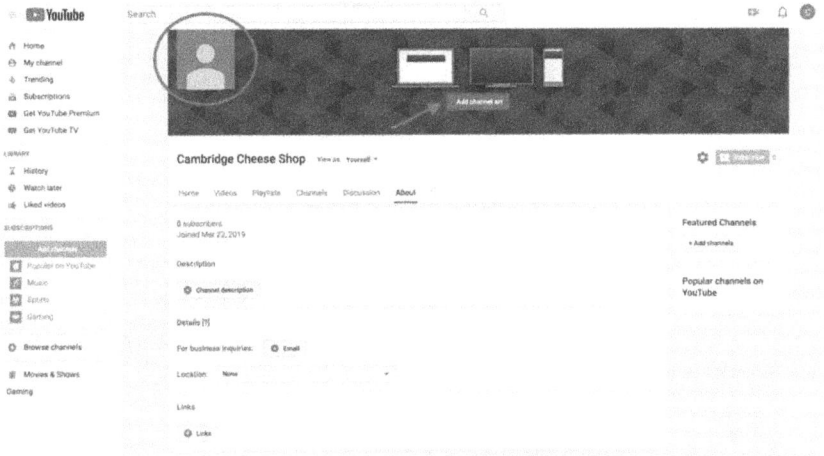

To add a channel icon, click on the default blue profile picture in your channel's upper left-hand corner and upload an image. Note: It may take several minutes for your channel icon to appear after uploading. Next, upload your channel art. Click on the blue "Add channel art" button in the center of your channel. **Check out YouTube's channel art templates** for specific design guidance.

After you upload your channel icon and art, add a channel description, a company email, and links to your company website and other social platforms under the "About" tab.

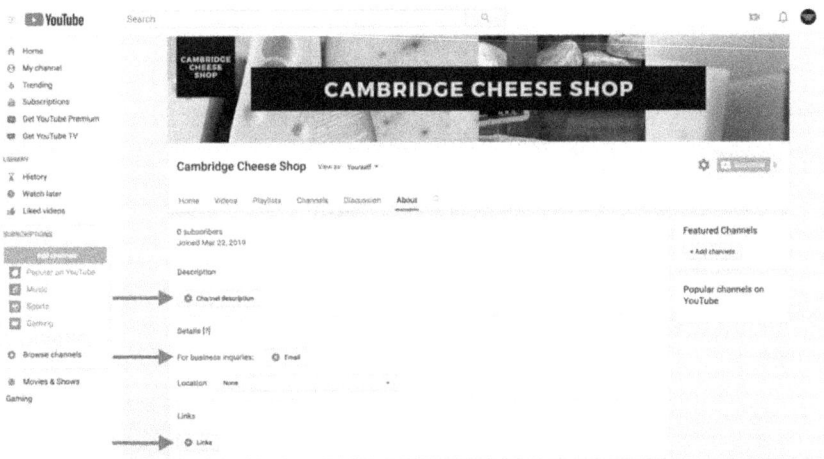

With the basic profile complete, it's time to add a few finishing touches! Before we move on, it is important to get one thing straight — you can customize the way your YouTube channel looks to subscribers and unsubscribed visitors. This means that unsubscribed viewers would see different featured content than dedicated, subscribed viewers. Pretty cool, right?

One of the main ways you can take advantage of this feature is by **creating a YouTube channel trailer**. A channel trailer is the video version of your description and is shown to all your unsubscribed viewers.

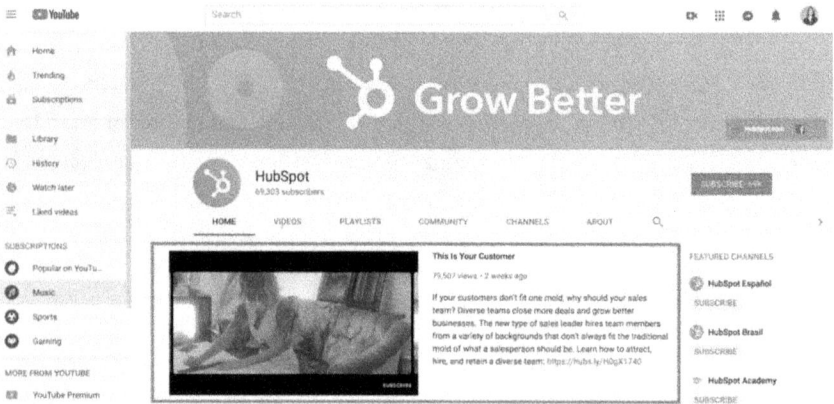

Ready to get started? First, make sure channel customization is turned on. To do this, click on the gear icon next to the red "Subscribe" button in the upper right-hand corner of your channel.

Next, make sure the option to "Customize the layout of your channel" is turned on and press "Save."

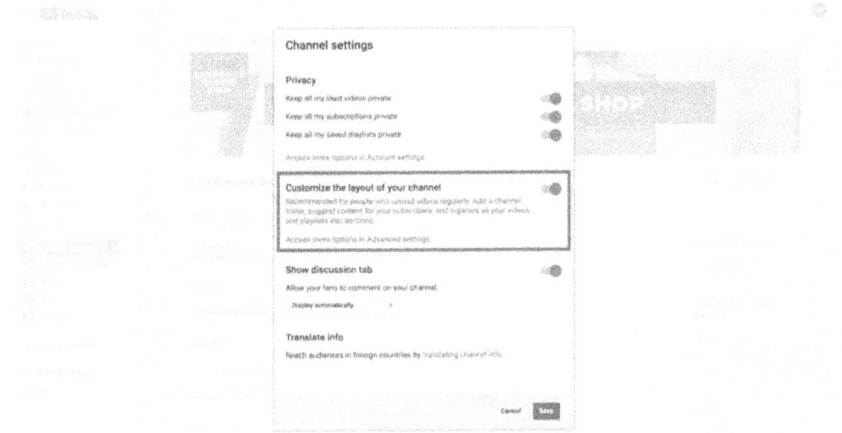

Now that your channel is set up for customization, upload your trailer. Click the arrow upload button in the upper right-hand corner and select your video file. Remember to add keywords to your trailer name and description.

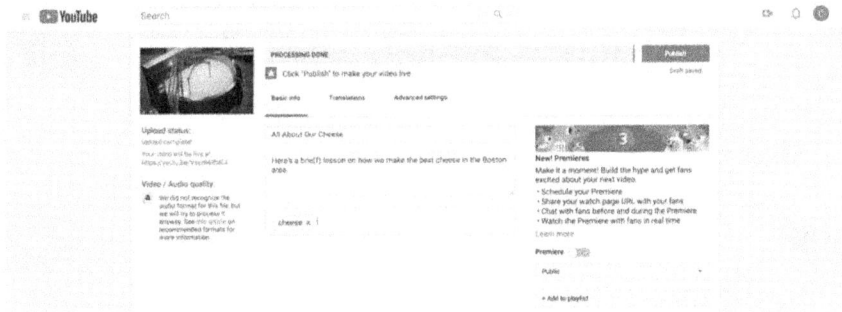

Once your video uploads, click on the "For new visitors" tab on your channel homepage. Then click "Channel trailer."

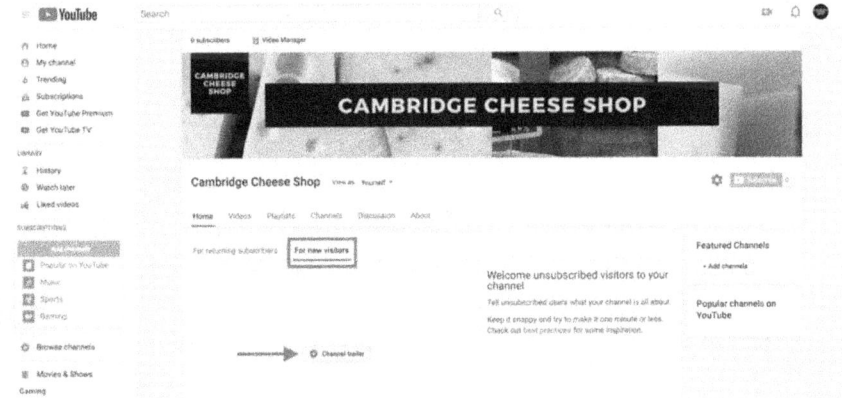

Finally, select your uploaded trailer, or enter a URL to a video you would like to feature, and press "Save."

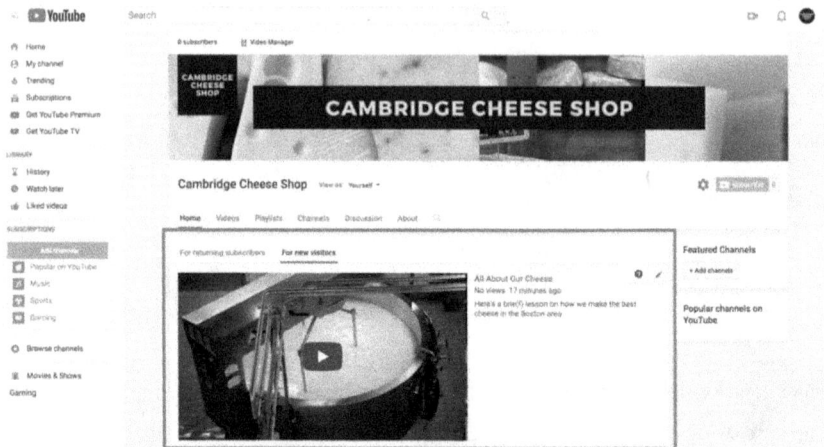

Setting Permissions for Your YouTube Brand Account

Before you start implementing your YouTube marketing plan, you should decide who on your team will need access to the account. Granting access to team members will allow them to help manage the channel through their own Google accounts.

When you grant access to a Google account, there are three options for roles:

- **Owner:** Owners have full editing power over all company Google properties. They can add or remove managers, edit business information, respond to reviews, and more.

- **Manager:** Managers have the same editing powers as owners, except they cannot add or remove page roles or remove listings. Anyone editing a YouTube channel must be a manager or an owner.

- **Communications Manager:** Communications Managers can respond to reviews and do several other actions, but they cannot use YouTube's video manager, upload content, or view analytics.

To add individuals to your account, tap your Google account icon in the upper right-hand corner to open the drop-down menu and go to "Settings."

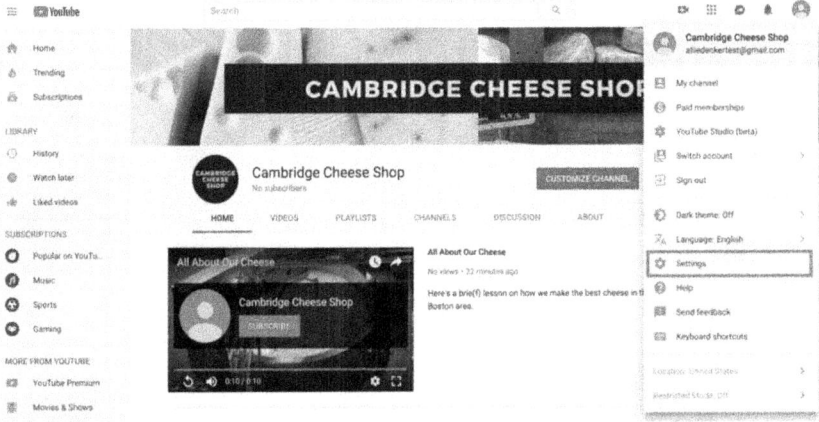

Click "Add or remove managers."

Click "Manage Permissions."

Then, select the people icon in the upper right-hand corner to invite new users. To grant permission to a person, enter their Gmail address and indicate their role.

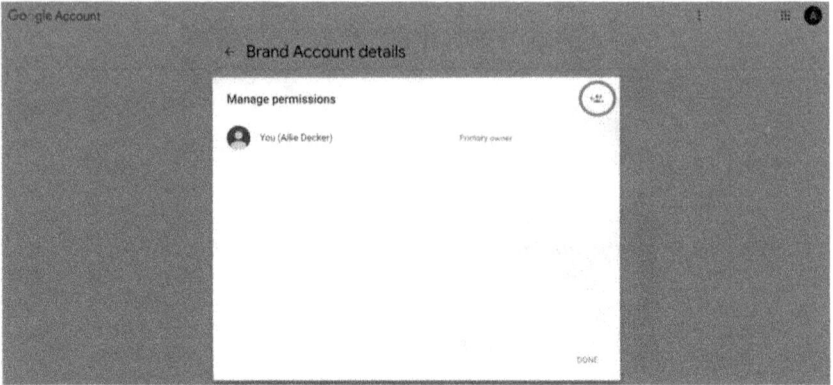

How to Create a Second YouTube Channel

Are you looking to create another channel from the same Google account? Perhaps you want a separate channel for personal videos, or you would like to start a second brand under the same business entity. Either way, the process is easy. Here's how:

- Go to your YouTube Studio account and open Creator Studio
- Classic.
- Click your account icon in the top right-hand corner and tap the gear icon next to "Creator Studio."
- Under "Your account," click "See all my channels or create a new channel."
- Click "+Create a new channel."
- Create and customize your new Brand Account (per our instructions above)

YouTube Brand Guidelines

Your YouTube channel is an extension of your brand, and it should be treated as such. As you create and customize your channel, follow these YouTube brand guidelines to properly establish your channel's identity and begin to attract subscribers.

- **Channel name:** Your channel name is associated with every single video you publish. Make sure it is correct and consistent with your other social media sites and overall branding.

- **Channel icon:** Google recommends uploading an 800 x 800 px square or round image. Your channel icon is like a Facebook profile picture. This image will be used across all of your Google properties, such as Gmail and Google+. Consider using a company logo or, if you are a public figure, a professional headshot.

- **Channel art:** Upload a 2560 x 1440 px image that will scale well across a desktop, tablet, mobile, and TV. You never know where your audience will be viewing your videos.

- **Channel description:** Your description should provide more information on your company and explain what type of video content you plan on sharing. Search engines look at your description when determining how to rank your profile, so incorporate relevant keywords in your overview. We'll talk more about how to optimize specific video descriptions below.

- **Channel trailer:** Your trailer should be short and sweet (30 to 60 seconds). Focus on showing visitors what your channel is about and what they can expect to see in your videos. Don't forget to encourage them to subscribe. Your trailer won't be interrupted by ads, which will keep the user focused on why they should subscribe and watch your videos.

- **Channel URL:** Your channel may be eligible for a custom URL if you have over 100 subscribers, a channel icon, channel art, and is more than 30 days old. Learn more about custom YouTube URLs here.

- **Channel links:** Link to all other social media accounts and relevant websites from the "About" section of your channel. Make it easy for subscribers to connect with you elsewhere.

How to Optimize Your Videos for SEO

Now that your YouTube channel is up and running, let's talk about search optimization.

Remember how we mentioned that YouTube is the second largest search engine? While creating engaging content is a must, it's not the only factor for success. You can do several things to optimize your videos to rank highly on both YouTube and Google search results. The first step to becoming a YouTube marketing pro is creating and improving your video's metadata. Simply put, metadata gives viewers information about your video, which includes your video title, description, tags, category, thumbnail, subtitles, and closed captions. Providing the right information in your video's metadata ensures that it is properly indexed by YouTube and appears when people are searching for videos like yours. Be brief and straightforward when filling out your metadata — your content could be removed if you try to promote it with unrelated keywords. Check out the video below to learn more about optimizing your video for search

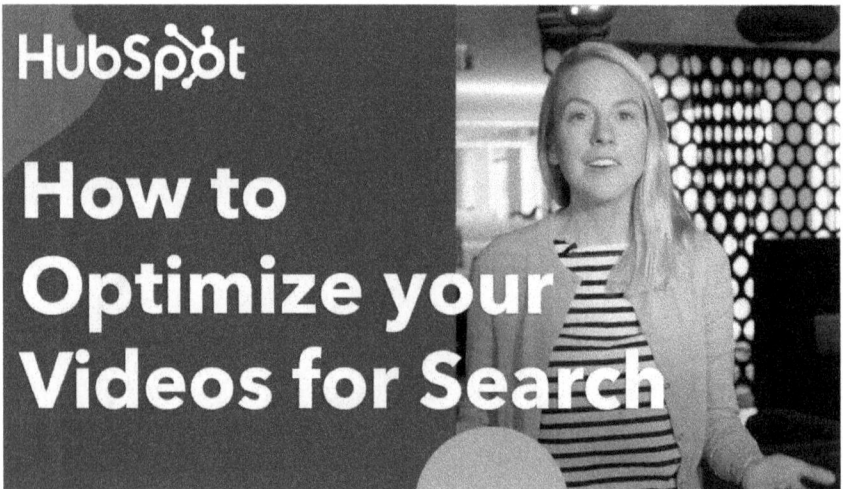

Title

Just like with on-page SEO, it's crucial to optimize your video's title and description. Titles are what people first read when scrolling through a list of videos, so make sure yours is clear and compelling. It should make it evident that your video will give them the answers they seek.

Do some **keyword research** to understand what viewers are searching for. Include the most important information and keywords at the beginning of your title. Lastly, keep titles to around 60 characters to keep text from being cut off in results pages.

Description
YouTube will only show the first two to three lines (about 100 characters) of your video's description. To read beyond that, viewers will need to click "Show more" to see the rest. For that reason, always include essential links or CTAs at the beginning of your description and write the copy to drive views and engagement.

Below this, include the video transcript. Video transcripts can significantly improve your SEO because your video is usually full of keywords. Add a default channel description that includes links to your social channels, video credits, and video-specific time stamps. You can also have #hashtags in your video titles and descriptions — just be sure to use them sparingly.

Tags
Next, highlight the main keywords in your tags. Tags associate your video with similar videos, which broadens its reach. When tagging videos, tag your most important keywords first and include the right mix of more common keywords and long-tail keywords.

Category
After you upload a video, YouTube will allow you to choose a video category under "Advanced settings." Video categories group your video with related content on the platform.
YouTube allows you to sort your video into one of the following categories:
Film & Animation, Autos & Vehicles, Music, Pets & Animals,
Sports, Travel & Events, Gaming, People & Blogs, Comedy,
Entertainment, News & Politics, How-to and Style, Education, Science and Technology, and Non-profits and Activism.

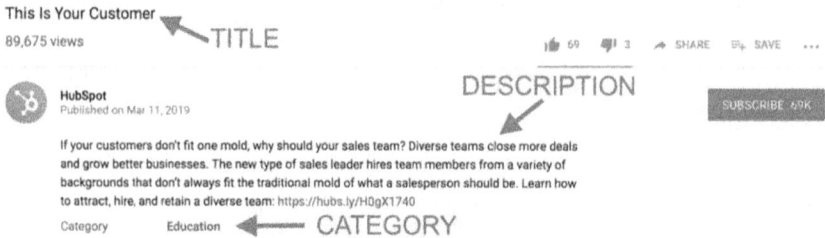

This Is Your Customer
89,675 views ← TITLE

👍 69 👎 3 ↗ SHARE ⤓ SAVE ...

DESCRIPTION

HubSpot
Published on Mar 11, 2019

SUBSCRIBE 69K

If your customers don't fit one mold, why should your sales team? Diverse teams close more deals and grow better businesses. The new type of sales leader hires team members from a variety of backgrounds that don't always fit the traditional mold of what a salesperson should be. Learn how to attract, hire, and retain a diverse team: https://hubs.ly/H0gX1740

Category   Education ◄————— CATEGORY

Thumbnail

Video thumbnails are the main images viewers see when scrolling through a list of video results, and yours can have a large impact on the number of clicks and views your video receives. YouTube will autogenerate a few thumbnail options for your video, but we highly recommend uploading a custom thumbnail. YouTube reports that "90% of the best performing videos on YouTube have custom thumbnails". When filming, think of high-quality shots that accurately represent your video. YouTube recommends using a 1280 x 720 px image to ensure that your thumbnail looks great on all screen sizes. Note: You must verify your YouTube account to upload a custom thumbnail image. You can do this by visiting youtube.com/verify and entering the verification code YouTube sends you.

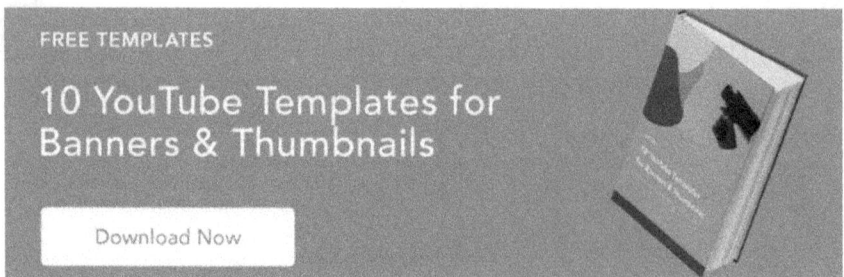

FREE TEMPLATES

10 YouTube Templates for Banners & Thumbnails

Download Now

SRT Files (Subtitles & Closed Captions)

Not only do **subtitles and closed caption**s help viewers, but they also help optimize your video for search by giving you another opportunity to highlight important keywords. You can add subtitles or closed captions by uploading a supported text transcript or timed subtitles file. You can also provide a full transcript of the video and have YouTube time the subtitles automatically, type the subtitles or translation as you watch the video, or hire a professional to translate or transcribe your video. To add subtitles or closed captions, head to your channel and click on "YouTube Studio," YouTube's replacement for Video Manager.

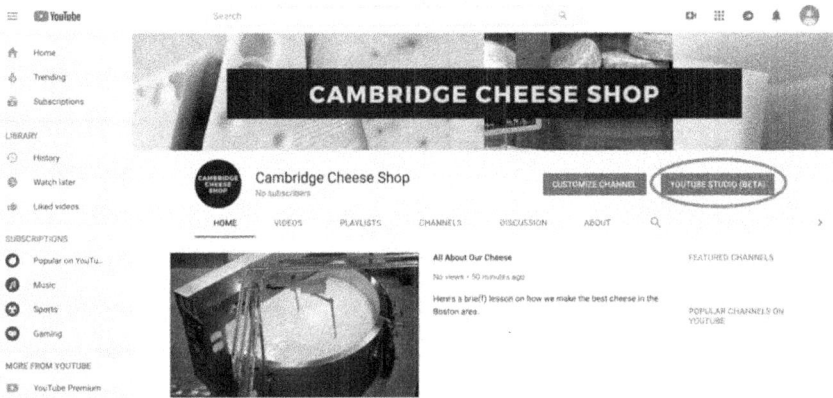

Once inside your YouTube Studio, click "Videos" from the menu on the left. Find the video you want to add subtitles or closed captioning to and click on the title to open the video settings.

Open the "Advanced" tab and choose the video language. Once you select a language, the option to "Upload Subtitles/CC" should become available. Click that option and choose to upload your subtitles or closed captioning with or without timing.

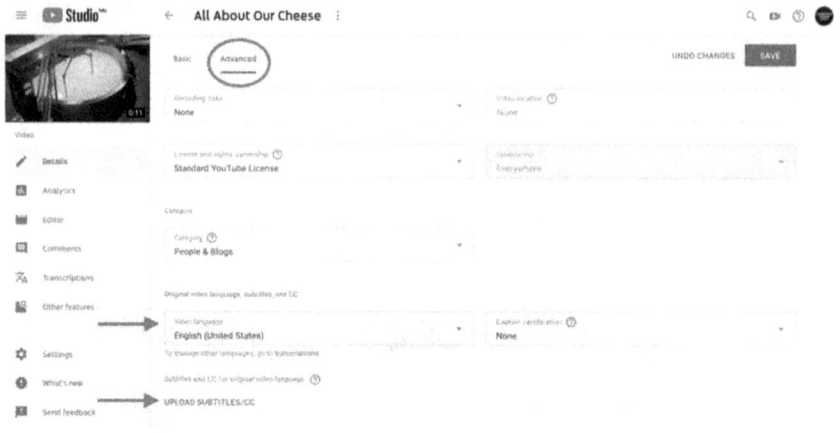

Cards and End Screens (Annotations)

Instead of annotations (which they sunsetted in May 2017), YouTube encourages users to incorporate cards and end screens in their videos to poll viewers, link to external sites, or direct people to other videos. Thankfully, cards and end screens are as easy to add as annotations. Cards are small, rectangular notifications that appear in the top righthand corner of both desktop and mobile screens. You can include up to five cards per video, but if you include multiple cards, be sure to space them out evenly to give viewers time to take the desired action.

Cards aren't yet available on YouTube Studio. To add cards, click "Creator Studio Classic" from the menu on the left and follow these steps.

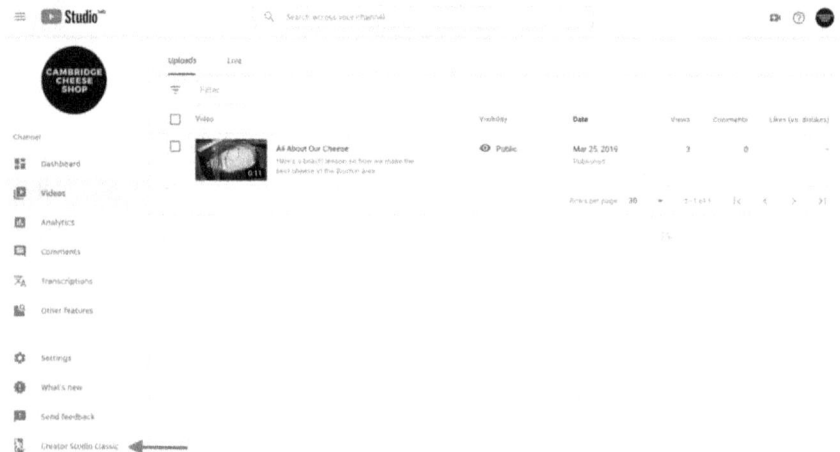

Once in the Creator Studio, click the drop-down edit arrow next to your video and choose "Cards."

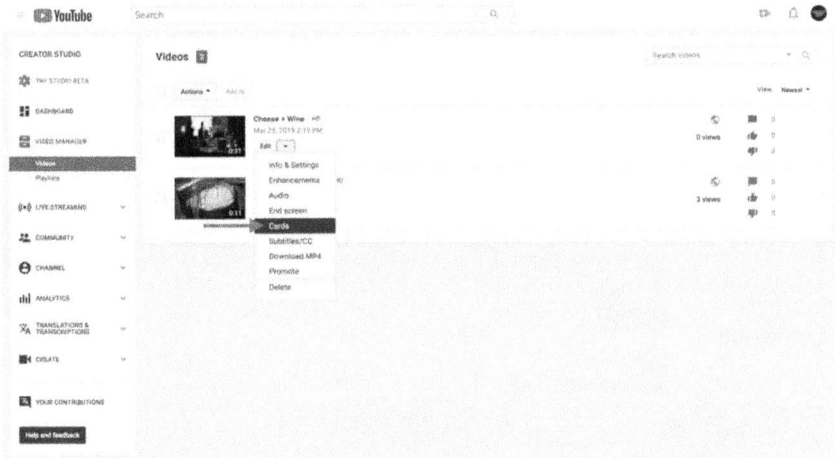

Then, click on "Add Card" and choose to create a Video or Playlist, Channel, Poll, or Link card. (Below is a video card featuring a suggested link to another video on the channel.)

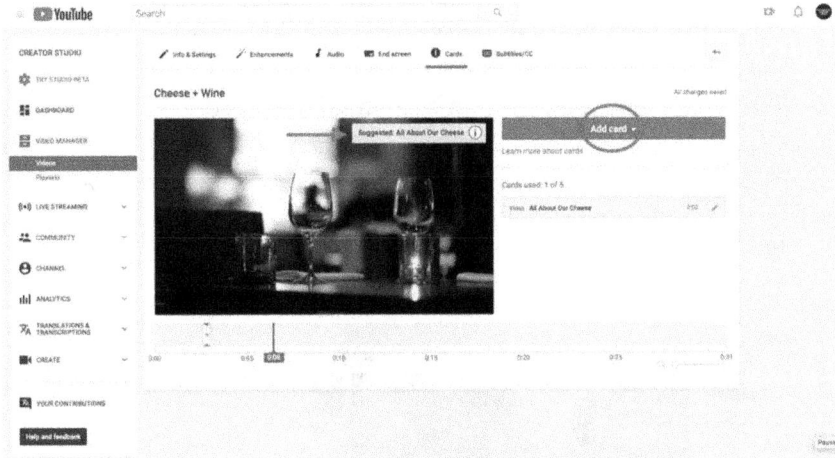

Once you have created your card, drag it to where you want it to appear. Your changes will be saved automatically.

End screens allow you to extend your video for 5-20 seconds to direct viewers to other videos or channels on YouTube. This encourages viewers to subscribe to your channel or promote external links, such as ones that direct them to your website. End screens encourage users to continue engaging with your brand or content.

To add an end screen, head to your video manager, click the drop-down edit arrow, and choose "End screen."

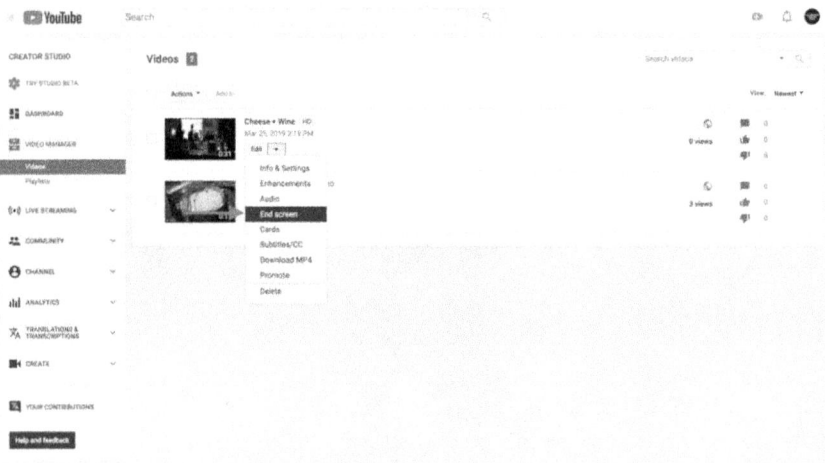

Then choose which elements you would like to add to your end screen. You can add elements by importing an end screen you used in another video, using a template, or creating elements manually.

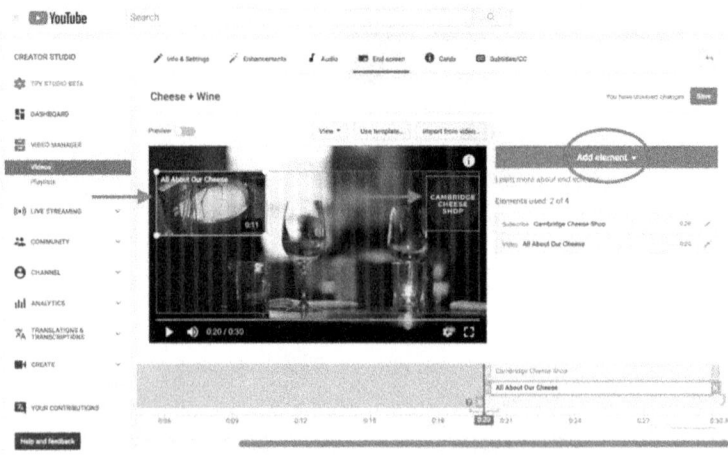

Note: YouTube requires users to promote another YouTube video or a playlist in part of the end screen.

Playlists

Are you creating videos around a few specific themes? Playlists might be the perfect tool for you! Playlists allow you to curate a collection of videos from both your channel and other channels. Not only do playlists help to organize your channel and encourage viewers to continue watching similar content, but they also show up separately in search results. Creating playlists provides you with more discoverable content. To create a new playlist, go to a video you would like to add and click "+Add to" under the video. Next, select "Create new playlist." Type in the name of the playlist you want to feature and click "Create."

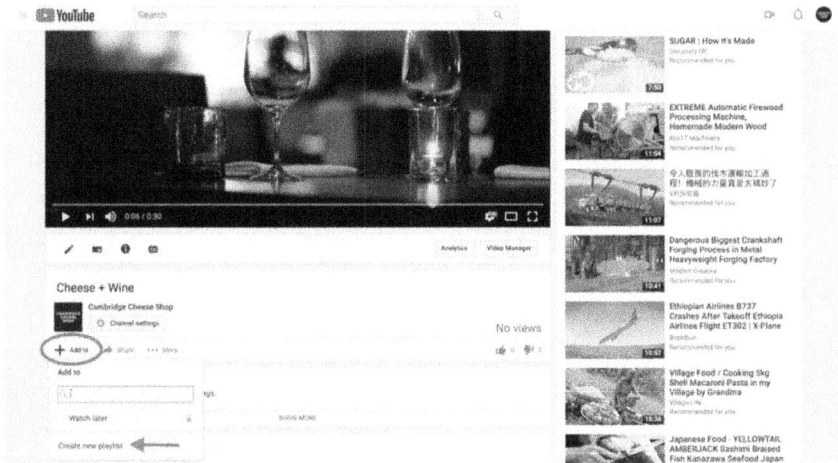

How to Create Videos for YouTube

Now that your YouTube channel is set up, it's time to start populating it with content. This is where the fun begins!

In this section, we will talk about some different types of videos you can create and how to film and edit them. Overwhelmed? Feeling uninspired? Check out our list of **great video advertising and marketing campaigns** for creative ideas to inspire your next project.

Eight Types of YouTube Videos to Create

Before you start filming, decide what type of video would help you achieve your goal. In a recent **article from the Huffington Post**, companies seeing the greatest YouTube success ranked different videos by their importance and effectiveness. Below, we cover these videos as ranked in the article.

Before brainstorming on filming and editing your videos, consider this list of video types:

#1 Customer testimonials

Customer testimonials are short-form interviews with satisfied customers. Customer testimonials can help build company and product credibility.

#2 On-demand product demonstration videos

Demonstration videos are short pieces of content showing the benefits and proper use of a product.

#3 Explainer and tutorial videos

Explainer videos are in-depth videos explaining how to use a product or various parts of a product or service. Tutorials can be used to answer customer support questions or explain a new product feature.

#4 Thought leader interviews

Interviews with experts or thought leaders can help amplify your company's credibility in an industry.

#5 Project reviews and case studies

Project reviews or case studies recap a successful campaign or project and often include statistics and results.

#6 YouTube Live

YouTube Live allows users to broadcast live content to viewers. Live video allows you to share unfiltered moments easily and lets your audience participate in real-time comments and reactions. Live videos on YouTube are recorded and appear like any other video upload. Go Live from your YouTube channel by clicking the camera+ icon in the top right corner and choosing "Go live."

#7 Video blogs
Video blogs are daily or weekly videos documenting daily life or events. You could also record a video that summarizes or highlights a blog post, so your audience has multiple ways to digest the content.

#8 Event videos
Event videos feature in-person experiences at a conference or expo and can be a great way to show a crowd's excitement.

Writing Your Video Script

1. Define your goal
It is important to establish what you want to accomplish with your video before getting into the nuts and bolts of bringing it to life.

Do you want to increase awareness of your brand? Drive inbound website traffic? Add subscribers to your channel? Increase social shares?
Or do something else entirely?

Establishing a singular goal at the start of the production process is crucial and will allow you to focus the video's script and strategy on accomplishing it. It is perfectly okay to have multiple goals for your YouTube channel, like increasing brand awareness and adding subscribers. The best practice is to focus on one goal per video.

2. Create a storyboard and write the lines
Once you have established your video's goal, get creative and start working on your storyboard. A storyboard is like a blueprint for your video and

serves as an outline for the shoot.

You have probably even seen one before. Storyboards look like comic strips and include rough sketches of different scenes paired with short descriptive information about the location, camera position and motion,
and dialogue. They vary in the level of detail included, but your storyboard should, at the very least, include:
- A frame for each major scene or location change.
- Basic descriptive information about the scene (time of day, weather, the mood of the characters, etc.)
- Lines for each scene.
- Camera direction for motion and shot details (i.e., tight, medium, or wide shots).

3. Decide on additional multimedia elements
If your video includes graphics, title slides, or other multimedia elements, you should plan the placement and content for those pieces in advance. These elements can be incorporated into your storyboards so that the video's content flows seamlessly.

4. Determine the video length
As you create your storyboard, you will also want to decide how long your video should be. On YouTube, videos under two minutes receive the highest levels of engagement.

Your video should be just long enough to deliver the key messages that align with its goal. If you create a longer video, experiment with how you present content — the pacing, story arc, and visuals — to keep viewers interested throughout.

5.Pick a filming location (or multiple)
You've determined your video goal, created a storyboard and decided on the ideal video length needed to deliver your message. Now it's time to find your filming locations.

In the film industry, this step is called location scouting, and like every other step in this process, it is an integral part of creating a compelling video. To get started, envision your storyboard, and create a list of the different locations each scene requires. Depending on your video concept, you may only need one location. Or you may need a new location for each scene.

Friends, co-workers, and even family can be great resources here for finding the locations you need. Remember that you will need permission from the owner to film for some locations, like businesses and other private property. To keep things simple, it's best to find your locations through people you know — at least for your first few productions.

Visit each location before the shoot. On your scouting trips, make sure you'll be able to capture the kinds of shots you want for your video.

Typically, it's better to have more space so you can adjust the camera position as needed. You should also check for any loud or ambient noise like busy roads or air conditioning units that could interfere with your audio when filming. The lighting and time of day are also important factors to consider. While the room might have sufficient light in the morning, you may need to bring a lighting kit in to film during the afternoon or evening.

Six Essential Tips for Shooting Quality Videos

After the prep, it's finally time to start filming your video. Don't worry if you don't have a fancy camera, with the advances in smartphone technology, it is completely possible to film great content with just your phone.

If you are filming with a phone, be sure to turn it sideways and film in landscape mode. This will prevent awkward cropping or framing when you upload the video to YouTube, which natively supports the landscape format. No matter what you're filming with, these tips can help your videos look professional and stay engaging for your viewers.

Use a tripod
You want viewers to focus on your story, not the shakiness of the camera. For static shots, be sure to place your camera on a tripod or any other level

surface.

Set your camera to manual mode
Suppose you're able to set your camera to full manual mode. This will allow you to adjust the focus and other settings as needed to expose and focus your shots properly.

Shoot from different angles and distances
For each scene, make sure you film from a few positions to edit between the clips. For an interview or video focused on a single individual, this may mean moving the camera from facing the scene head-on to filming from a 45-degree angle.

head-on to filming from a 45-degree angle.

You can also try to move the camera closer and further away or zooming in and out for more variety. Cutting between different angles and distances will keep your video visually interesting and engaging.

Film more than you think you need
Less is not more when it comes to filming. It's better to have too much than too little. With too much, you can condense what you have recorded down to the best bits. With too little, you will have to try and film more which can be frustrating after already doing so. To make sure you have the clips you need, shoot multiple takes of each scene. Make sure you don't miss a moment and count down from five before starting the action and before you finish recording.

Introduce motion
If you have a slider or Steadicam, try including camera movement in your video. Even subtle movements from left to right or in and out can add intrigue to your clips.

Use a good microphone
If you plan on speaking in your video, be sure to use a high-quality microphone to capture the audio. Many different microphone choices

record audio separately from the camera. There are even **mics you can plug into your smartphone** for better audio on the go.

Editing Your Video Content

Tools

There are many options for editing tools and software. Your computer may come with free editing software such as iMovie or Windows Movie Maker, depending on your operating system. These programs provide basic editing tools, like cutting clips together, adding tiles, and adding limited effects and color correction.

There are also higher-end, more expensive Final Cut Pro X or Adobe Premiere CC options, which offer various editing tools. YouTube even has its own online editing platform you can use to compile your clips and edit your videos together.

Video Thumbnails

Once your video is ready to upload, YouTube allows you to select the video thumbnail that will appear on your channel, in search results, and on the right-hand column. We recommend uploading your own custom thumbnail — as we talked about above.

Watermarks

You can also add a custom watermark to all your videos. To do so, navigate to the branding section of the Creator Studio. The watermark serves as a customable subscribe button that viewers can click anytime when watching your videos.

To add a watermark, go to your YouTube Studio and click on "Settings."

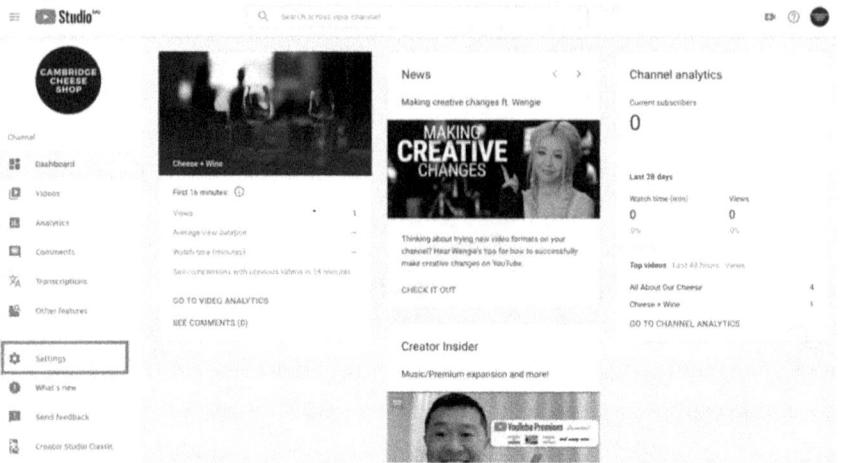

Tap "Other settings" > "Channel branding."

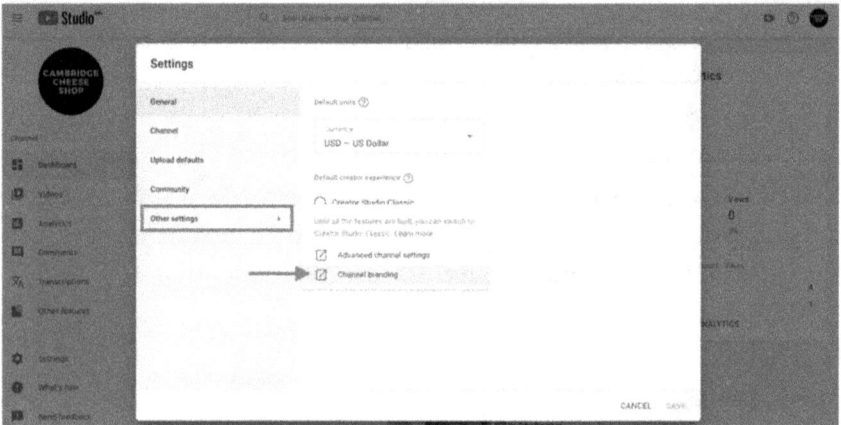

You should be directed to a screen where you can select "Add a watermark." Follow the instructions to upload a file.

Music & Sound Effects

Professional quality music and sound effects can differentiate between a successful video and a seemingly amateur one. Fortunately, cinema quality sounds are now readily available, even if your videos don't have Hollywood-size budgets.

When selecting music for your video, first consider the overall mood you would like to create. Music is one of the most valuable tools for setting a video's tone and often dictates the editing style, camera movement, and on-camera action. If you're introducing your brand to a new audience, you probably want to select music that is upbeat and catchy.

The second key part of picking music is obtaining the necessary permissions to use the song. What you're looking for here are songs marked as "royalty-free. This doesn't mean the music will be free, but it does mean you only pay a flat rate to use the music and won't have to pay additional royalties or licensing fees on top of that.

YouTube has a **library of free sound effects and music** to use in your videos. Some other great resources for royalty-free music are Pond5, **Epidemic Sound,** and **PremiumBeat.** Both services include thousands of professionally recorded and produced songs in various genres at varying lengths and tempos. PremiumBeat and Pond5 both include a large library of sound effects to add texture and depth to your videos.

Sometimes, it only takes a subtle sound effect layer in the background of a scene to elevate the production quality of your video and really pull your audience into the story.

YouTube Marketing Strategy

Now that you have produced a video and optimized it for search, let's talk about how to market your YouTube channel. While ranking high in search results and having a large subscriber base are ideal, those goals can be difficult to achieve when you're just starting out.

That's why it's important always to spread the word about your YouTube channel and videos across other platforms. Fortunately, YouTube and other platforms make it easy to do this.

Below are some **tips for how to best promote your YouTube content** on other channels.

Social Media

Sharing your videos on social media is an easy way to engage with viewers. YouTube makes it incredibly simple for you and others to promote your video across other social networks. To **share a video,** just click the "Share" tab underneath the video. There you can select where to send the video. YouTube even provides a shortened URL to your video for convenient posting.

Consider what is the best marketing strategy to use when promoting your YouTube channel or videos on your social media sites. Simply sharing the video on your timeline may not be the most effective option. Why did you make the video? Maybe you created a tutorial because users were asking many questions about how to use your product.

In that case, it might be best to respond to those questions with a link to your video. If you created a video as part of a larger campaign or global trend, be sure to include relevant #hashtags (where appropriate) to ensure your video is included in the conversation. If you created a video to build awareness around your brand, consider posting the link in your profile bios.

Blog Posts and Website

Market your YouTube channel and videos on your website and blog. First, add a YouTube follow icon to your website and blog so your audience can easily find your channel. Second, embed relevant videos on your website or in blog posts. Consider creating a YouTube video to accompany a specific blog post or sharing customer video reviews or case studies on your website. Not only will this help market your YouTube channel and videos, but it will also **drive traffic to your website.**

To add a YouTube video to your blog or website, copy the embed code under the video you want to feature.

To add a YouTube video to your blog or website, copy the embed code under the video you want to feature.

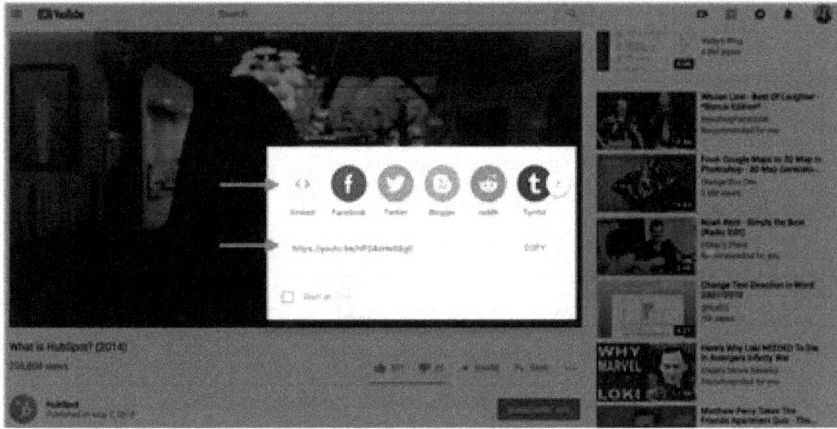

Email

While you're on the quest to find and attract new customers and leads, don't forget about the ones you already have. Share your video content and channel with relevant email lists. Encourage your contacts to check out a blog post you've in which embedded a video to increase both the video and website traffic. Sending an email newsletter with valuable information and video content is another great way to keep your contacts engaged.

Q&A Sites

Do your videos help solve a problem or answer a question? If so, engaging with popular Q&A sites like Quora might be a great marketing technique for your business. Monitor questions and share video content users will find helpful.

Collaborate With Others

Does your company have a relationship with another company that has a great YouTube presence? Ask them to collaborate! Collaborating with others is a fun way for both channels to gain exposure to other audiences. Create a video or playlist together. There are many options to collaborate with other brands creatively; just make sure that their audience and goal are similar to yours. The partnership should align with your marketing strategy.

Engage With Viewers

Finally, be sure to engage with your viewers. Respond to comments, answer questions, ask for feedback, and thank viewers for their support. This is an easy task to forget so try to choose a dedicated time to check video interactions and respond to users.

8 Tips to Market Your YouTube Channel and Videos

Above, we touched on some components to build a high-level marketing strategy for your YouTube videos. In this section, we will discuss some tips on how to promote your YouTube content best.

- Keep your channel branding consistent with your other social media accounts.
- Optimize your title and description for SEO and searcher intent.
- Feature real people or animated faces in your videos, not just words or B-roll.
- Choose a video thumbnail that accurately represents your video content.
- Include calls-to-action (CTAs) in every video.
- Make it easy for others to share your content.
- Create playlists that feature your videos.
- Produce videos regularly and consider doing a video series.

Understanding YouTube Analytics

You have put a lot of time and effort into your YouTube channel. You've created interesting content, optimized it for SEO, and shared it across different platforms… now, it's time to measure your success.

YouTube Analytics can seem daunting at first. Let's face it, interpreting a bunch of numbers and strange-looking graphs can be pretty challenging.

Thankfully, understanding YouTube Analytics is fairly straightforward once you know your way around it.

Determine Your Goal

First things first, you can't measure your success without **determining your goal.** If you've filmed, edited, uploaded, optimized, and shared your video and still don't know what goal you're trying to achieve, we have an issue. Your goal should drive your video strategy from beginning to end.

You should focus on targeting one goal per video. Some of the most common video goals are to increase brand awareness, views, clicks, or inbound links. Depending on how you use the video in your marketing material, the goal could be to increase an email series' open rate or improve the conversion rate on a landing page. YouTube is an excellent platform for growing brand awareness.

As the world's second-largest search engine, YouTube allows your videos to be seen through organic search or paid advertising.

Video is a great way to humanize your brand by showcasing real employees, customers, or partners. It also allows you to build credibility by publishing informational content that helps your target buyer. Promoting your videos through paid advertising versus organic search can impact the type of video you create. If you're planning to increase awareness organically, consider filming your company's history, customer reviews, or product tutorials.

Key metrics to track

Now that we've talked about why determining a goal is so important, we can discuss how to measure success effusively. At first glance, YouTube analytics can be overwhelming. On the flip side, it's frustrating when you post a video and don't receive as many views or as much engagement as you were expecting. YouTube analytics shows you how viewers find your content, how long they watch it for, and how much they engage with it. Let's start by going over what exactly you can measure and how to find it.

First, head to youtube.com/analytics. You should be directed to an analytics dashboard that shows an overview of how your videos have been performing during the past 28 days. You can adjust the analytics timeframe by clicking on the drop-down menu in the upper right-hand corner. The overview report features some top-line performance metrics, engagement metrics, demographics, traffic sources, and popular content.

You can also filter your results by content, device type, geography or location, all video content or playlists, subscriber status, playback type, traffic by different YouTube products, and translations. In addition to filtering results, YouTube allows you to display your results in various charts and even an interactive map.

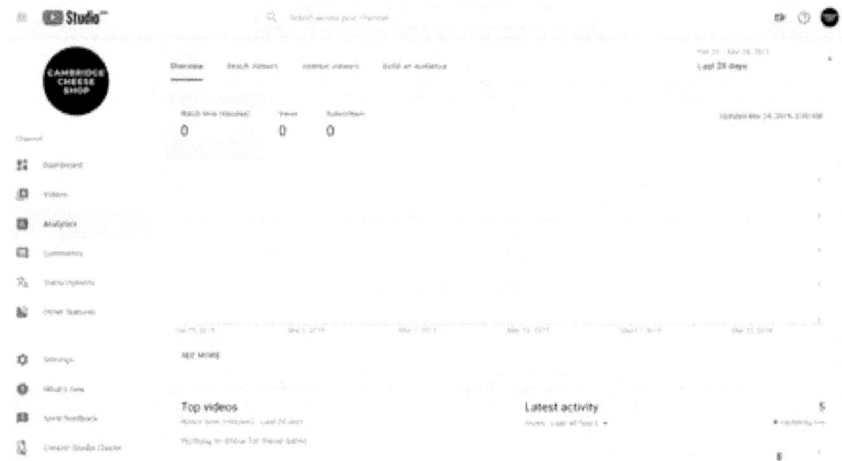

While there's no one-size-fits-all approach for reporting and measuring a campaign's success, below are a few key metrics that you should special pay attention to.

Watch Time and Audience Retention

Watch time reports. These show the total number of minutes your audience has spent viewing your content on your channel as a whole, and by video. This helps you see what pieces of content viewers are actually consuming instead of just clicking on and navigating away from.

Watch time is important because it's **one of YouTube's ranking factors.**

A video with a higher watch time is more likely to rank better in results. YouTube provides a line-item report on watch time, views, average view duration, location, publish date, and more.

A video's average percentage viewed, or **retention rate,** indicates the average percentage of a video your audience watches per view. A higher percentage means there is a higher chance that your audience will watch that video until the end. Try placing cards and end screens in videos with a higher average percentage viewed rate to improve the number of views your calls-to-action receive.

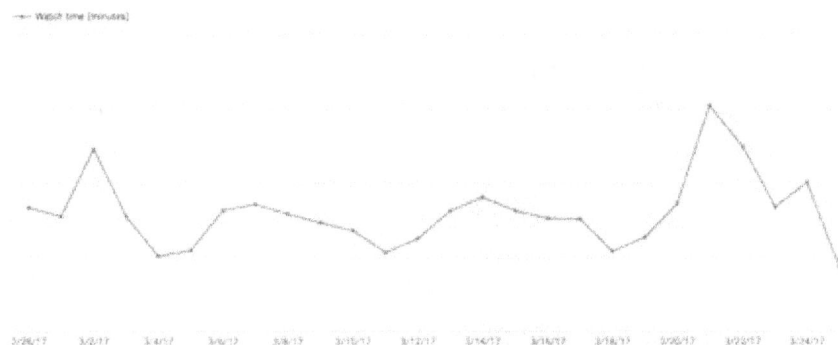

Sample watch timeline chart

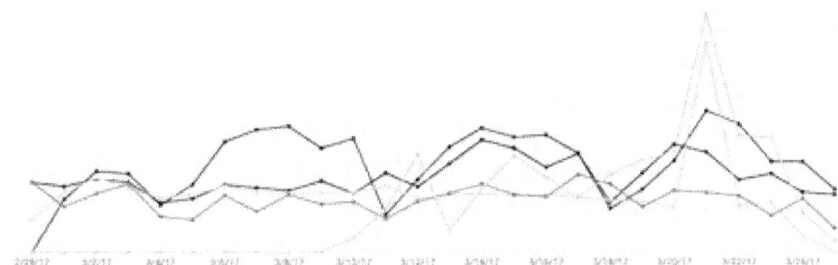

Traffic Sources

The traffic sources report shows how viewers are finding your content online. This provides valuable insight on where to promote your YouTube content. For example, you can see if viewers are finding your content through YouTube, Facebook, or Twitter. To view more in-depth traffic reporting, click on the overall traffic source category. This data can help refine your YouTube marketing strategy. Be sure to optimize your metadata based on your findings.

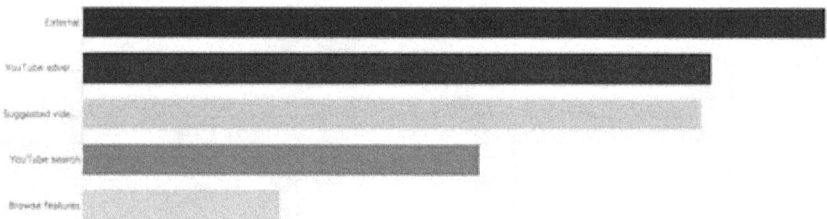

Sample traffic sources overview bar chart

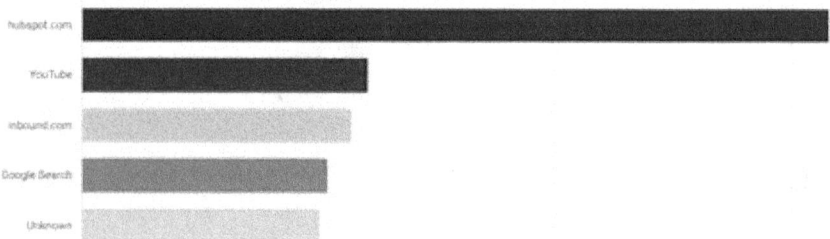

Demographics

The demographics report helps you understand your audience by reporting their age and gender. You can then break down age groups and genders by other criteria such as geography. This report will help you better market to your YouTube audience and understand if your content is resonating with your established customers.

Make your video marketing stronger with buyer personas. Download our **free Persona Templates here.**

Engagement Reports

Engagement reports help you learn what content is resonating with your audience. Here, you can see what viewers are clicking, sharing, commenting, and promoting. You can also see how your cards and end screens are performing in your engagement reports. Cards and end screens reports help you learn what your audience is engaging with so you can optimize your calls-to-action in future videos.

How to Run a YouTube Advertising Campaign

In addition to driving organic traffic to your content, several paid options are for promoting your video on YouTube. In this section, we'll dive into some of the basics of how to run a YouTube advertising campaign.

Cost of Advertising on YouTube

YouTube uses a cost-per-view (CPV) model, which means you only pay when someone engages with your ad. If your ad is skipped, you are not charged for that view. The exact cost per click varies on keyword competitiveness, but on average it's around $0.06. Once you set your daily campaign budget, YouTube will display your ad until the daily budget is spent.

Types of YouTube Ads

#1 Video Discovery Ads

TrueView video discovery ads appear on the YouTube homepage, within search results, and as related videos on YouTube watch pages. When a user clicks on one of these ads, they are redirected to the promoted video.

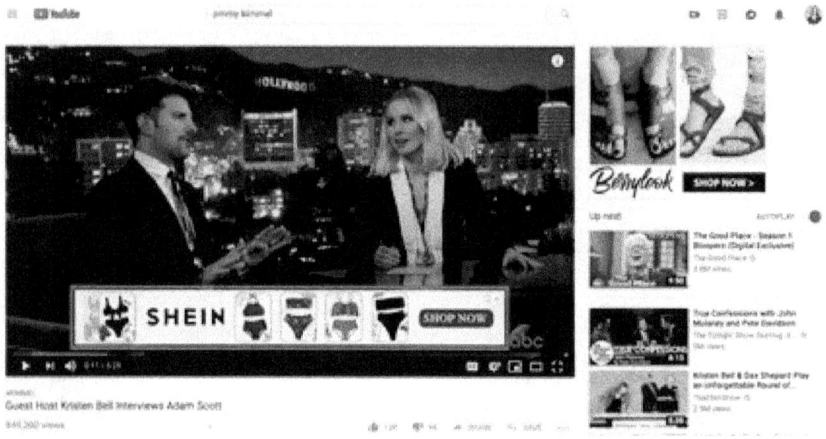

#2 In-Stream Ads

In-stream ads refer to ads that play within a YouTube video. TrueView in-stream ads play before a viewer watches the video they've selected. These ads can be customized with different overlay text and CTAs, and viewers usually have the option to skip the ad after watching the first five seconds. In addition to the pre-roll in-stream ads that play before the video, there are also mid-roll video ads that appear halfway through YouTube videos that are 10 minutes or longer.

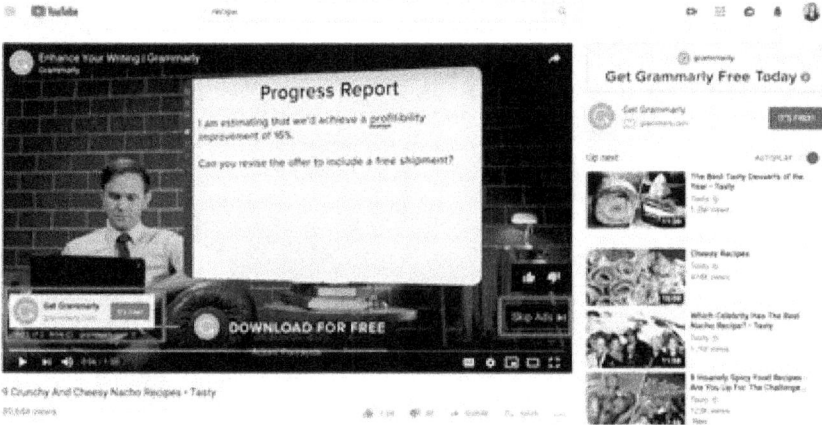

See a full list of the **advertising options on YouTube here.** Setting Up Your YouTube Ad Campaign

You can **create a campaign** using any video you've uploaded to your YouTube channel.

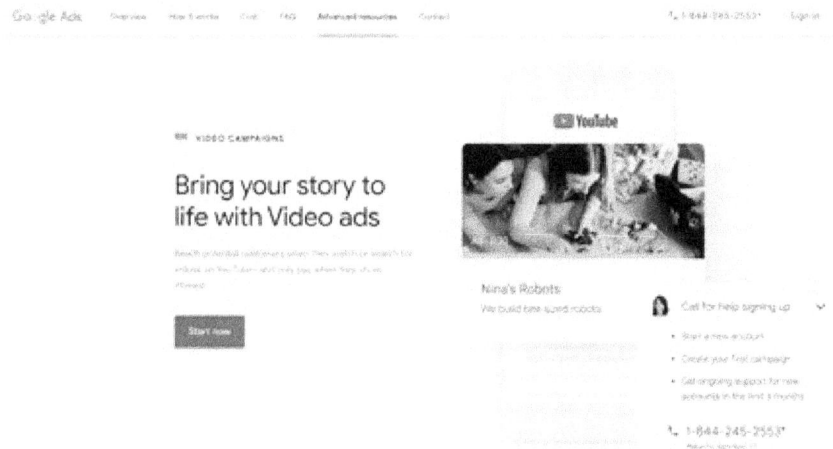

First, go to **your Google AdWords account** and select "New Campaign" to get started.

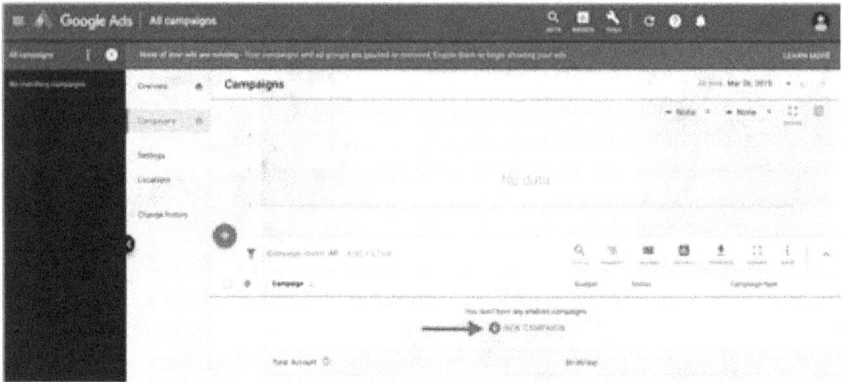

Select "Video" as your campaign type.

Next, select a goal to access suggested campaign settings as you walk through the setup process. You can choose Sales, Leads, Website traffic, Product and Brand Consideration.

Sales, Leads, and Website traffic require **conversion tracking**. Product and Brand Consideration offer campaign subtypes to further customize your campaign's goal.

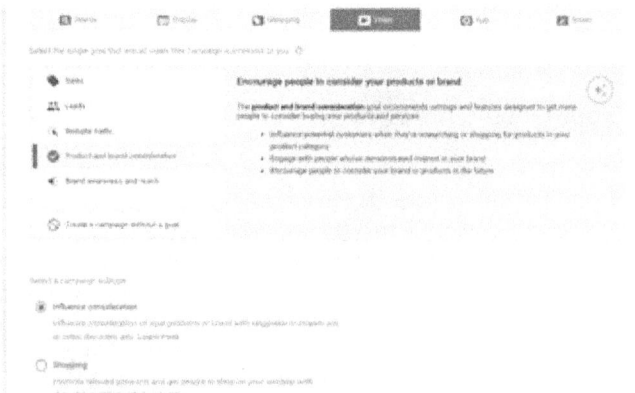

Note: You can also proceed without a set goal, although Google Ads won't provide step-by-step suggestions.

Next, choose a name, budget, and timeline for your campaign. You will also choose your bidding strategy, ad networks, target languages, and locations in this step.

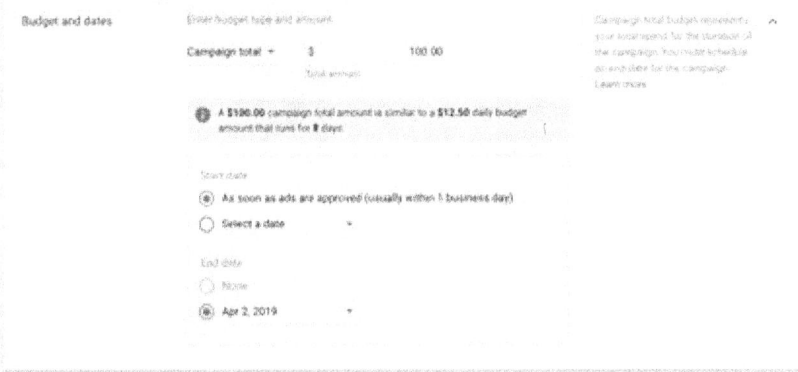

Scroll down to build your ad. Name your ad group and set your audience's demographics. You can also set keywords, topics, and placements to narrow your campaign and reach further. Finally, decide on a bid for your ad.

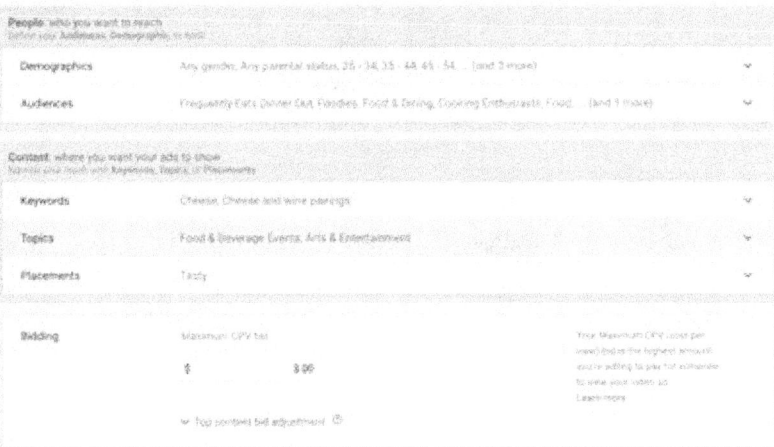

Lastly, create your video ad. Input the URL for your video and choose your video ad format. Indicate where you want your viewers to go if they click on your ad — and don't forget a CTA.

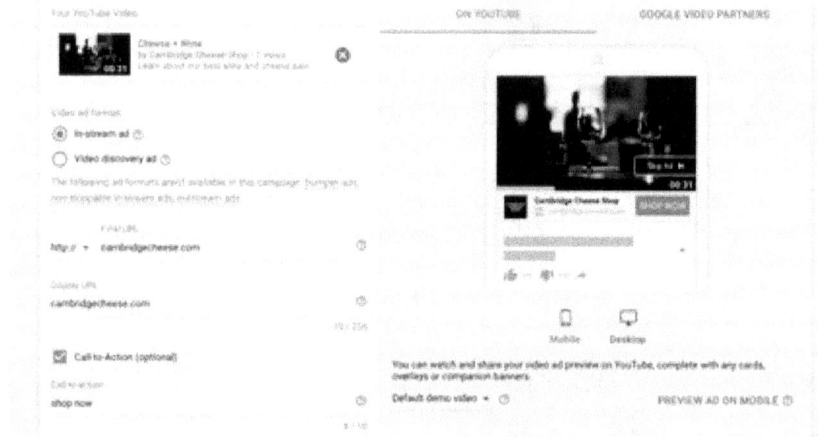

Click "Save & Continue" to review your ad. Congratulations! Your YouTube ad campaign is ready.

Ready, Set, Action

With **more than a billion active users,** YouTube is not merely a home for funny videos anymore. Video drives a 157% increase in organic traffic from search engines. YouTube is a serious marketing platform that provides your brand with the opportunity to promote content in a visual and engaging way.

It's essential to practice inbound marketing techniques when marketing your YouTube channel and videos. Create content that shares an interesting story and provides your viewers with valuable information. Then, market that content across different platforms, including social, email, and your company blog or website. Optimize your content by including cards and end screens with clear CTAs.

YouTube may seem overwhelming at first, but it makes it very easy to share and digest content. Your audience wants to learn, be entertained, and engage with your brand through video.

Stay tuned for guides on how to use YouTube business manager on the Akylles Facebook Group and channels.

Conclusion

Your start-up, E-Commerce, or project is your baby, and just like a baby, it needs care, attention, and nutrients to grow. Your nutriments are data and followers, and your care is constant attention to the branding, content, and community you are building around it.

I am giving you a sheet of tools to use for your business, tools that will make your life much easier on all levels. Make sure to have accounts on these platforms to push your business forward.

Disclaimer: This is not a paid promoted list. You can trust that the list will be greatly beneficial for you because they are my genuine suggestions.

SCAN ME

9. Raise Money Fast.

Money is your fuel, so for me as a petrolhead, when I started my journey as a founder, money became my petrol. I wanted to generate as much money as possible and become a money head for Lexyom. As I told you before, I raised a lot of money in the first few months. It was rewarding to experience growing a business from scratch, with people trusting you and giving you financial support. This thrill alone, pushes you to hustle further. You will have this neurological drive to continue raising funds.

Fundraising Psychology Hacks You Need to Know

Charitable giving is admirable, but it is also a puzzling phenomenon to many psychologists. The same concepts apply in raising funds for start-ups. What motivates a person to put aside their own interests and give money (or other resources) to someone else, often someone they don't even know?

Luckily, research allows us to understand what motivates people to donate and what organizations can do to encourage philanthropy. Here are some critical findings non-profits can use to optimize their fundraising strategies.

1.Identifiable Victim Effect

The identifiable victim effect is one of the most important psychological concepts for fundraisers to understand. Experiments indicate that people are more likely to donate to a cause when presented with a single, identifiable victim instead of when presented with a group of victims.

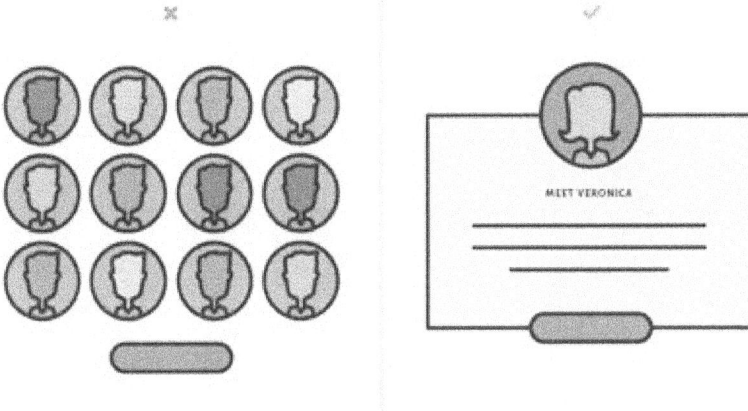

Give your audience a main character to root for, a single person they can emotionally connect with. Include identifying details, like their name, job, or hobbies, to help potential donors get to know the person.

Of course, only share someone's story with their permission.

2. Psychic Numbing

Many organizations try to convey the scale of the problem they work on by highlighting the vast number of people in need, but this can backfire.

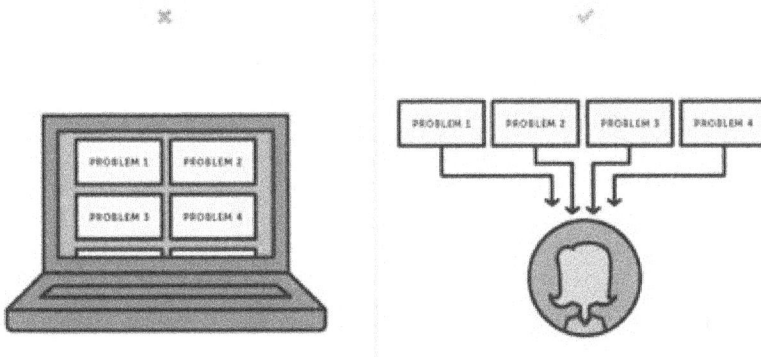

The problem with telling donors about 10,000 people in need is that it leaves them feeling overwhelmed. They can't know and connect with thousands of people, so it's easier to tune out. Present individual stories so your audience can relate and imagine providing aid on a smaller scale.

3. The Time-Ask Effect

When it comes to fundraising, it can be useful to ask for your audience's time before their money.

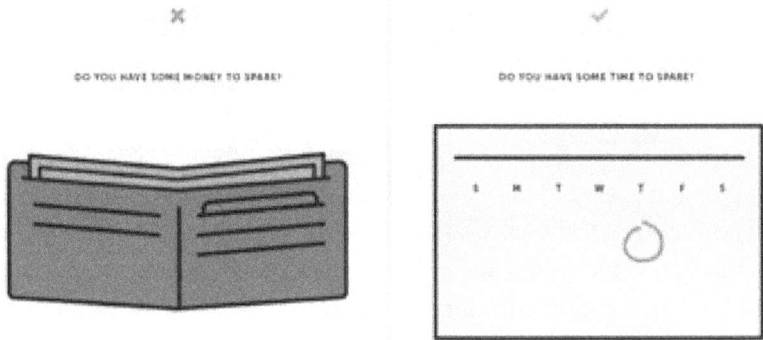

In several studies, the research found subjects who were first asked to give their time to a non-profit donated more money than subjects who were immediately asked to make a monetary contribution. Starting the conversation asking for money puts people in a transactional, utilitarian mindset. Whereas, asking people for time focuses on their experience and how good it can feel to give back.

When you interact with potential supporters, invite them to talk and learn more about your cause and volunteer opportunities. Instead of immediately thinking about their wallet, they will consider how the gift of their time could make a difference. Even if they don't actually volunteer, your audience may give more when you ask for a donation.

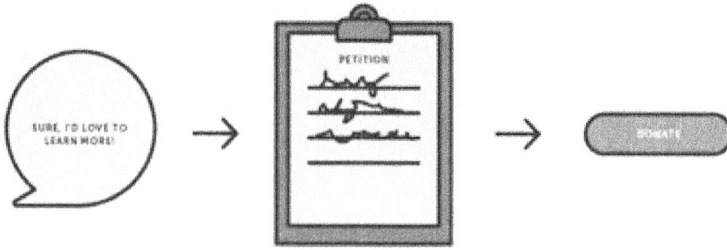

An ask for a small time commitment also taps into the concept of consistency, which psychologists say leads people to take into account their past actions when making decisions. For example, signing a petition is a small step someone can take to align themselves with your cause. If you later ask for a donation, they may be more likely to give as that behavior is consistent with their past support.

TAKEAWAY: You should focus on cultivating investors and developing a robust advisory program. Asking advisors for their time first may lead to larger gifts down the line.

4.Emotion and the Decision to Give

People who feel more sympathy for others in need are more likely to give. To get your investors to invest, you need to help them feel something for the people and market you serve. Presenting an identifiable victim is an important step.

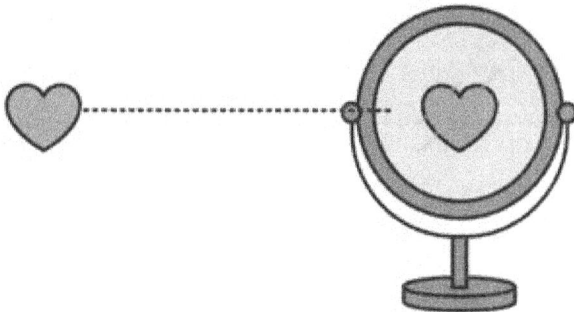

The potential investor's similarity to the person in need can also motivate them to give. For example, a mother who reads about an impoverished woman who cannot feed her children might identify with the victim and donate. At Lexyom, we approached investors touched by topics like refugees and injustice and started a FREE legal advice campaign for the people most in need.

Part of the reason people donate to charity seems to be to subdue the negative feelings that arise when they see others suffering. This is one reason you must show donors that their contribution makes a difference. If they don't think their gift will help the situation, a donation will seem futile. It is the same for early stage start-up investments. It fulfils some investors who relate to starting up a business, the struggles, and the fights.

5.Goal Proximity Effect

The closer you are to your fundraising goal; the more likely people are to give.

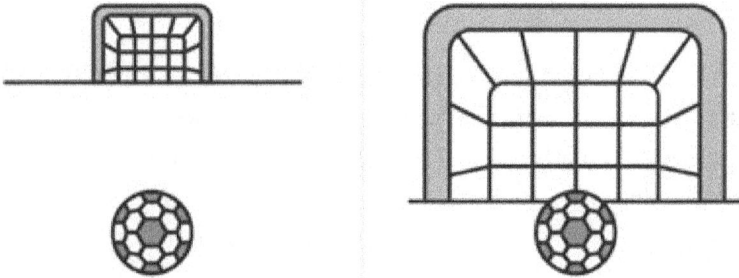

The goal proximity effect happens because people want to be part of a winning team. When you are closer to your goal and seem likely to reach it, people are happy to help you cross the finish line.

Therefore, you should call on your most devoted supporters early on in your fundraising campaign. When they donate and create fundraising pages, you'll gain momentum toward your goal. For your start-up, call on family and friends to encourage you and then show the investors that you are very close to reaching your funding goal. The more the goal is attainable, the easier it is to raise.

6.Martyrdom Effect

People tend to feel more satisfied by accomplishments they work hard for. This suggests that potential donors can derive more meaning from contributing to your cause if it requires a certain amount of effort. This is one reason endurance events are famous for fundraising campaigns. It is the same for your start-up or E-Commerce. If the investor feels that they have to put some effort in, like advising, PR, or any other effort to get on board, this will push them to consider you for their portfolio.

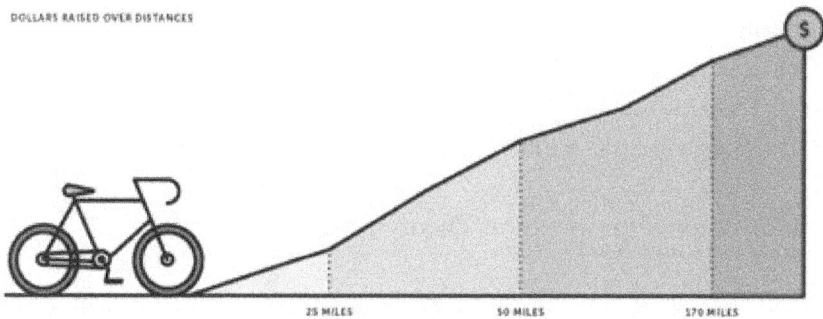

In a study of participants in a bicycling event with three races of different lengths, those who committed to longer events tended to raise more money for the cause.

To sum up, if you want to raise money and bring people on board, you have to convince yourself that you want to convince people. Be ready to answer any question, anytime, anywhere, in any circumstance. If you are caught in a moment, you should be able to respond without hesitation, without panic, without showing a lack of confidence or security.

So, what Neuro-strategies can you use to convince people?

1.Amplification Hypothesis

When you express with certainty a particular attitude, that attitude hardens. The opposite is true as too. Expressing uncertainty softens the attitude. The more you amplify your certainty, the more you can convince others. It does not mean you lie but means you stress on the relevant and significant points.

2.Conversion Theory

The minority in a group can have a disproportionate effect on influencing those in the majority. Typically, those in the most susceptible majority are the ones who may have joined because it was easy to do so, or who felt there were no alternatives. Consistent, confident minority voices are most effective. So, make sure you let them raise their voices, especially when sitting in front of a jury. Analyze the jury, look at them, and determine who would identify with you and the who would oppose you. There is a rule in Poker I keep repeating: "If you are not able to identify all the personalities on the table within 15 minutes of playing, you have lost the game ".

3.Information Manipulation Theory

This theory involves a persuasive person deliberately breaking one of the four conversational maxims. These are the four:

Quantity: Information is complete and full.

Quality: Information is truthful and accurate.

Relation: Information is relevant to the conversation.

Manner: Information is expressed in an easy-to-understand way and non-verbal actions support the tone of the statement

4. Priming

You can be influenced by stimuli that affect how you perceive short-term thoughts and actions. Here's a really smart example from Changing Minds:

A stage magician says 'try' and 'cycle' in separate sentences in priming a person to think later of the word 'tricycle.' Check Priming in Chapter 2.

5.Reciprocity Norm

Reciprocity, an everyday social norm, involves our obligation to return favors done by others. When you start by giving to investors you will have more chances to get something back from them. Offer them things; offer them some product you sell, some discount, some access, or anything that would make them more involved in your start-up, e-commerce, or project.

6.Scarcity Principle

You want what is in short supply. This desire increases as you anticipate the regret you might have if you miss out by not acting fast enough. Ensure you do this very decently and in a very, very subtle way.

7. Sleeper Effect

Persuasive messages tend to decrease in persuasiveness over time, except messages from low-credibility sources. Messages that start with low persuasion gain persuasion as our minds slowly disassociate the source from the material (i.e., a presumably sleazy car salesman and his advice on what car is best).

8.Social Influence

We are influenced strongly by others based on how we perceive our relationship with the influencer. For example, social proof on web copy is persuasive if the testimonials and recommendations are from authoritative sources, big brands, or peers.

When you give your Instagram Username to someone, it will change all the conversations if they see 1,000 followers or 10,000 followers.

9.Yale Attitude Change Approach

Based on multiple years of research by Yale University, this approach found several factors in persuasive speech, including being a credible, attractive speaker, the ideal demographics to target, and when it's essential to first or last. A Yale University multi-year, multi-project research into persuasive communication showed (amongst other things):

Who (source of communication):

The speaker should be credible and attractive to the audience.

Says what (nature of communication):

Messages should not appear to be designed to persuade. Present two-sided arguments (refuting the 'wrong' argument, of course).

- If two people are speaking one after the other, it is best to go first (primacy effect).

- If two people speak with a delay between them, it is best to go last (recency effect).

To whom (the nature of the audience)

Distract them during the persuasion
Lower intelligence and moderate self-esteem help. The best age range is 18-25.

Example: Watch politicians. They do this wonderfully well. They look great. They talk through the other side's argument, making it seem reasonable and highlighting all their problems. It all seems to be just common sense spoken by a nice person.

10. Ultimate Terms

Certain words carry more power than others. This theory breaks persuasive words into three categories:

- God terms those words that carry blessings or demand obedience/

sacrifice. e.g., progress, value.
- Devil terms: those terms that are despised and evoke disgust. e.g., fascists, paedophiles.

- Charismatic terms: those terms that are intangible, less observable than either God or Devil terms. e.g., freedom, contribution.

How to write for what we all crave

We all know how important food, water, shelter, and warmth are to survival. Any ideas what is next most important?

The Hierarchy of Needs pyramid, proposed by psychologist Abraham Maslow in the 1940s, shows the advancing scale of how our needs layout on the path to fulfilment, creativity, and the pursuit of what we love most. The version of the pyramid you see below (shared by the Doorway Project) shows the five different layers of needs.

The three steps in between the physiological needs and the fulfilment needs are where marketing most directly applies

- Safety
- Belonging Esteem

In Maslow's pyramid, the descriptions for these needs don't exactly have a marketing perspective to them, so it requires a little creativity to see how you can tailor your message to fit these needs.

Without these three essential keys, a person cannot perform, innovate, be emotionally engaged, agree, or move forward.

The more we have of these three keys, the greater the company's success, the relationship, the family, the team, and the individual.

- "What if." This phrase removes ego from the discussion and creates a safe environment for curiosity and brainstorming.

- "I need your help." This flips the dominant and subordinate roles, engaging the other person and providing a transfer of power.

- "Would it be helpful if?" This phrase shifts the focus from the problem to the solution.

How to win friends and influence your audience

When you talk about influencing people, our ears perk up at Buffer. Our company culture and values are based on Dale Carnegie's book called How to Win Friends and Influence People. Remove your ego. Default to happiness and positivity. Be welcoming to others.

A discussion on persuasion and influence could begin and end with Carnegie's book in many ways. Here is just a segment of the book's table of contents, filled with ideas on kindness, generosity, and partnership. **Win people over to your way of thinking:**

The only way to get the best of an argument is to avoid it. Show respect for the other person's opinions. Never say, "You're wrong."

If you are wrong, admit it quickly and emphatically. Begin in a friendly way.

- Get the other person saying "yes, yes" immediately.
- Let the other person do a great deal of the talking.
- Let the other person feel that the idea is his or hers.
- Try honestly to see things from the other person's point of view.
- Be sympathetic with the other person's ideas and desires.
- Appeal to the nobler motives.
- Dramatize your ideas.
- Throw down a challenge.

Be Clever but Not Manipulative
A fun way to look at persuasion is as a playground slide.

The idea comes from Roger Dooley of the blog, Neuro-marketing, who uses a person's variables on a slide to show how different factors affect the outcome of influence. Here's the graphic he created to explain the idea:

Essentially, here's how it works: You give a customer a **nudge** (a tweet, a blog post, a phone call, an ad).

Gravity, that customer's internal motivations, help move the customer down the slide.

The additional motivation you provide (the angle of the slide) can enhance gravity. If a customer has low internal motivation, it will take a steeper angle to get them down the slide.

Friction, seen here as the difficulty (real and perceived) in converting, causes the slide to slow down to varying degrees.

The nudge could be anything persuasive, for example, a couple of psychological theories that we outlined above. Amplification could mean that the customer further cements his values and attitudes as he propels down the slide. Social proof could be a stronger push down the slide, resulting in faster conversion.

Liking
One way people exploit this is to find ways to make themselves like you. Do you like golf? Me too. Do you like football? Me too. Although often these are genuine, sometimes they're not.

Liking is similar enough to the consistency that it bears, pointing out the difference here. Someone might say, "Do you like having more visitors to your blog?" They aren't necessarily looking for a connection with you (as in liking), but instead, they're seeking consistency. Of course, you'll say yes, and in theory, you'll have a harder time backing off that statement when you are pitched a product or service later.

Authority
Something as simple as informing your audience of your credentials before

you speak, for example, increases the odds you will persuade the audience.

Noah Kagan does this for each guest post he publishes at OK Dork. He writes a quick intro on how he connected with the guest writer and all the amazing credentials the writer has.

Social proof
People will more likely say yes when they see other people doing it too. Social proof is not all bad. It is one of the main ways we learn in life.

Two others that are worth pointing out are consistency and scarcity.

Personally, consistency is the one I find myself most susceptible to. I identify a lot with how Parrish describes the effect:" If you ask people to state their priorities and goals and then align your proposals with that in mind, you make it harder for people to say no." Parrish connects this to the IKEA effect, the way you love your IKEA furniture because you're invested in it from the beginning, as you are the one who puts it together.

As for scarcity, Visual Website Optimizer wrote an extensive post on all the different ways you can use scarcity to increase e-commerce sales. Have you ever noticed that Amazon tells people there are only a certain number of products left? That is scarcity at play.

Disrupt, Then Reframe
You can disrupt routine thought processes by mixing around the words and visuals that a user uses to see, then reframing your pitch while still figuring out the disruption. Researchers tested this technique by pitching a product as costing $3.00 versus 300 pennies; the penny pitch was the clear winner.

A unique implementation of this is on a pricing page. Instead of standard names for pricing tiers, you can go with a disruption technique with the copy and then reframed the pitch with the pricing info below.

The Key to Good Storytelling
We mentioned above the theory about ultimate words, and we've written

recently about the power of storytelling in your content. Make sure that you are telling the right story. Here are the three stickiest and most memorable story plots.

1. **The Challenge Plot:** A story of the underdog, rags to riches, or sheer willpower triumphing over adversity

2. **The Connection Plot:** A story about people who develop a relationship that bridges a gap. Whether racial, class, ethnic, religious, demographic, or otherwise; think of the film "The Blind Side."

3. **The Creativity Plot:** A story that involves someone making a mental breakthrough, solving a long-standing puzzle, or attacking a problem in an innovative way

10. Control Your Design Theory

The words 'design theory' might make you freeze up. Trust us, it's not as complicated as it sounds, and designers should get to grips with it. To help you out, we have written this definitive guide to help answer the question, 'what is design theory?

To start, let's break down the two words separately. Graphic design is the effective visual communication of an idea or concept, and theory is a system of ideas intended to explain something. So, put simply, design theory is a system of ideas that explains how and why a design works. Designers need to know how everything they put on a page communicates, influences, invites, entices, and excites an audience.

Design theory can be broken into several theoretical approaches for understanding, explaining, and describing design knowledge and practice. Next, we're going to break these down. Shillington London teacher, Andy Lester who is a designer, explained what design theory means:

"Design theory is the asking and answering of the question 'why am i designing it this way?' If you can't answer that question at every stage of the design process, you probably need to do a bit more thinking…"

So, What Exactly Is Design Theory?

Here are the fundamentals of design theory:

Design Principles

The five design principles should be used in every design project you work on. Each principle is an essential part of a design but working together is the most critical thing to consider when communicating a message to a specific audience.

Alignment: Aligning elements on a page creates visual connections and creates a unified design. It allows the viewer's eyes to see order, which makes for easier, more comfortable viewing.

Repetition: Repeating elements creates associations and familiarity—certain elements of a design, if they are repeated, can be used to identify a brand quickly and easily.

Contrast: Contrast can be created when you use two elements that are complete opposites, like a classic and contemporary font or cool and warm colors. Using it makes an impact and emphasis on design.

Hierarchy: Grouping similar things close to each other implies that they are related to each other somehow—hierarchy is fundamental in creating organization in a design.

Balance: Balance is the weight distributed on a page by how things are placed. There are two kinds—symmetrical balance and balance by tension. It gives design stability and structure.

Working together, all five design principles create a design that is visually appealing and structured so users can be more focused on the elements and content being conveyed.

Color Theory and Color Technical

The color theory breaks down how and why to use a specific color or color palette in a design. It explains how color can be a powerful tool; it can entce or persuade, create a specific emotion, or convince. For example, red can be associated with passion or strength—they demand attention.

The color theory also considers how the different factors must be contemplated when colors are chosen for a design, though how color is received differs person-to-person.

Being able to choose a color and harness its potential correctly is the mark of a successful designer.

On the other hand, color technical is a series of technical considerations about applying color in a finished design. These considerations alter depending on many things, like whether a design is digital or printed. Color technical includes color mixing (additive or subtractive), color systems (RGB, CMYK, etc.), and color gamut.

Design Thinking

Also known as human-centered design, design thinking is all about putting the user first and creating a design for a specific intended audience.

In other words, it's about the designer putting themselves into the shoes of the person who is going to interact with their design.

Design thinking can be broken down into five key stages:

Empathize: They need to understand this person, their likes, dislikes, and what they will respond well to.

Define: They then need to define the problem that needs to be solved through their design.

Iterate: They need to brainstorm several ideas on how to solve these problems.

Prototype: Decide what these ideas will look like and build them.

Test: The intended audience tests the design to discover what did and did not work.

Stages do not need to be in this order, but it's essential to always start with empathy. You can always go back and revise stages if your test is not successful.

Graphic Elements

Designers should know how to identify a graphic element and be able to use them in a design.

Graphic elements are a combination of forms, lines, and shapes—some examples include line work, pattern, texture, and type. Used sparingly, graphic elements can be used to provide variation and interest in a design or create a hierarchy to guide the viewer through a design. The difference between a graphic element and illustration is that graphic elements are purely decorative, while illustration aims to communicate a concept or message.

Okay, So What Are the Benefits of Knowing All This?

Design theory gives you the knowledge and ability to combine form (the design principles etc.) and function (the design purpose), which, according to Bauhaus theory, is the basis of any successful design. In layman's terms, you need both design theory and practical design knowledge to create effective design solutions.

Being a good designer is more than just knowing the software; it's about understanding the theory behind it and how this should affect your decisions and outcomes.

Additionally, design theory also enables a designer to talk eloquently about their designs. They can explain how theoretical decisions lead to their chosen outcome, rather than hollow explanations.

When you understand the importance of design theory, you can create more effective, appealing, and valuable work for your project.

Designers have been creating with design theory long before software and Adobe CC. If you're using a pencil or illustrator, these principles should be a part of your design process and design critique."

How Is Design Theory Used in the Real World?

When a new exciting project lands, the creative juices tend to flow faster. The adrenaline can often lead you down many rabbit holes, and after a while, you soon start to wonder where on earth all this is leading to.

Coming back to colors, this is a list of the meanings of colors you can take from to use in your branding, design, structures.

Warm Colors

Warm colors include red, orange, and yellow, and variations of those three colors. These are the colors of fire, fall leaves, sunsets, and sunrises and are generally energizing, passionate, and positive.

Red and yellow are both primary colors, with orange falling in the middle (making it a secondary color), which means warm colors are all truly warm and aren't created by combining a warm color with a cool color. Use warm colors in your designs to reflect passion, happiness, enthusiasm, and energy.

Red (primary color)

Red is a hot color. It's associated with fire, violence, and warfare. It is also associated with love and passion. In history, it's been associated with both the Devil and Cupid. Red can have a physical effect on people, raising blood pressure and heart rates. It has also been shown to enhance human metabolism.

Red can be associated with anger and associated with importance (think of the red carpet at awards shows and celebrity events). Red also indicates danger (the reason stop lights and signs are red and that warning labels are often red).

Outside the western world, red has different associations. For example, in China, red is the color of prosperity and happiness. It can also be used to attract good luck. In other eastern cultures, red is worn by brides on their wedding days. In South Africa, however, red is the color of mourning. Red is also associated with communism.

Red has become the color associated with AIDS awareness in Africa due to the popularity of the [RED] campaign.

In design, red can be a powerful accent color. It can have an overwhelming effect if used too much in designs, especially in its purest form. It's a great color to use when power or passion wants to be portrayed in the design. Red can be very versatile, though, with brighter versions being more energetic and darker shades being more powerful and elegant.

Examples

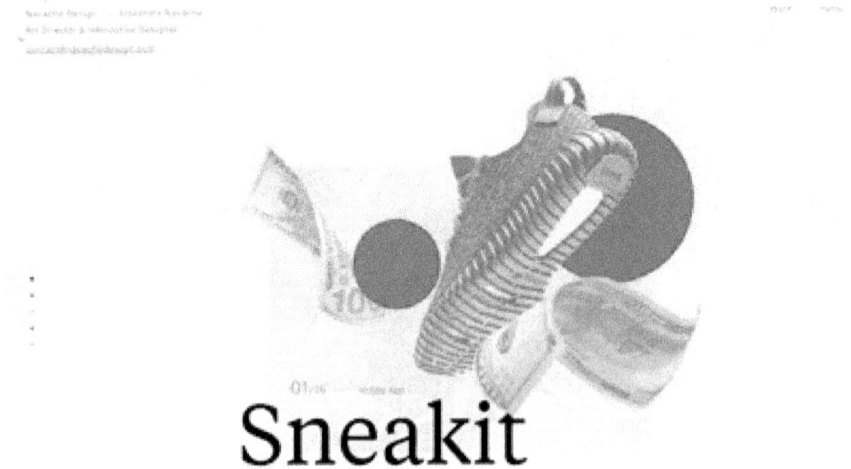

Sneakit

The bright-red illustration on Nacache Design's site homepage gives the page a ton of energy and vibrancy.

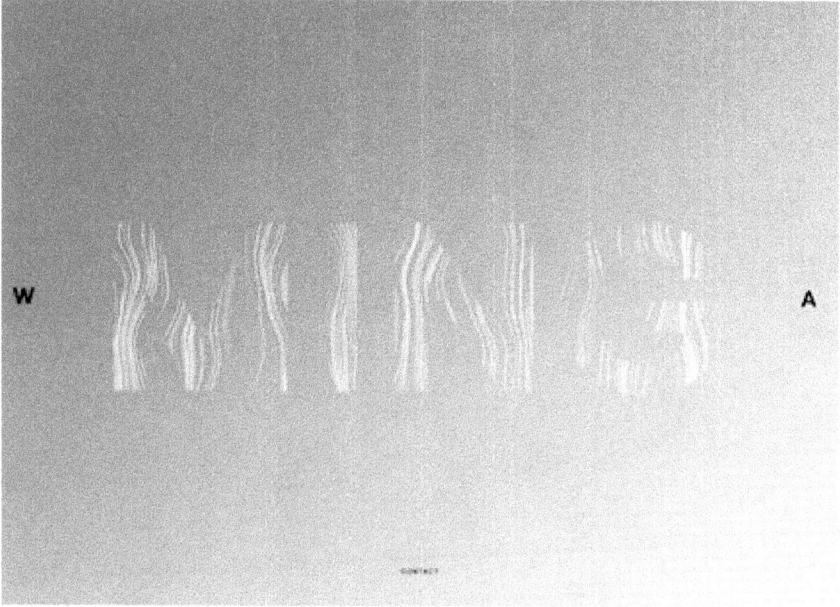

The bright pinkish-red of the background on Ming Lab's website is inviting and passionate.

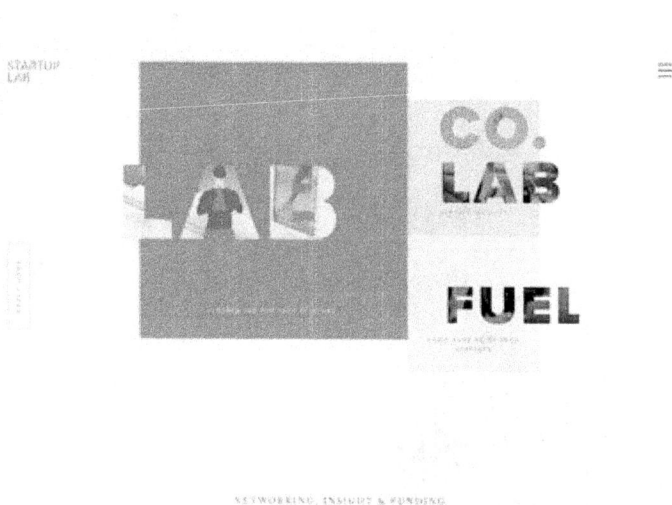

The muted red on the website is energetic without being aggressive.

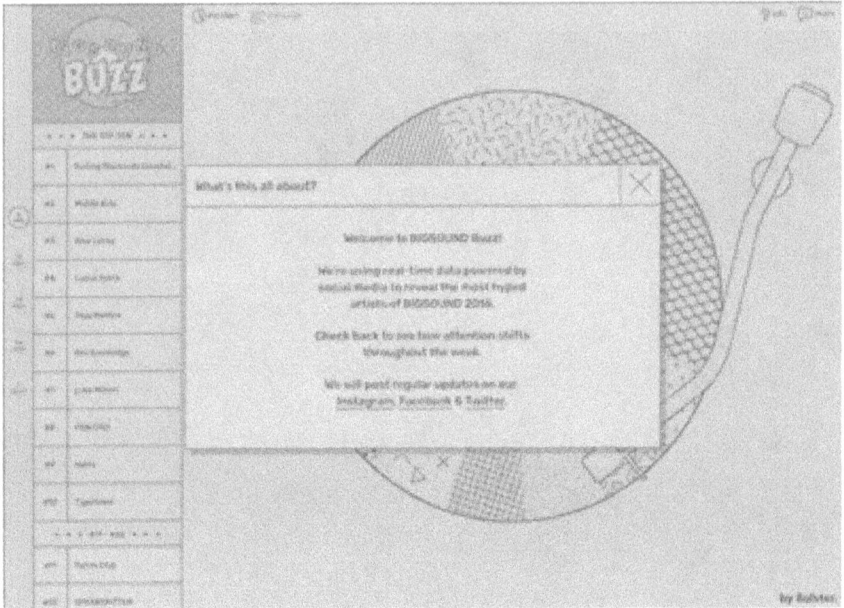

This website uses a monochromatic design of various shades and tones of red, which in this instance, gives a poppy, retro vibe.

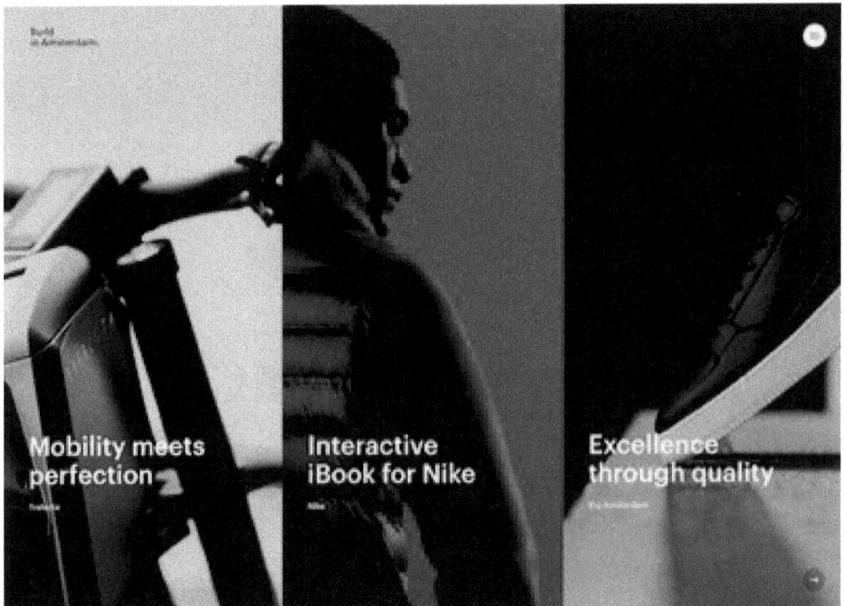

Build-in Amsterdam's website uses a vibrant red accent color that draws your eyes to the middle of the page immediately.

Orange (secondary color)

Orange is a very vibrant and energetic color. In its muted forms, it can be associated with the earth and with autumn. Because of its association with the changing seasons, orange can represent change and movement in general. Orange is also strongly associated with creativity.

Because orange is associated with the same name's fruit, it can be associated with health and vitality. In designs, orange commands attention without being as overpowering as red. It's often considered more friendly and inviting and less in-your-face.

Examples
Bitter Renter's bright and bold home page takes full advantage of the energy that orange can provide to a design.Examples

We Are Not Sisters' dark orange; oversized typography makes an immediate impact.

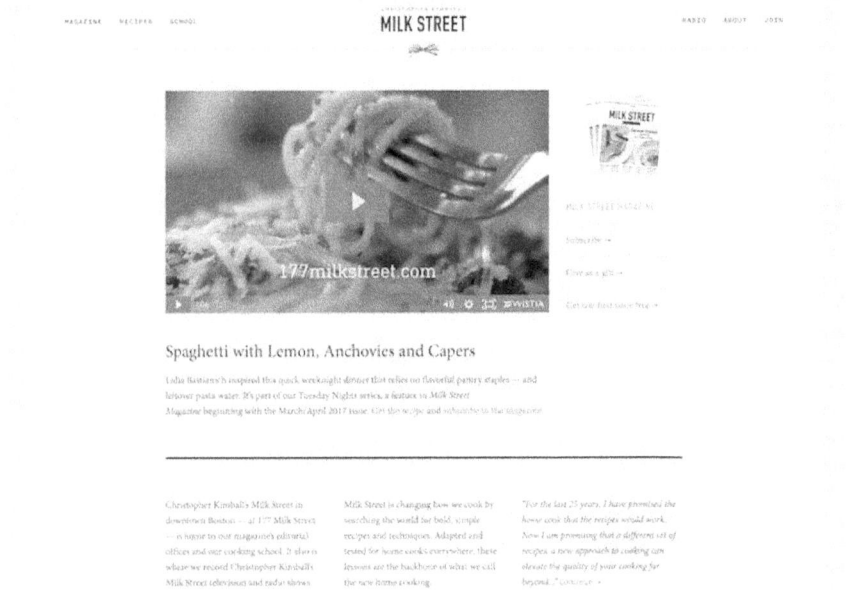

Spaghetti with Lemon, Anchovies and Capers

Christopher Kimball's **Milk Street's** subtle use of orange as an accent color shows it can be used in more elegant and conservative designs.

Sbjct mixes a subtle peach color with a dark orange for a more monochroma ti c design with a lot of energy.

Robin De Niro also uses a very light peach background with two orange shades for the typography in a much more understated design.

Yellow (primary color)

Yellow is often considered the brightest and most energizing of the warm colors. It's associated with happiness and sunshine. Yellow can also be associated with deceit and cowardice though.

Yellow is also associated with hope, as seen in some countries when yellow ribbons are displayed by families who have loved ones at war.

Yellow is also associated with danger, though not as strongly as red.

In some countries, yellow has very different connotations. In Egypt, for example, yellow is for mourning. In Japan, it represents courage, and in India, it's a color for merchants.

In your designs, bright yellow can lend a sense of happiness and cheerfulness. Softer yellows are commonly used as a gender-neutral color for babies (rather than blue or pink), and young children. Light yellows also give a calmer feeling of happiness than bright yellows. Dark yellows and gold-hued yellows can sometimes look antique and be used in designs where a sense of permanence is desired.

Examples

Kettle's not-quite-true-yellow is lively and vibrant without being overwhelming.

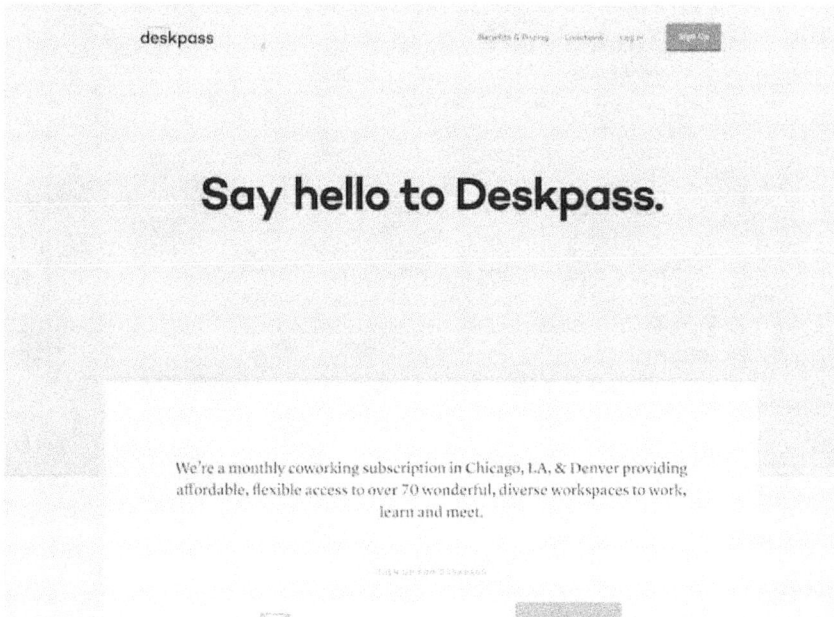

Deskpass uses a slightly darker yellow, giving it an eye-catching but slightly muted look.

Toyfight uuses a bright goldenrod background but **Toyfight** uuses a bright goldenrod background but otherwise keeps its

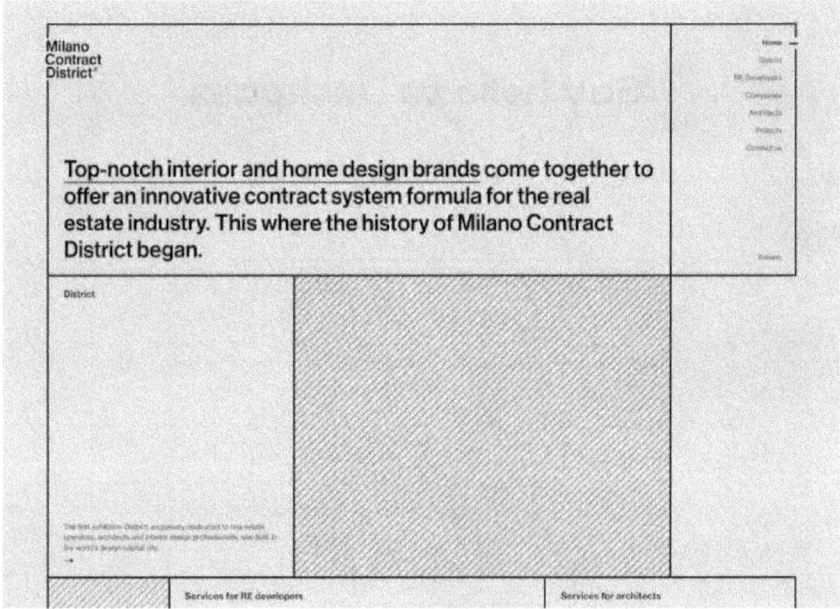

Milano Contract District's website is straightforward and minimalist, with the design's impacts coming from the bright yellow background.

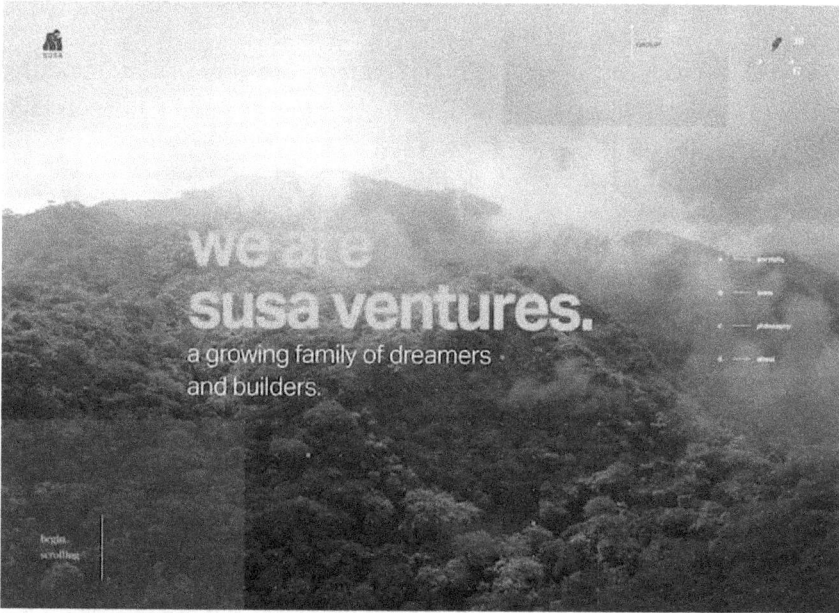

Susa Ventures uses a goldenrod hue as an accent color in their typography to significant effect.

Cool Colors

Cool colors such as green, blue, and purple, are often more subdued than warm colors. They are the colors of night, water, and nature, usually calming, relaxing, and somewhat reserved.

Blue is the only primary color within the cool spectrum, which means the other colors are created by combining blue with a warm color (yellow for green and red for purple).

Thus, green takes on some of the yellow attributes, and purple takes on some of the red attributes. Use cool colors in your designs to give a sense of calm or professionalism.

Green (secondary color)

Green is a very down-to-earth color. It can represent new beginnings and growth. It also signifies renewal and abundance. Alternatively, green can also represent envy or jealousy and a lack of experience.

Green has many of the same calming attributes that blue has, but it also incorporates some of the yellow's energy. In design, green can have a balancing and harmonizing effect and is very stable.

It's appropriate for designs related to wealth, stability, renewal, and nature. Brighter greens are more energizing and vibrant, while olive greens are more representative of the natural world. Dark greens are the most stable and representative of affluence.

Examples

The site for **Memory is Our Homeland** uses a blue-green hue that's energized by the yellow typography without being too bright.

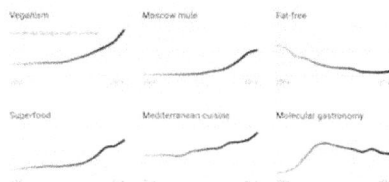

The **Rhythm of Food's** site uses a bright kelly green that's ideal for a site that test food and information together.

Rich, hunter green makes a great accent color on an elegant restaurant website like Le Farfalle Osteria's.

Anna Rosa Krau's website has a soft sage green background, which works almost as a neutral for this portfolio.

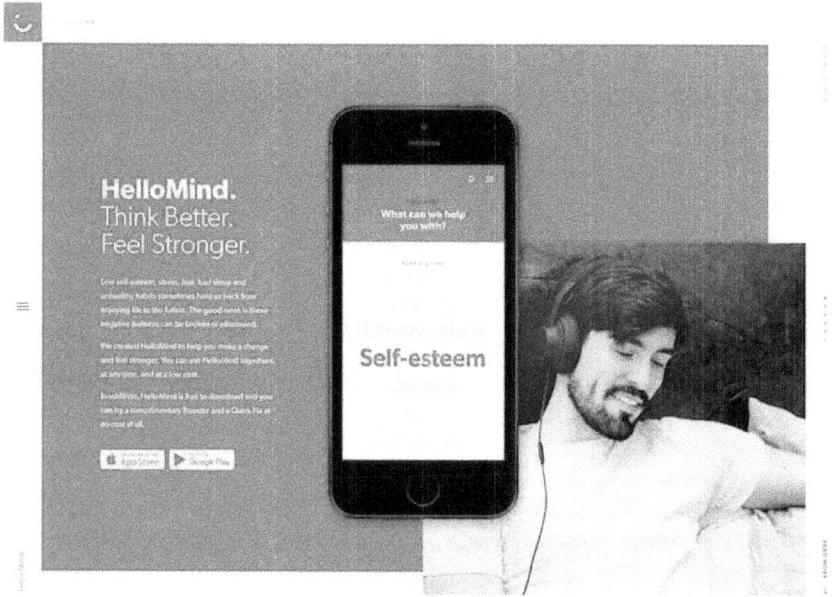

HelloMind's bright green background is youthful and gives a sense of growth (in line with their product for improving your brain function).

Studio Farquhar's lime green accents are punchy and modern, and they stand out in their minimalist layout.

Blue (primary color)

Blue is often associated with sadness in the English language. The color is also used extensively to represent calmness and responsibility. Light blues can be refreshing and friendly. Dark blues are more robust and reliable. Blue is also associated with peace and has spiritual and religious connotations in many cultures and traditions. For example, the Virgin Mary is generally depicted wearing blue robes.

The meaning of blue is widely affected, depending on the exact shade and hue. In design, the exact shade of blue you select will significantly impact how your designs are perceived. Light blues are often relaxed and calming. Bright blues can be energizing and refreshing. Like navy, dark blues are excellent for corporate sites or designs where strength and reliability are essential.

Examples

bright blue background of the Future of Design Survey results homepage stands out and is used as an accent color throughout the rest of the site.

Versett is a product design and engineering studio.

Versette uses a bright blue as the primary color on their website and several other bright hues to differentiate different sections.

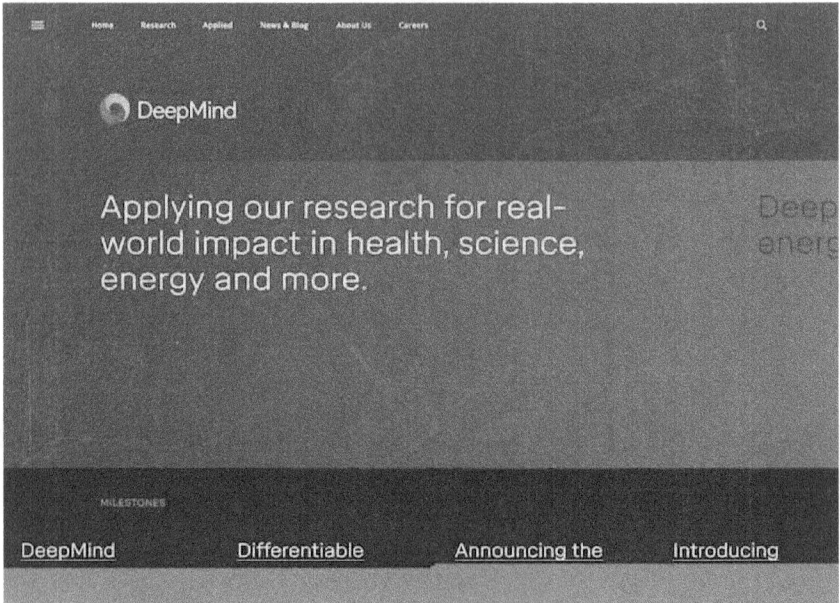

Deep Mind'ws ebsite uses various blue shades for its background, giving it a trustworthy, authoritat iv e feel.

Purple (secondary color)

In ancient times, the dyes used for creating purple hues were extracted from snails and were awfully expensive, so only royals and the very wealthy could afford them.

Purple is a combination of red and blue and takes on some attributes of both. It is associated with creativity and imagination, too.

In design, dark purples can give a sense of wealth and luxury. Light purples are softer and are associated with spring and romance.

In design, dark purples can give a sense of wealth and luxury. Light purples are softer and are associated with spring and romance.

Examples

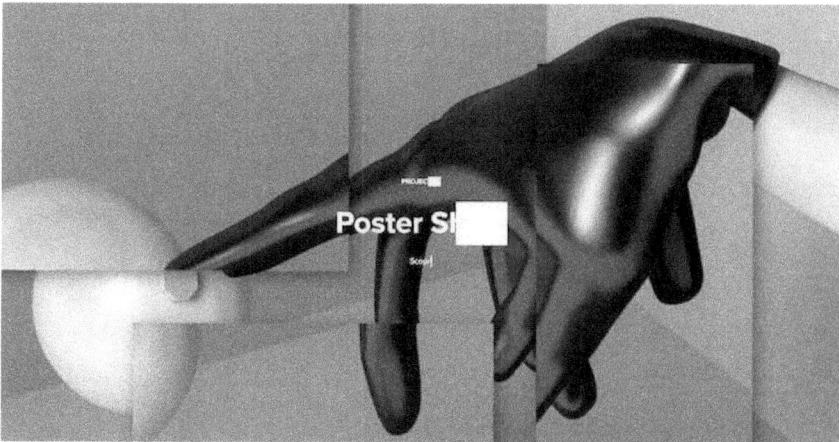

The first project in **Filippo Bell o 's po rt foloi** uses a purple color scheme that adds to the sense of creat iv ity.

The **One Shared House** documentary site uses a vibrant shade of purple and hot pink accents to give a sense of energy, creativity, and imagination.

On Content Stack, reddish-purple works great as an accent color against a neutral background and draws attention to essential page elements, like buttons.

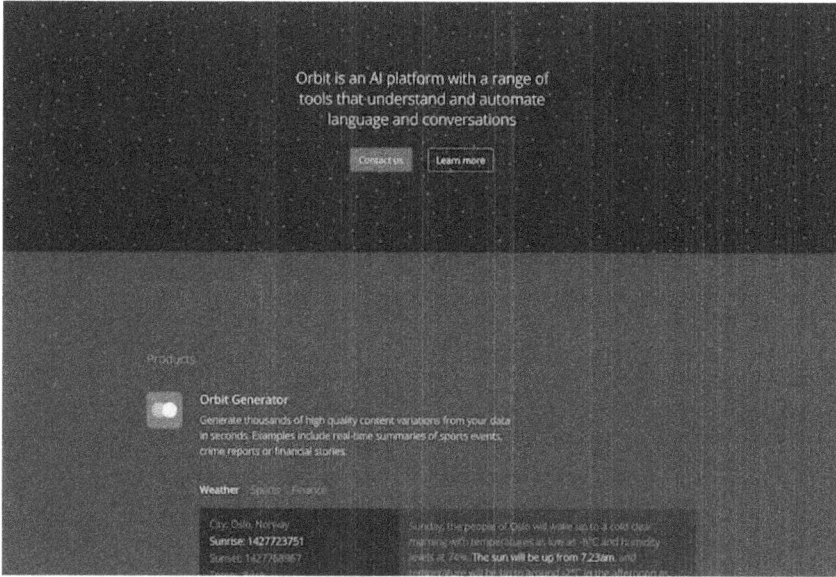

The dark purple hues of **Orbit's** website give a sense of sophistication fitting their AI.

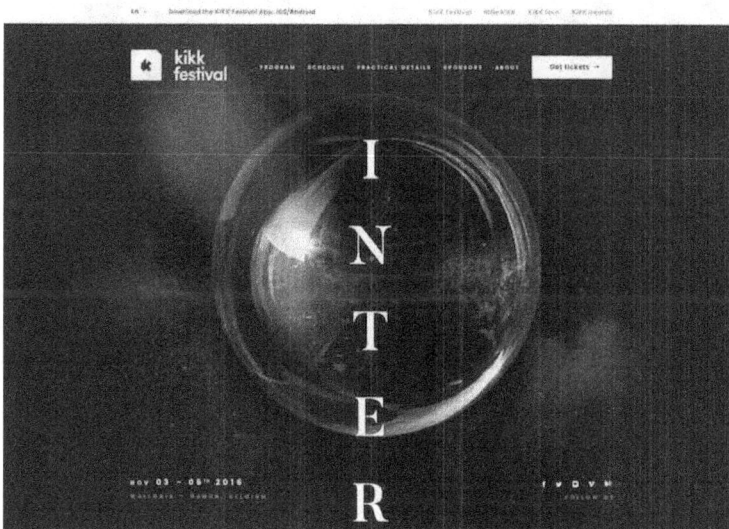

Purple is the perfect hue for a creative endeavor like KIKK Festival 2016.

Neutrals

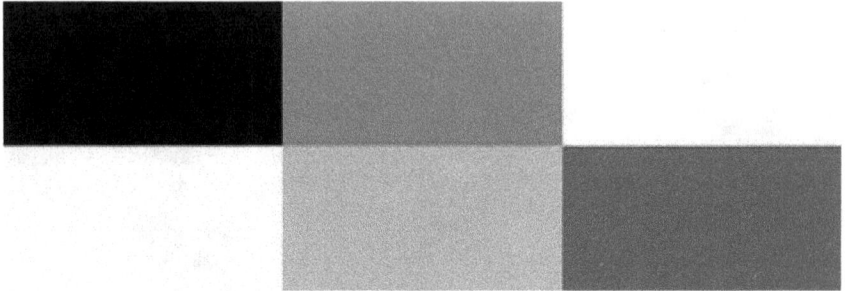

Neutral colors often serve as the backdrop in design. They are commonly combined with brighter accent colors. They can also be used on their own in designs and can

create very sophisticated layouts. The meanings and impressions of neutral colors are much more affected by the surrounding colors rather than warm and cool colors.

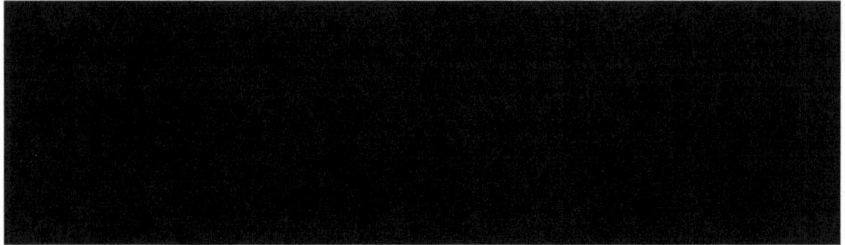

Black is the strongest of the neutral colors. On the positive side, it is commonly associated with power, elegance, and formality. On the negative side, it can be associated with evil, death, and mystery. Black is the traditional color of mourning in many Western countries. It is also associated with rebellion in some cultures and is associated with Halloween and the occult.

When used as more than an accent or for text, Black is commonly used in edgier and exquisite designs. It can be conservative or modern, traditional, or unconventional, depending on the colors it is combined with. In design, black is commonly used for typography and other functional parts because of its neutrality. Black can make it easier to convey a sense of sophistication and mystery in a design.

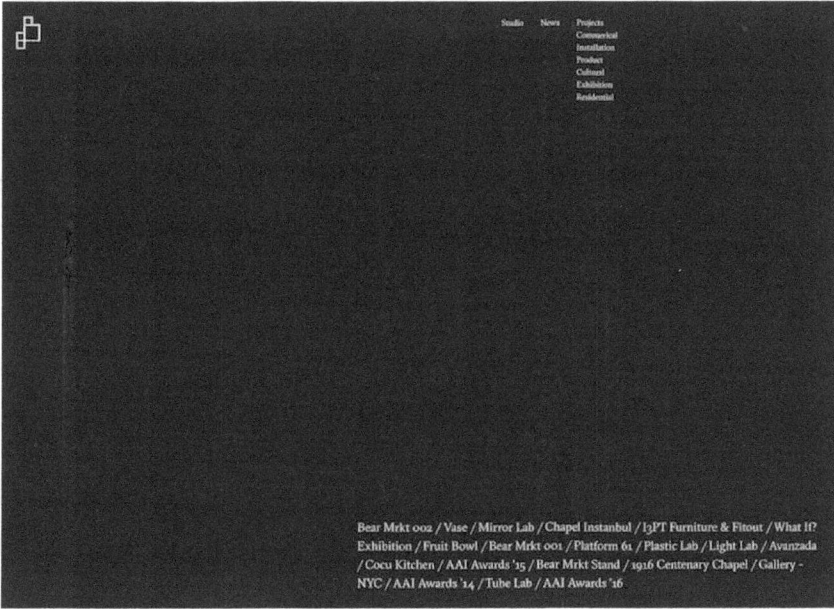

The faded black (technically dark gray, but close enough to black that it

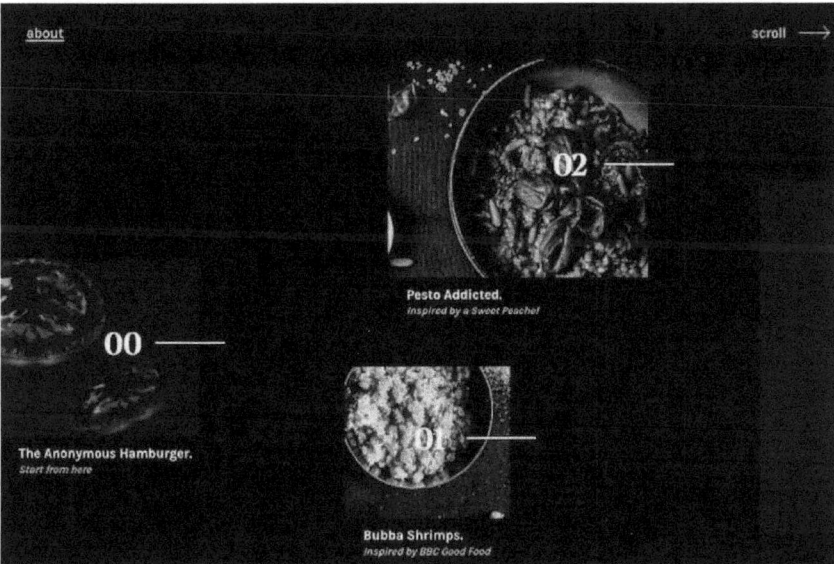

Anonymous Hamburger Society's black background is a perfect canvas for the amazing food photos on the site.

Many of the images on **Timothy Saccenti's portfolio** are dominated by black, which is also the transparent menu color, giving the entire site an edgy, modern feel.

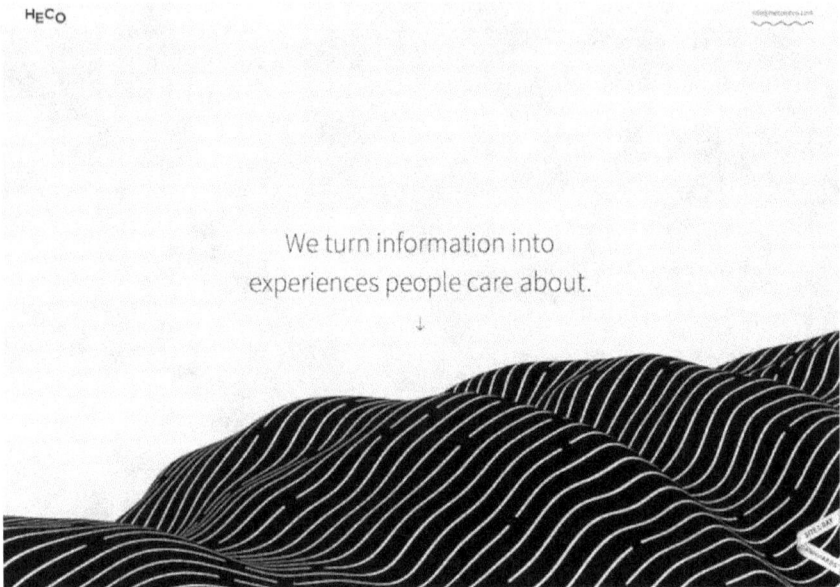

Minimal design with black used as an accent color gives Heco's site a super modern feeling.

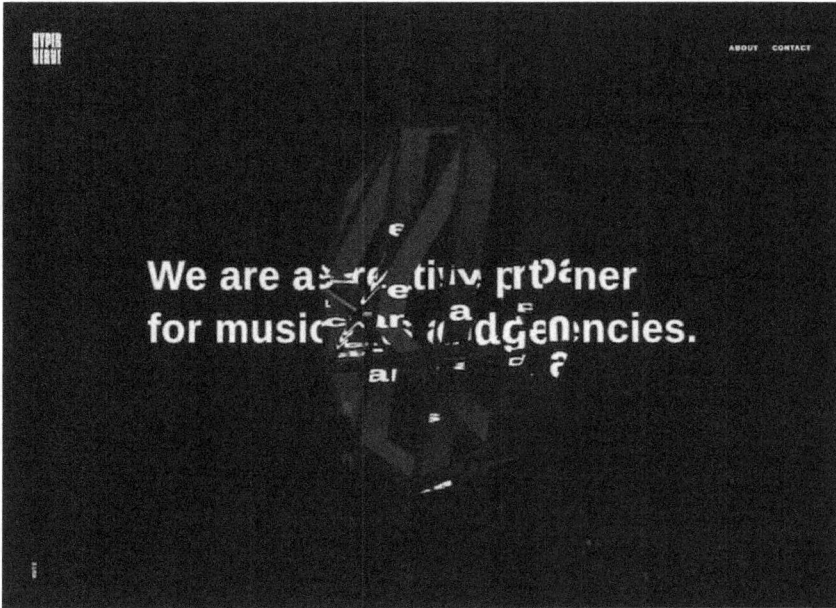

The black hue used here, along with the animation, gives it an edgy, almost creepy feel.

White

White is at the opposite end of the spectrum from black, but like black, it can work well with just about any other color. White is often associated with purity, cleanliness, and virtue. In the West, white is commonly worn by brides on their wedding day. It is also associated with the healthcare industry, especially with doctors, nurses, and dentists. White is associated with goodness, and angels are often depicted in white.

In much of the East, however, white is associated with death and mourning.

In India, it is traditionally the only color widows are allowed to wear.

In design, white is generally considered a neutral backdrop that lets other design colors have a larger voice. It can help to convey cleanliness and simplicity and is popular in minimalist designs. White designs can also portray either winter or summer, depending on the other design motifs and colors surrounding it.

Example

Black & Wood uses white as both a background and an accent color (in their typography, for example), giving the site a streamline and clean feel.

I'm Nuno, a product designer based in Tokyo.

Currency is an incredibly simple currency converter for iOS. Download it for free on the App Store.

The mostly white background of Nuno Coelho Santos's website contributes to the modern aesthetic.

Skylark's website uses white typography to lend the site a cleaner feeling without minimalist design.

Spent uses white typography to lend a modern yet soft look to the site.

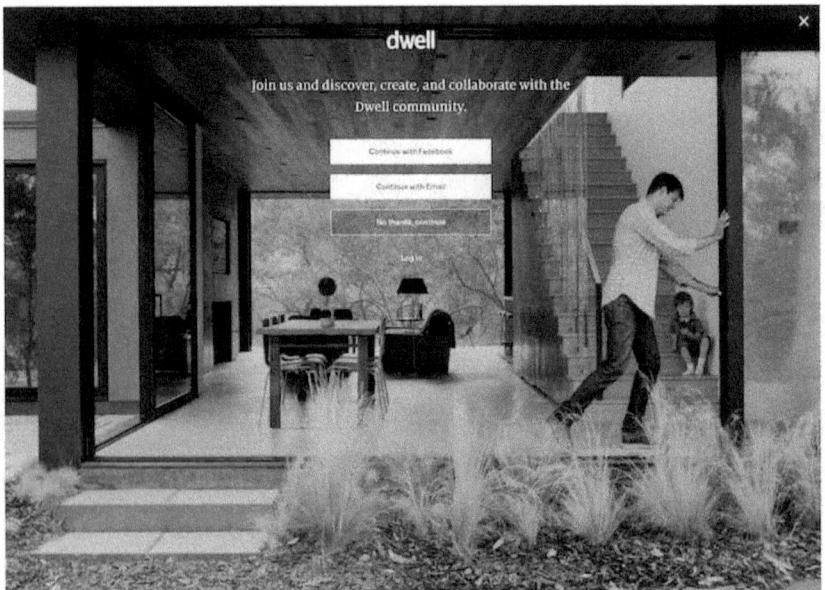

Dwell uses white as an accent color on their splash page, an incredibly unique and effective choice for something that includes a CTA.

Gray

Gray is a neutral color, generally considered on the cool end of the color spectrum. It can sometimes be considered moody or depressing. Light grays can be used in place of white in some designs, and dark grays can be used to replace black.

Gray is generally conservative and formal but can also be modern. It is sometimes considered a color of mourning. It is commonly used in corporate designs, where formality and professionalism are essential. It can be a very sophisticated color. Pure grays are shades of black, though other grays may have blue or brown hues mixed in. In design, gray backgrounds are quite common, as is gray typography.

Examples

Refugee Legal:
Defending the rights
of refugees.

Giving hope this
Christmas

Round is a design practice that harnesses culture and creativity to transform brands.
We're based in Melbourne, but our people come from many places. We're a team of creative thinkers and strategic designers. We recognise that change is inevitable. Together, we design remarkable experiences that engage people and enable organisations to grow.
more

The **Round** website is very modern, with various gray shades used to delineate different site sections.

For Office Use Only is a graphic + digital design studio

The For **Office Use Only** website's gray background is so subtle it almost appears white and gives the site a very modern feel.

Gray takes on a sophisticated yet down-to-earth feeling on the Shinola website.

When mixed with modern typography, gray takes on a modern feel.

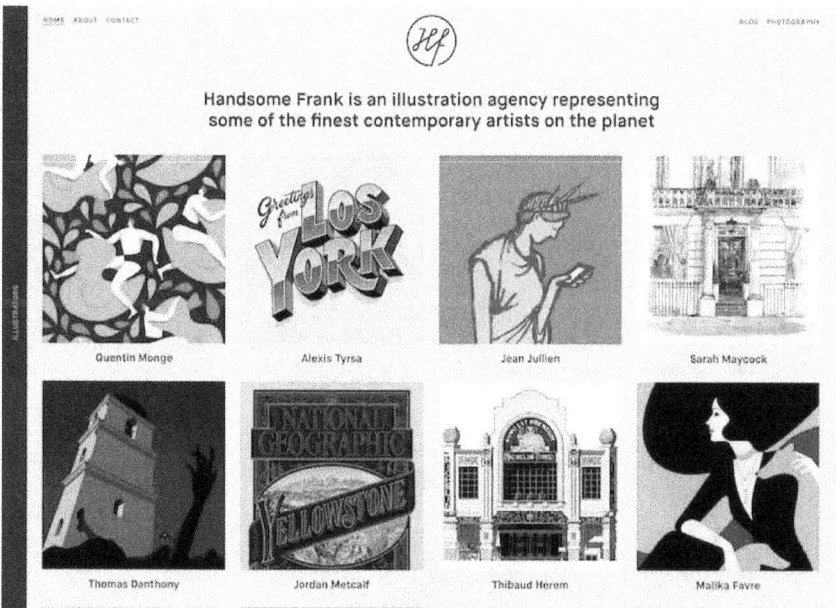

Gray is a perfect background color for a portfolio of illustrations and it allows the pictures to stand out.

Brown

Brown is associated with the earth, wood, and stone. It's a completely natural and warm neutral color. Brown can be associated with dependability and reliability, steadfastness, and with earthiness. It can also be considered dull.

In design, brown is commonly used as a background color. It is also seen in wood textures and sometimes in stone textures. It helps bring a feeling of warmth and wholesomeness to designs. It is sometimes used in its darkest forms as a replacement for black, either in backgrounds or typography.

Examples

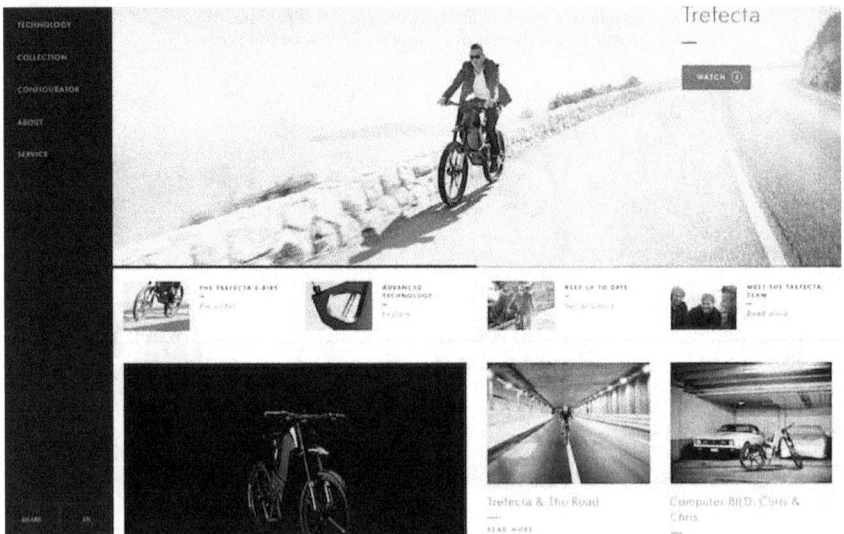

Trefecta uses a warm brown as an accent color for buttons and CTAs, an unexpected choice given the rest of the design's modernity.

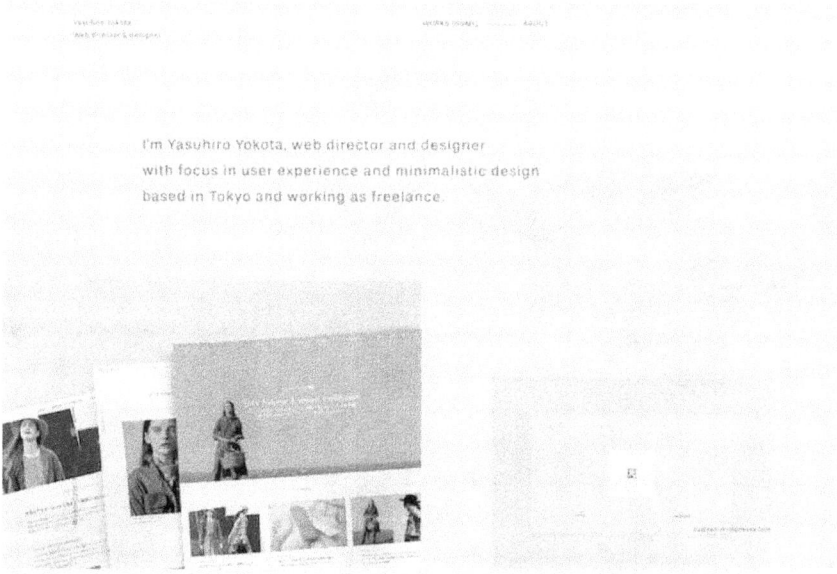

The cream background and brown typography of Yasuhiro Yokota's portfolio site are warm and earthy while still serving as a good backdrop for design work.

Off & On Barber Shop uses various brown elements for the bulk of their site, giving it an old-fashioned feeling.

Umbert Cessari's website uses various shades of brown for accent colors throughout, giving it an earthy appeal.

Green Rebel's website uses brown for much of its typography and graphics throughout and in some textures, lending an organic feel.

Beige and tan

Beige is somewhat unique in the color spectrum, as it can take on cool or warm tones depending on the surrounding colors. It has the warmth of brown and the coolness of white. Like brown, beige is sometimes seen as dull. It is a conservative color in most instances and is usually reserved for backgrounds. It can also symbolize piety.

Beige in design is commonly seen in backgrounds with a paper texture. It will take on the characteristics of colors around it, meaning it has little effect on the final impression that a design gives.

Examples

People Map's website uses a more gold shade of tan, giving the site an upscale feel, especially when combined with the site's typography.

Plane Site's warm tan background color feels modern without feeling minimalist.

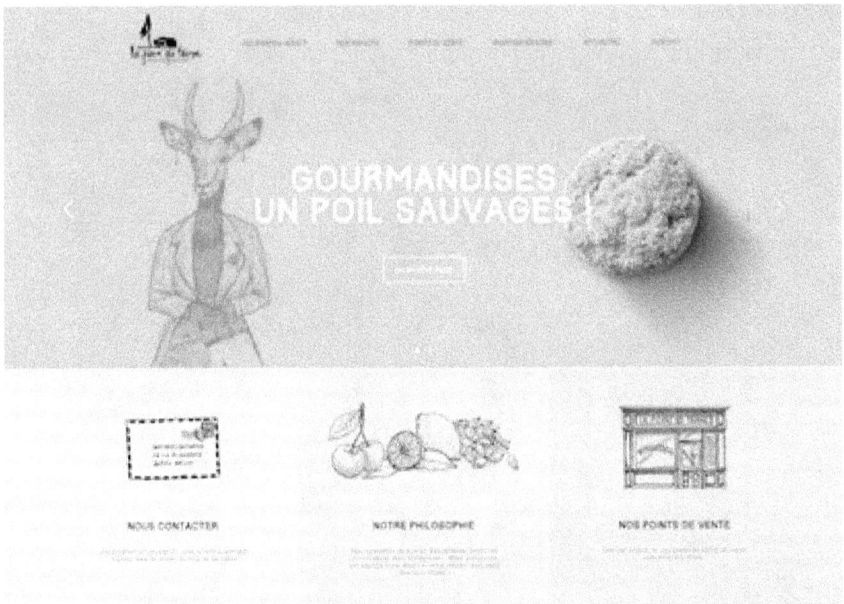

La Pierre qui Tourne's website uses various tan shades for their primary color palette, alongside some great bright colors for an entertaining design.

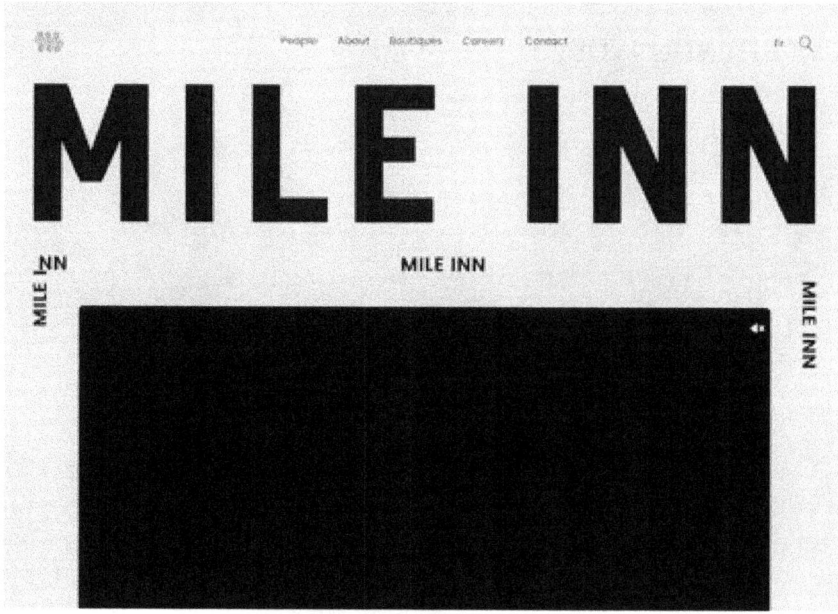

The Mile Inn site combines modern typography with a beige and black color palette for a site that feels retro and hip.

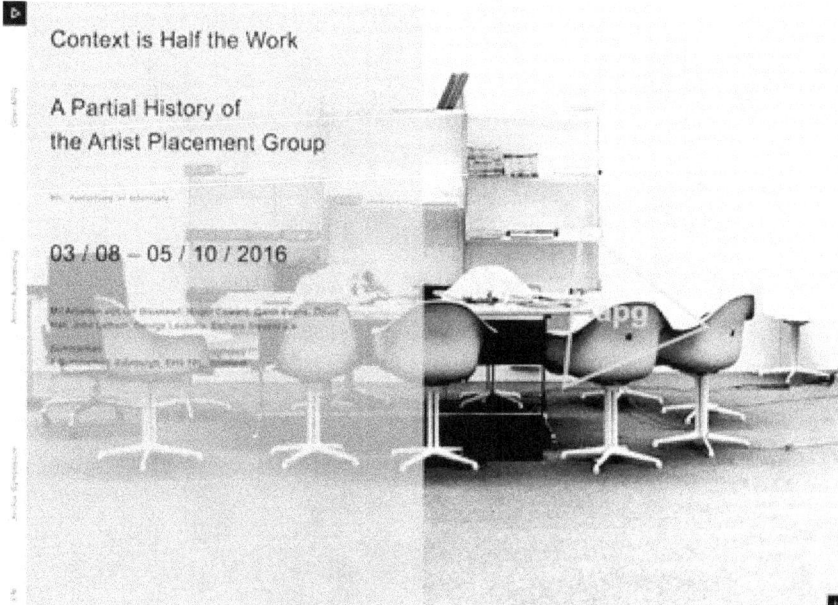

The tan accent color used on this site is entirely unexpected and gives it a Mid-Century Modern look.

Cream and ivory

Ivory and cream are sophisticated colors, with the warmth of brown and coolness of white. They are generally quiet and can often evoke a sense of history. Ivory is a calm color, with some of the pureness associated with white, although a bit warmer.

In design, ivory can lend a sense of elegance and calm to a site. When combined with earthy colors like peach or brown, it can take on an earthy quality. It can also be used to lighten darker colors without the stark contrast of using white.

Examples

Stefanie Bruckler's portfolio site's barely-there ivory background is a welcome change of pace from the typical neutral gray, giving it a timeless look.

Rich cream feels like a very modern and even edgy accent color when used with a black background.

The cream is an unexpected background color of choice for a **website focusing on the tech industry** but gives it a warm, human touch.

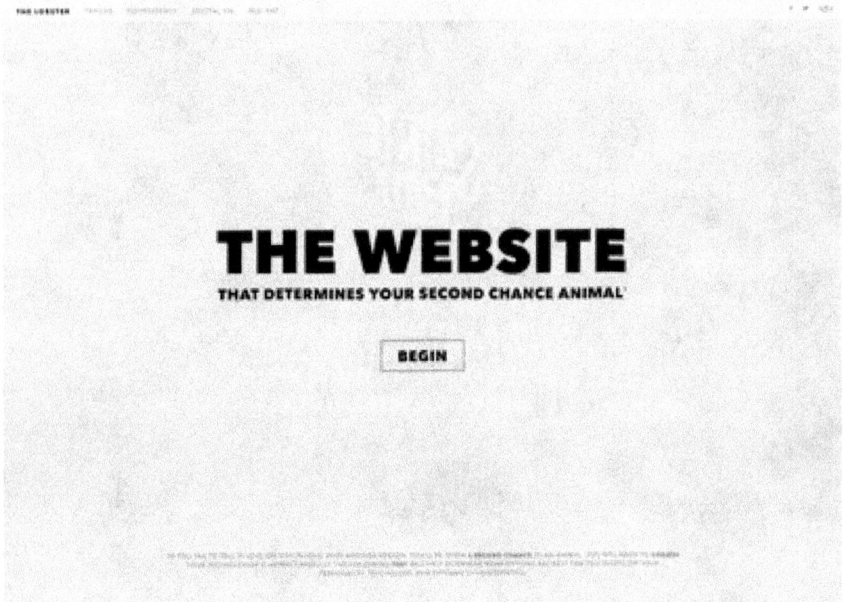

Considering how odd the film **The Lobster** is, their use of a pale off white background for the website is an unexpectedly subdued choice that feels very modern.

Sweet Magnolia Gelato's rich cream background is a perfect neutral for a warm and inviting design.

In Brief:
While the information contained here might seem just a bit overwhelming, color theory is as much about the feeling a particular shade evokes as anything else. But here is a quick reference guide for the common meanings of the colors discussed above:

Red: Passion, Love, Anger
Orange: Energy, Happiness, Vitality
Yellow: Happiness, Hope, Deceit
Green: New Beginnings, Abundance, Nature
Blue: Calm, Responsible, Sadness
Purple: Creativity, Royalty, Wealth
Black: Mystery, Elegance, Evil
Gray: Moody, Conservative, Formality
White: Purity, Cleanliness, Virtue
Brown: Nature, Wholesomeness, Dependability
Tan or Beige: Conservative, Piety, Dull
Cream or Ivory: Calm, Elegant, Purity

After understanding design theory and the meaning of colors, we will focus on rules users experience, which completes the puzzle for product design and should be targeted towards creating the best product and experience for the user.

User Experience

So, what is User experience, and what are the rules to be applied. We had already discussed part of it previously, especially in chapter 2, when we discussed priming and other ways to simplify things for the user to purchase your product/service.

The first thing to understand in user experience is the goal. The goal is to immerse the user in the easiest, fluent, friendly, and attractive experience to enjoy going through pages and actions to reach the purchase page or subscription and buy the product/service. So how can we reach this objective? There are many ways to do so. I personally do not believe in specific objective systems; however, some techniques have been tried, tested, and retested to generate results and push users to actual purchases. You hear many speakers, influencers, and gurus who prone systems, but it all comes down to each business, product, and vibe the business wants to give to its community

1.Involve Your Users

Users naturally gravitate to websites that they like. To best determine what people, want on a website, just ask them. When you involve your users in the design process, you organically create a better UX. Though intuition is often a useful tool in a design project, what is intuitive to a site designer might not be intuitive to your customer base. Reaching out to users will give you ideas that you can count on.

How you choose to communicate depends on your customer demographic. Create a Twitter survey, start a Facebook quiz, initiate a survey after purchase, or ask Snapchat users for a snap of what they like/dislike. Not only will this help you develop insight into your users, but it could also boost your business's social media presence. Find them where they are, get their advice, and offer an incentive for their help. A 10% coupon or first access to sales may be just the reward; a guest needs to spend a few minutes explaining how you can improve your UX.

2. Consider the cognitive load

The UX will be poor if someone has difficulty interpreting what you ask them to do, so consider what is happening in your customer's mind when you design UX. One way of approaching this is through science. Consider cognitive load, a psychological term that describes the amount of thought a particular task requires of its doer. One of the most significant cognitive load types is intrinsic cognitive load, which refers to the difficulty with which a user completes a prompted step or instruction on a website or application. Knowing what to do next should come naturally. If users struggle to understand how to take the next step, you have lost them. Keep the instructions short and easy to interpret, but most of all, make sure they are intuitive.

Another type of cognitive load is germane cognitive load, which focuses on processing information and constructing schemas. On websites and applications, there are often discernible design patterns that a user can recognize. The UX will be better if the user can recognize your website's schema or application, as they will understand it faster rather than using an entirely new design pattern.

3. Keep things simple

No one wants to feel dumb when they approach a website. If your users do, they will bounce. People tend to have little patience for situations they cannot understand, but that can be doubly true for technology – where their fuse may already be short. When designing for streamlined UX, it is essential to keep things simple. Overly complicated wording or overwhelming decorative touches will not do your site any favors.

People tend to make choices online fast, so give them the space to do that by offering clear options. Omit excess attributes and focus on the most crucial part of your website or application so they can make a quick and easy decision. Confusing UX can make users feel like they are the problem.

When a consumer feels like the design is too smart for them to navigate, they will find a site where they feel more comfortable.

4. Be consistent

Being consistent is one of the most important rules when designing an effective UX for your website. First, it will make your website clearer. If a user can get a feel for your style and not have to adjust their thinking, it will be easier for them to navigate. If they can quickly navigate your site, they are less likely to bounce. More than increasing UX, developing a clear style will strengthen your brand and make it easier for people to recognize and remember your organization.

5. Design intentionally

Though UX should feel familiar, it should not seem dull. Insert some unique or creative elements into your website or application design to attract users and make them want to spend time on your site. Be intentional with your creativity; too many unique moments may make the site feel inconsistent and frustrating. Break with convention just enough to make your website memorable.

Additionally, be intentional with your site's overall design style. There is an endless number of design conventions, but they are not all interchangeable. If you choose the wrong style, your website or application could be less appealing to users. Having a strong UX for your digital service relies partially on your overall style fitting your brand and pleasing users.

6. Focus on function over aesthetics

Though it is essential for your website to be visually appealing, it is more important that it functions well. Before investing large amounts of time into making your website or application appealing to the eye, ensure that it functions quickly and easily.

7. Know where you are in the design process

UX design is an extensive and complicated process. It often takes a long time to achieve the stellar UX that everyone strives for. As the process is long and complicated, it is easy to get caught up in each small step and forget to look at the overall project.

If you are looking for feedback from users, it is essential to have an idea of your overall position in the process. Feedback will be far less useful if you have extensive details about one small part of the project and only a vague description of the overall goal. It also helps you determine which questions to ask when trying to get user feedback. Instead of asking about each step individually, ask questions that analyze the design's overall effectiveness. Each step works on getting your website to the end goal, so having information about how the design functions is most important.

8. Personalize the experience

People are exponentially more likely to connect to a website or application design if they can get a sense of the person behind the screen. Developing a connection with users strengthens their experience with your platform and leads them to build loyalty to your brand. If your website looks like every other one online, it will likely be quickly forgotten. Lifeless, impersonal designs do not appeal to potential clients or customers. If you can design your website so that the user imagines a group of people behind the site instead of a machine, you will attract more people and improve the UX on your website.

9. Leave room for user error

Design your digital experience so that it still functions when someone makes a mistake. Consider how some search engines autocorrect for spelling; if they did not, many people would not get far in their online searches. Designing empathetically may help you circumvent problems your user will make, but you cannot foresee all errors. When a box pops up telling the user there was an error, be sure to include instructions. Instead of merely saying "an internal error occurred," say that an error occurred and provide directions for the user on how to resolve it. If your website or application becomes unusable after a user error, you will lose a lot of interest

Many designers leave out the most critical piece to create the ultimate website or app – those who will be using and engaging with it. Spend some time improving your UX design, and see more traffic, increased conversions, and lower bounce rates.

This brings us to complete the product design puzzle that includes design thinking, colors, and user experience. Whatever you are trying to develop, you will use these strategies and techniques to build an amazing product and remember that the client/customer/lead or whatever you want to call them are kings.

11. Relationships 2.0

If you have reached this far, then you are definitely on the road to success, and you have so much knowledge at your disposal. You are now at a stage in this process where you know how to start a business, the legal implications, the managements, the Neuro-Theory of things, and how things are related to psychology and mental priming. You know the ins and outs of social media, the tools available to you, digital marketing, and all other channels you can use to market your product. You know how to raise funds and how to make people believe in your business. You know how to design your product, your platforms, use techniques to grow your business and how to hire talent.

Lastly, I want to talk to you about relationships 2.0 and how to build amazing relationships in the 21st century combined with keeping a positive and excited attitude. I will divide this chapter into two parts: the 4 Ps [Positivity, Passion, Purpose, & Productivity]; and Relationships 2.0.

The Four Ps

The four Ps are what will guide and push you to making a relationship succeed. Positivity, Passion, Purpose, and Productivity are the key pillars to succeed in anything you are trying to do and trying to achieve. Whether it is in your relationships, in your personal life, in your getaways, at work, in college, or wherever you are around the world. As I am writing this, I am immersed and thinking about every one of you struggling and pushing to make it in this world. Try to do the same,

putting a piece of background music and look afar. You will start thinking of the amazing people around you and the great-hearted people looking to make it and succeed in whatever they are doing, whether in Dubai, Hong Kong, New York, Los Angeles, Buenos Aires, Libreville, Sidney, Bangalore or anywhere around the world.

Keep focusing on these four pillars and start with positivity. What does positivity mean? Well.

1. Positivity

Let's start by getting something clear in our minds. We all have problems. We all have our struggles, issues, fears, and complications. I was born clinically blind, and God gave me the gift of relative eyesight through the eyes, but total eyesight through the heart and mind. When I look at things, I focus on the small details, on the beauty of things, on the uniqueness of each human being, object, and situation. Positivity does not mean having positive things around but rather forcing positivity on yourself and others. It involves steps that, if done repetitively, can generate energy, an energy that can translate to positive situations and outcomes. I was always the eternally positive person in any group I was in, but that does not mean I was not sad. I understand life, whether fortunately or unfortunately, there is a thin line between understanding and over understanding life.

When you reach a point in your life where you really get it, you are sad. You are really sad, but then you make peace with this sadness and the subtleness of life. You realize that it is all about experiences, journeys, relationships, and added value to this world, in which we are temporary. We all grow and become older, but what is most important is to keep playing, keep enjoying, and moving around to create value, love, and passion for others.

There are a few steps you take to keep the positivity high:

1. **Keep saying positive words** even when you talk to yourself, discuss with others, and interact with anyone you see. Instead of saying no, say yes, and instead of negating, confirm and add to the sentence. I shared a few sentences below that show you how to say things more positively. I am a true believer in something in French called "Pollution Sonore" or noise pollution. This means that whatever you hear, whether from yourself or others, makes its way to your ear and, therefore, your head. I push my analysis even further to say that whatever a not-yet-born child hears from exterior surroundings DOES affects how the kid will grow. Hence, the debate about genetics versus education becomes much narrower when you factor in this element.

2. **Keep listening to positive things:** Yes, keep listening to positive people, positive podcasts, omics videos, and, most importantly, positive news. Do not get sucked into some people's negativity, and do not push towards situations that make you feel sad. With sadness there is a feeling you get that can be satisfying to some people and sometimes addictive, so try to look the other way and take it seriously doing so.

3. **Stay in a positive environment:** Another part of forced positivity is to push yourself towards people and situations that are positive and exciting. I always have this mindset when heading to amazing events and gatherings. This is where you will grow, network, meet amazing people, and get access to amazing opportunities.

My family and I come from a suburb. We did not have things easy, but I wouldn't say that we had it rough either. However, staying where you are will not make you win; staying in the same environment will not make you grow. To be practical, let's say you are born in a suburb of any city around the world; think about where you would make it more? You can stay where you are or find any way to get on a plane to New York City and hustle and grow there? Think of the opportunities, of the target market, of the people, of the wealth that you can benefit from, and the international exposure that is there. Come on, jump. Go to events, go to gatherings, change your attire, your profiles on social media, and integrate. When you want to be with wealthy, this is a step-by-step guide:

Understanding: Rich people do not like exposure. Real rich people are quite secretive, choose a secretive location, and even their usernames on social media are pretty complicated on purpose to keep it niche. The next trend worldwide is communities and small groups based on particular interests. Look at Porsche Groups on Facebook and the engagement levels on posts; it is simply crazy. Look at Twitch and the relationships gamers and the likes have built. All the small circles are the next big thing. So, what you should do is:

1. **Choose interests** you might like and that align with your image and goals. If you are a guy, cars are a good start but know that each car club has a specific type of profile, and people that like Porsches do not necessarily assimilate themselves with Lambos and exotic cars. If you are a girl, being part of a fan club or being in touch with women groups tends to get you there.

2. **Revamp your social media profiles:** Make sure you are on the trendiest social media platforms and are always on the lookout for new trends. By the end of 2021, you need to be on Instagram, LinkedIn, Facebook, TikTok, Twitter, Snapchat, and in some cases and countries, more niche social media platforms.

3. **Choose events that matter:** Choose the best events to attend and get together with people. Also stop looking at your phone every couple of minutes.

4. **Create an Identity:** Create an identity you can describe yourself with and live that identity. You are like any brand; you are a brand - you are a special purpose vehicle for your ideas and the crowd.

"In public - no phone! In elevators discuss, in cafes discuss, in public discuss. Meet people and interact..."

2. Passion

What is passion?

Entrepreneurial passion is essential for success. It is required to convince a team to devote themselves to the venture, investors to back the venture, and customers to pay for the product or service. Passion can therefore be a differentiating factor between success and failure for an entrepreneur.

Passion defined

Entrepreneurial passion is a motivational construct characterized by positive emotional arousal, internal drive, and engagement with personally meaningful work that is salient to the entrepreneur's self-identification.

The passion effects

Entrepreneurs who convey passion are more persuasive, motivated, have larger social networks, and have more social capital [1]. As a result, they have more income, sales revenue, and earnings growth than entrepreneurs who are less passionate [2]. Passion is, therefore is critical to an entrepreneur's success.

Passion is palpable

Passion affects how customers, investors, and employees view the entrepreneur and their product. When they can feel the entrepreneur's passion, they may be more persuaded by it, and for a good reason. To these individuals, passion is a strong indicator of:

Degree of motivation

Level of commitment

Confidence in their vision
If they will persevere in the face of obstacles
How well they can lead people in their venture

Persuasion skills
Therefore, it is necessary to display passion when communicating with customers, employees, and anyone making funding decisions as it will help persuade them to support the venture or vision.

Passion and decisions
Entrepreneurs must be passionate when pitching to an investor making funding decisions, selling to a customer, or hiring new employees. Passion will boost their confidence in evaluating the business plan, product, company, team, and entrepreneur.

However, passion alone is not sufficient to influence decisions. When passion is integrated with a concrete business plan, product, or service, the entrepreneur will be evaluated more favorably. When a passionate entrepreneur's business plan lacks substance, their product fails to deliver as promised, or their service is insufficient. The entrepreneur will likely be viewed as fake, manipulative, and insincere.

The passion sweet spot
The amount of passion displayed also affects decisions. If the entrepreneur displays too much passion, it may appear as if they are not genuine, desperate, or pretentious. Of course, too little passion can result in being perceived as not being completed invested in the venture or not confident about the product, service, company, or team. It is essential that entrepreneurs display an appropriate amount of passion and that their passion is supported by an amazing product, service, or business plan. Passion will facilitate persuasive arguments, the buying process, and funding decisions. Entrepreneurs who convey passion will sell more, earn more and convince more, all contributing to their venture's success

3. Purpose

What is Purpose?

Purpose has to come in a very detailed way. It must have a clear scope, be clearly identifiable, and, most importantly, assessable. Look at any KPI [Key Performance Indicator]. It must be clearly and thoroughly assessable so that know how and when you reach your results.

I will lay down for you 12 KPIs you should know for your start-up to get going. It is critically important for the founders of a company to understand its key performance indicators (KPIs) intimately. Founders cannot hope to grow a company in any meaningful way without an almost obsessive focus on its KPIs.

Why? If constructed correctly, KPIs give management and potential investors a cold, analytical snapshot of the company's state, untainted by emotion or rhetoric. This focus must not be limited to the KPIs themselves, for they are merely measurements of outcomes. We look for founders to understand what levers can be pulled and what tweaks can be made to improve the business, which will then be reflected in its KPIs.

The focus should not be on the KPIs themselves, but their meaning and knowing what impacts each one.

Let's review some of the KPIs that are important for founders to understand thoroughly and for which they should have a strategy, or set of strategies, for optimizing. Please note that some KPIs are not relevant to some types of businesses. Finally, I will not go into very much detail on each metric, and how to calculate it as, (a) that is beyond the scope of this book and (b) that information is readily available from other sources.

Customer acquisition cost (CAC): CAC is the amount of money you need to spend on sales, marketing, and related expenses, on average, to acquire a new customer. This tells us about your marketing efforts' efficiency, although it's much more meaningful when combined with some of the other metrics below and compared to competitors' CAC.

Acquiring new customers is one thing but retaining them is even more critical. Your customer retention rate indicates the percentage of paying customers who remain paying customers during a given period. The converse to retention rate is churn (or attrition), the percentage of customers you lose in each period. When we see high retention rates over an indicative period, we know the company has a sticky product and keeps its customers happy. This is also an indicator of capital efficiency.

Lifetime value (LTV) is the measurement of an average customer's net value to your business over the estimated life of the relationship with your company. Understanding this number, especially in its relation to CAC, is critical to building a sustainable company.

We consider the **ratio of CAC to LTV** to be the golden metric. This is an accurate indicator of the sustainability of a company. If a company can predictably and repeatedly turn x into 10x (note: 10x is just an illustration and not meant to imply any minimum or standard), then it's sustainable.

The most successful founders tend to have an obsessive focus on their KPIs and the drive to experiment and optimize them constantly.

CAC recovery time (or months to recover CAC). This KPI measures how long it takes for a customer to generate enough net revenue to cover the CAC. CAC recovery time has a direct impact on cash flow and, consequentially, runway.

Whereas CAC measures the variable expenses attributable to acquiring customers, **overhead** measures the company's fixed expenses incurred irrespective of the number of customers acquired. Overhead relative to revenue reflects the capital efficiency of a company (i.e., all things being equal, a company that generates $1 million in revenue on $200,000 in overhead is twice as efficient as one that generates $1 million in revenue on $400,000 in overhead).

Understanding your revenue and monthly expenses (fixed and variable) enables you to calculate the company's **monthly burn**. This is simply the net amount of cash flow for a month when net cash flow is negative. If the company starts the month with $100,000 in cash and ends the month with $90,000 in cash, its burn rate is $10,000. If a company's monthly net cash flow is positive, it is not burning cash.

A keen focus on a runway is critical to the survival of any start-up. A **Runway** is the measure of the amount of time until the company runs out of cash, expressed in months. A Runway is computed by dividing the remaining cash by monthly burn. We prefer to view a conservative estimate of a runway that calculates the monthly burn utilizing current revenue and projected expenses (after accounting for the increased expenses incurred post-investment). We require an absolute minimum of 12 months of the runway but have a strong preference for 18 months or more. Short runways cause entrepreneurs to be myopic and not have the liberty to tweak and iterate when necessary. It also forces them to almost immediately focus on the next fundraising project instead of growing the company.

Expressed as a percentage, profit margin tells us how much your product sells for above the actual cost of the product itself. Put another way, it reveals how much of the selling price is "**mark-up**." This invaluable metric allows us to consider the return of investment on the product's cost and is significant in understanding its scalability and sustainability.

We consider the **conversion rate** to be a very telling KPI. It reveals a combination of its ability to sell its products to its customers and customers' desire for the product. It is particularly instructive to track and review conversion rates over time and regularly run experiments to improve them.

Certain businesses find that revenue may not be the most informative indicator of their financial performance. This is especially true for marketplaces for which revenue (i.e., their take rate) represents a small

Gross merchandise volume (GMV) can be a useful KPI in these cases. GMV is the overall dollar value of sales of goods or services purchased through a marketplace.

For companies with apps, online games, or social networking sites, **monthly active users (MAU)** are an important KPI. MAU is the number of unique users who engage with the site or app in a 30-day period. Understanding MAU helps determine the revenue potential of a company or how well it is currently monetizing.

When we speak to founders to learn more about their companies, we ask them for these KPIs, along with their narrative and other information. It is a quick way for us to understand the business's current state. We have serious concerns about founders who do not know their KPIs.

I find that the most successful founders tend to be those who have an obsessive focus on their KPIs and the drive to experiment and optimize them constantly.

4. Productivity

With productivity comes efficiency, and with efficiency comes smart work. Setting up and running a start-up is no easy task. Entrepreneurs, businessmen, and women worldwide come across many challenges daily. Funding and finding the right talent and time management are only some of the issues they face. But sometimes, all it takes are a few small changes to processes to increase the level of productivity and efficiency in a business.

Be as efficient as possible

Do you ever come out of a meeting and think, "gosh, this could have been an email!" While I agree with that, a lot of the time, I find that a quick face-to-face conversation allows us to get things done more efficiently. Often, what could be a two-minute discussion with a colleague can turn into a two-hour waiting game over emails. Of course, other alternatives use technology, allowing us to minimize face-to-face meetings—options like Microsoft Teams, for example, can be used to call, text, and share files with team members at a much faster pace than an email would, and does not restrict us to a physical location or meeting room.

Be as digitally-savvy as possible

Use all the platforms you can. I shared a few earlier that can save you a lot of time. Look at Trello, Slack, which will soon become part of Salesforce if all goes well on this transaction.

Join an Accelerator

Do not underestimate the power of joining an accelerator. These specialized organizations can expand your growth by offering access to investment, office space, and mentorship from industry leaders. An accelerator scheme offers everything needed to help you thrive, including access to mentors in the local and international tech ecosystem.

Location, Location, Location

You have heard this before, but location is one of the most significant assets you can invest in as a start-up – not just in terms of physical space, but more broadly, the market from which you operate. It is critical for your start-up to understand your criteria, what exactly it is that you want to do, and which location will best help serve your needs. Ultimately, you need to understand the specific tools needed to be put in place for your idea to flourish, and the location is a critical component in that. Most of all, though, don't feel limited by geographies, go out and find the right place; I guarantee you, it exists.

Create structure

Leaving roles undefined, especially in small start-ups, can create confusion, and even worse, lead to duplicate efforts and tons of wasted time. Defining roles and tasks gives the team a sense of responsibility and promotes accountability, both of which are crucial to any start-up's success.

Invest in the culture

Whether in a start-up or a large organization, a management team must promote trust, open communication, and access to information. Early on in your journey, you need to find out exactly what kind of culture and values your start-up stands for and how you plan to communicate that to your team and your customers.

Invest in marketing smartly

Many start-ups pour a significant amount of their capital into marketing their products and services. It is not necessarily a bad thing, but you must be smart about it. Identify your targets and what channels and tools would help you effectively and efficiently drive your message through. Don't be afraid of thinking outside the box—what works for one company may not work for another

Encourage autonomy, don't micromanage

The best way to encourage productivity and creativity in your team is for the managers (and founders) to step back. Let your team manage their tasks freely and independently; you trusted them enough to join your start-up, so you should be able to give them a task and let them fly with it. This increases motivation, and you'll find that the more ownership someone can take off their role, the better job they will do at it.

This brings us to a conclusion. Relationships 2.0 are relationships that are adapted to the new modern era. Today, you cannot approach relationships like you would have 50 years ago. Today employees are no longer employees, founders are no longer founders, investors are no longer investors, and clients are no longer clients. Relationships 2.0 redefines what each relationship is and adapts it to the modern era to stop struggling with what once was and focus on what will be.

Founders are no longer business partners; they must be friends, lovers in one instance, and close people who respect each other and take things most credibly from others. Founders now have to continually communicate with each other, lease, and interact in the most interactive and convergent way. You can no longer consider that you have two lives: one personal and one work. You have to blend when it comes to start-ups. Choose people you have fun with, you interact with, and you can build long-lasting friendships with.

Employees are no longer employees; they are friends, freelancers at times, partners at other times, and project-based helpers. Resources inside the company can no longer sustain themselves. Even big conglomerates will move to work more and more with a workforce operating remotely, operating on a project basis, as freelancers maybe and in an Uber-like way. Uber is one of the biggest companies worldwide and look at its workforce. Just 20 years ago, you would assess a company's size by its employees; today, it is no longer the case. Uber has freelance drivers; Amazon is gearing towards a revolution in logistics working with solopreneurs, small entrepreneurs in local areas to help deliver. They are even helping people invest in their own trucks, logistics material, and solutions to deliver products for amazon. Law firms are gearing to an enormous revolution where software and freelancers will cover most of the corporate requirements in corporate legal services and investment rounds.

Investors are no longer Investors:
They are more friends, advisors, partners, and sometimes customers and suppliers. Look at your investors like friends and partners. Have a party with them, show them your weaknesses, show them your weak spots, and share personal stuff with them.

Customers are no longer customers:
Today, customers are friends, fans, part of your community, part of your group of loyalists, defenders, and brand ambassadors. Today customers reviews are the most amazing business generators; they are no longer this passive comment that no one reads. People will come to you to join a community. Think of ways to build your community and not be afraid to think outside the box and share your stories, bloopers, and content. Remember, even in your YouTube content and your business videos, people want to see natural and candid.

Lastly, relationships 2.0 does apply to personal relationships as well, and you cannot think of your personal relationships like you used to before. Relationships nowadays have to be more and more free, libertarian, more expressive, and simply more fun. You do not have obligations, boundaries, struggles, limits anymore. You do not need to abide by any rules, timeframes, timelines, or other limitations. Each of you chooses your own types of relationships.

12. A Country Is A Startup

Today, in a world with clearly broken traditional boundaries, preconceived norms, and policies that once were the pillars of governance, we find ourselves bound for change, bound for transformation and disruption on the public policy level. From an incredibly young age, I was infatuated by politics and governance. I did not know why and did not analyze the reasons behind this attraction even though it was and still is a major attraction. I studied Law, studied Finance, worked at the United Nations, and got involved with many political parties in the Middle East, France & the United States.

The Covid crisis and the overall economic situation that hit the young generation, coupled with the massive growth in access to Media, News, and Information, contributed to awakening at most societal levels. People became more aware, more skeptical, and much more investigative when hearing certain speeches, promises, projects they were asked to adhere to, and more. Don't get me wrong; there is still a lot of blurriness, lies, and even scams out there, but overall, people are more and more aware of things simply because the information is out there. One could debate that even though the information is there, its excess leads to effective misinformation. There might be some truth in that, especially with fake news being seen on major platforms nowadays.

Nevertheless, I still believe that the net result is more information, more data, and much more informed decisions down the line. For example, consider the different wars that happened throughout the 20th century compared to wars that happened post-2010 [Social Media Era]. When a battle would be fought, opposition oppressed, communities wiped out, the media would discuss what they had in the information. Post-2010, with social media, phone cameras, and more data shared in different forms; people could see more details and make informed conclusions about different situations

Add to that Technology, Automation, and Robotics, and oh boy, how this creates a mix that can be mind-blowing when it comes to disruption.

During the frontier conference held in Pittsburgh by the White House in 2016, President Obama argued that you could not run a country, especially the United States, as a start-up. He argued that government could not act like a start-up because it must worry about many aspects not included in a start-up's agenda like welfare, veterans coming home [in the case of the United States] and/or healthcare and others. He gave examples of specific policies that cannot be decided on swiftly and without considering risk and contingency plans. I would agree that governance is the complexity involved in articulating projects and the adversity involved in innovating.

As Plato said, "The heaviest penalty for declining to rule is to be ruled by someone inferior to yourself." The dilemma is simple when it comes to ruling. The hard workers will not go through the effort and struggle to reach power which leaves the door open for less hard workers and less technical people to take the lead and govern.

However, where I would diverge from President Obama's statement lies in the evolution of modern society and politics overall. The world is gearing up for a considerable take-off from what once was and will be soon moved by amazing transformations related to government and power. The once appealing field of politics has lost a bit of its charm because it does not attract as much as it once did - the extensive work involved in reaching power, the funding required that puts candidates at funders' mercy. Most importantly, the income they get out of it compared to what politicians used to get makes it less appealing and less attractive. Let me explain. In the 1970s, a politician would get into politics with much less effort because of less competition. They would require less funding because there was no real need for ad spending, as there is today. For that, you can easily check the budgets of presidential candidates in the 2020 US presidential run.

Furthermore, candidates were not under scrutiny for what they did and did not do, what's happening in their private life, and what small mistake they did, or people interpret they did. In the early 20th century, a politician would naturally get rich not only through remuneration but also through the deals they would strike, commissions they would get, and office terms that would span for years and years. Today a politician is under the radar and literally cannot be rich. They cannot show wealth as it would be easily and naturally associated with potential corruption schemes or bad deals they have made. Add to that the swiftness of swings in public opinion, which could go from love to hate in a few weeks. Yesterday's ruling class is today's criticism and tomorrows despise.

Another considerable transformation is imminent in the way people interact with their respective countries. People are more and more country shopping choosing 50% of the vow for better but not necessarily for worse. With citizenship programs, institutions lending money for people to buy passports, and so many active immigration programs, the likes of Canada and other countries looking to attract people to their ever-aging population, people have more choice. Therefore, sticking to one's country has a limit that is far closer than what it was before. Do not get me wrong, immigration has been there for ages, and people would go from one land to another looking for resources. A better life and a better environment to live in, but access was not always available, and communities were much more interlinked in an era where long distance communication was not available.

Today, we have many choices, many prerogatives, many opportunities to change lands in the blink of an eye. Look at what has happened in a small country called Lebanon in the Middle East in 2019. It was hit by a huge crisis, which proved to be the worst Ponzi Scheme in history. Banks closed and limited withdrawals, the national currency rapidly devalued, and the country went into a huge economic crisis. A hundred years before, this situation would have created the worst humanitarian crisis, hunger, and violence bringing blood to the streets. However, what happened was different. Yes, a crisis was born, but many families sustained by either: fleeing to Canada, France, and the United Arab Emirates. Others kept receiving USDs from their children and siblings, making the diaspora the single strongest supporter of Lebanon at the time. These solutions would not have been available before.

So, if you add the digital transformation, the choices, the disruption in our professional world, the disruption in behavioral economics, in individual and communitarian aspirations and geopolitics subjected more and more with economic and trade benefits and interests; Yes, the country should be run like a start-up from the ground up, sorry Mr. President.

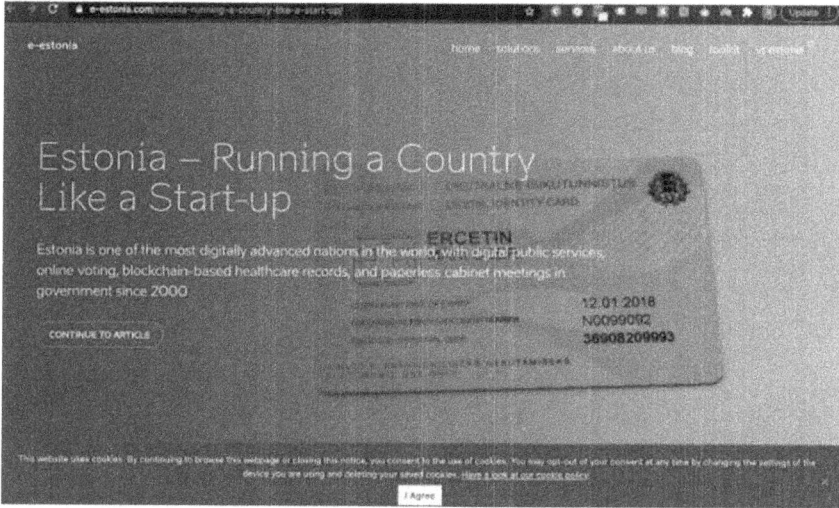

This is Estonia's web presence showing how Estonia moved to become a start-up nation quite fast. Singapore led this movement in the 60s and 70s, and many countries are currently starting to apply start-up concepts in governing.

So, to all Entrepreneurs, this is your chance to make a difference, move fast, change countries and ecosystems to succeed, and make it to the top. With Lexyom, we were the first legal tech/law firm to unite ALL major ecosystems unifying documentation, contracts, processes, and legal advice. We could advise a start-up in San Francisco in the morning and advise a start-up in Dubai in the afternoon. Both consultations would be radically convergent, although legal systems and laws would be drastically divergent. Understand that even the world is no longer your limit [Look at SpaceX].

For countries, it is the same, act like a start-up fast, and yes, find solutions with the Private Sector, with Entrepreneurs, with digital innovators, with disruptors. But how to do it?

To answer this question, we need to start with the conceptualization of a country. What is a country? What is government?

The word country comes from old French **contrée,** which derives from Vulgar Latin (terra) **contrata** ("(land) lying opposite"; "(land) spread before"), derived from contra ("against, opposite"). It most likely entered the English language after the Franco-Norman invasion during the 11th century. A country is a political state, nation, or territory which is controlled. It is often referred to as the land of an individual's birth, residence, or citizenship. This definition brings up three components of a country: The Land, The People, and the Government. We will be adding a 4th component, which would be crucial in the next phase of humanity working together to achieve specific goals.

The Evolution Of The State

I will touch base on the state's evolution as it is crucial to understand the transformation in concepts to grasp the trends that are evolving nowadays. I always saw evolution as a fascinating phenomenon and as a source to deeply understand the real reasons behind things. A state is the consequence of the people building and interacting with it, so it is only natural to evolve and transform over time. Nevertheless, this evolution is torn between two concepts that will soon become irrelevant, the superstate and the minimal state. The superstate controls most facets of power, social, economy, trade, security, and other aspects. It is the state that integrates on all levels and has led various episodes in history to some kind of tyranny. On the other hand, the minimal state is the state that is contrary to essential interventions, leaving the door open to the significant and active involvement of the private sector in determining and organizing certain aspects of society. This form has led several times to a weakened state controlled by private interest and corruption.

Throughout history, we moved through several forms of state. As stated by philosophers who focused on politics like Montesquieu, John Locke, or others, the fundamental principles of a modern state distinguish between the executive, the legislative, and the judicial powers [as added by Montesquieu in the Spirit of Laws [L'esprit des Lois]]. Suppose the United States constitution gets inspired by these philosophers and Samuel von Pufendorf's natural principles. In that case, this current will dissipate and have minimal effect moving forward both in the United States and in France.

These concepts of powers and counter-powers will lose steam as of the mid-19th century, especially with Elie Halévy, who sees this as a moral pessimism, a doubt in human beings' capacity to understand their real interest - that of the State. This led to the era of institutionalization destined to refine the people's thoughts and actions, obliging them to understand what "the other" is thinking. It builds on the concept of "reason," which is not purely abstract but feeds from a confrontation with reality, making laws not the commandments of a higher power but rather a set of inter-relations amongst community members. The State becomes an entity that does not have one ultimate ruler but hides many rulers within its structure.

This is especially important to understand, as it makes you see the actual structure you live in and what is ripe for disruption and ripe for evolution. We entrepreneurs have to understand these concepts to make sense of our surroundings and how things function in life.

Imagine France in the 1750s, François Quesnay, and the Physiocrats who conceptualized the idea of being governed by nature, considered that only agriculture would create the equilibrium with nature. Pierre Samuel Du Pont de Nemours forged the term Physiocracy by associating two Greek terms "Physis" [Nature] and "Kratos" [Force, Government]. The idea of wealth coming from the earth, that the only productive class is that of Farmers, and that there are no other laws, but the laws of nature based on freedom and private property, would be enough to create equilibrium, was just crazy considering what we know today.

Another philosopher Quesnay wrote in General Maxims of Government in a kingdom of agriculture: "The system of Counter Power in government is a pointless opinion that only highlights the divergences between big powers and the weakness of small powers. Indeed, this was the beginning of the conceptualization of a practical government that would have prerogatives to lead without consensus and obstacles in the name of democracy, freedom, and the concept of power to the people.

The state moved from being in control of everything under a superpower coming from God at the times of Richelieu, to a state that was more of a police state, controlling mainly security through the police, the army, and the judicial system; to a Welfare State heavily assisting on the social level and culminating with the Marxist and communist theory; to recently the Economic Support State creating an equilibrium in the economy to maintain growth. Different sub theories emerged to this concept with more economically involved state theories like the Keynes theory of major state projects that would fuel the economy; or other freer market theories pushing towards deregulation.

Tomorrow, the state will be a decentralized, delocalized, borderless state, regulating different government and state aspects. It has a more critical educational, welfare role, especially after countries start to adopt "Universal Income" and other policies to shield against acute poverty. Tomorrow's countries will be based on visions, missions, and goals like start-ups are taught to do today. Each country will have to challenge itself to deliver a vision that would contribute to humankind's growth and shield our race from dangers and threats coming our way within the next 200 years. Just like the Mayans were able to see thousands of years ahead, our culture will set the baseline to thousands of years to come.

We will have visions and cultures in the forms of countries promoting certain goods and services that would be unique to them but would converge with the interests of humanity.

The Startup Theory

Step 1: vision, mission, goals

Each country should start by defining their vision, their mission, and their goals. To do that, they would look at their assets, their resources, their geographical positioning, their culture, and all that constitutes their evolution to come out with a vision that would make the best use of all these aspects. A small country caught between major powers cannot aspire to be a major force in diplomatic struggles, just like a major state cannot be borderless as a first stage. Once this exercise is done, the start-up theory for a state begins at the bottom of the ladder, with municipalities, counties, villages, being given the right tools to implement this vision. Blockchain, decentralizing databases, creating a new educational center that would teach new techniques and skills people can use to make money online or throughout borders, a development plan for agriculture, industry, and/ or services depending on the county's resources, and much more.

Once we start working with small districts and elevating the results to the state level, we would reap results quite fast, considering that the vision is clear.

Step 2: giving the tools to small districts

Once this is done, all government parts must be synchronized under a unique central agency that I call "The Centralis." The Centralis is the epicentre of the state; it is a decentralized entity that is governed by the vision. This is not an easy concept to grasp but imagine you create a set of rules, borders, frontiers, and directions just like when creating a video game. These rules would be decentralized, and you would input actions into this system. If actions converge with the rules, they would be approved. Of course, our beloved Einstein emerges with his relativity theory here;

Indeed, these concepts would apply to significant actions and decisions and leave a margin for smaller actions to be taken.

Step 3: install centralis

Once we have a vision governed by Centralis with tools given to smaller districts, we would work on the different facets of our social, healthcare, and educational system. You would need a strong and forceful government to implement reforms, adapt to changes and work closely with all stakeholders to reach specific goals swiftly and accurately. Look at Estonia, Singapore, United Arab Emirates, and others who have flourished; what do they have in common? Don't be afraid to say it? They have a strong government, and the debate on politics is not that elaborate. This is what created their efficiency and success when no one has understood the concept of practically working in Centralis. Tomorrow things will change, and people will further understand that the point is to grow, work together and be practical in approaching government and ruling. Tomorrow people will understand that life is about other challenges, and most of the time, it's about the small things. Tomorrow's world is where everyone would be growing within their community, with small activities, interactions, and freedom within boundaries. It would also be a more organized world where the challenges would be to find an incentive for people to do things, to find purpose and goals for the individual to want to grow and stay alive, to push individuals to fake or altered realities where risk remains on the virtual level protecting the real dimension we know today, which one could argue is also a virtual dimension that was there yesterday.

Countries will be vision-based. We will have to compete to share their vision better. This mindset has been there for quite some time without really being identified as such. For the older ones, just remember how in your 20s, in university, you were more geared towards leftist movements. With age, work, and involvement in the professional world, you find yourself leaning more towards rightist movements. This generation is much more elaborate in assessing the reasons behind certain thoughts and ideas.

Once each of the 190+ countries have set out their vision, their mission, and their goals based on their overall resources and identity, we will have around 190+ major entities competing and working together to grow humanity into a healthier, more evolved, more curious species looking past Earth to discover the universe further. We will reach a point where humanity will be looking for further excitement in discovering the unknown universe, and all the problems and struggles we face today will be irrelevant and out of date. Call me crazy, but I see this era coming very soon, and I genuinely believe in the system that is put in place to reach specific outcomes; I am part of the system and do not refuse its aspects and forms.

Relationship 2.0

I would like to end the book by focusing on the concept I discussed in the previous chapter. Computer and communications technology seems to be impacting relationships the most. Mobile phones, texting, Facebook, and Twitter are just a few ways of how relationships are being redefined, established, and maintained by technology. We have entered a new era of Relationships 2.0.

Many of these changes, like relationships, have been positive and productive. Online communities based around shared ideas and passions are a vital wellspring of information and action. Causes have been fomented and movements launched by online communities. New technology has allowed people formerly disconnected, to establish relationships that have increased creativity, innovation, productivity, and efficiency. A personal example: I was the lead attorney/negotiator on a deal, and my co-counsel and I met over the Internet. We communicated through email and have never met in person and only spoke on the telephone once (to congratulate each other on its completion) through the entire preparation and publication process.

Relationships 2.0 is also a boon to maintaining already established relationships. If you have family or friends who live at a great distance, or if you travel a great deal (as I do), you no longer have to rely on the telephone to stay connected. You can be in constant contact through relatively primitive technology, such as email, or more advanced technology such as texting, Facebook, Flickr, Skype, and Twitter. Tech-savvy grandparents love this aspect of Relationships 2.0!

In exploring Relationships 2.0, I do not mean to devalue all manner of relationships that are now possible due to the recent revolution in computer and communication technology. We should embrace all the benefits that this new technology has to offer. But, as with all value neutral innovations, there are both benefits and costs, positive uses and unhealthy misuses, intended outcomes, and unintended consequences.

My concern focuses on the more personal and social aspects of Relationships 2.0. For example, I hear many people talking about all the "friendships" around the world they have made on the Web, whether through social networking, gaming, or dating sites, or sites that reflect their beliefs (e.g., political, or religious) or their interests (e.g., technology, sports). There is no doubt that the Web has enabled people everywhere to connect and communicate like never before, but I would argue that connection alone does not make a relationship.

Just like the use of the old term, virtual reality, many people in Relationships 2.0 have what I believe are virtual relationships yet consider them to be real relationships. Virtual relationships have all the appearances of real relationships. Still, they are missing essential elements that make real relationships, well, real, namely, three dimensionality, facial expressions, voice inflection, clear emotional messages, gestures, body language, physical contact, and pheromones. Virtual relationships are based on limited information and, as a result, are incomplete.

When connecting with others through technology, you get bits and pieces of people - words on a screen, two-dimensional images, or a digitized voice - almost like having some, but not all, of the pieces of a puzzle. You get a picture of them, but you lack the pieces you need to get a complete picture.

Virtual relationships can seem so real. I advise a group of mobile technology web sites. The email banter among the almost-exclusively male staff is no different from if many guys were sitting around drinking beer and watching football. Despite evident geographical and political differences, the camaraderie and support are amazing. However, would this group get along if they met in person? I don't think so. Perhaps that is both the beauty and the shame of online relationships.

These limitations don't mean that we shouldn't have virtual relationships; they can serve a valuable purpose in our personal and professional lives. But I worry that people are substituting real relationships for virtual ones. Rather than being just a small subset of their relationships, virtual relationships come to dominate their relationship universe. I often see groups of teenagers sitting together but not talking, only texting. I wonder if they are texting each other! So, what is the attraction of virtual relationships? We live in a society where families are no longer nuclear, communities are fragmented, and people can feel isolated and disenfranchised. Economic uncertainty, global unrest, and political polarization can create feelings of alienation and anxiety. Fears of inadequacy, rejection, and failure also add to the maelstrom of personal angst. Isn't it just safer to stay in your room and connect with people through your computer? Isn't it better to have the appearance of intimate relationships, but without all the risks, rather than put yourself out there and take the chance of being hurt?

People can fulfil many of their needs for connection and affiliation through virtual relationships. They can present their best faces to their online community. They can get support from a vast number of people. Virtual relationships are also comfortable and safe. Easy because you don't have to leave your room. Safe because of their anonymity and your ability to just hit end or delete when you want out. But they certainly lack the richness and satisfaction of real relationships. Technology limits what we can honestly know about someone. It prevents us from using the most deeply ingrained qualities that have allowed us to make connections for ages. Though there is a place for online relationships, they are no substitute for the depth and breadth of real, flesh-and-blood relationships. Relationships where you can see, hear, smell, touch, and sense the other person. Yes, real relationships can get messy, with hurt feelings, anger, frustration, and disappointment. But they are like two sides of the same coin; you cannot have the beauty of relationships - love, joy, excitement, and contentment - without also being willing to accept its occasional blood, sweat, and tears. And I challenge anyone who can show me that virtual relationships can provide that.

I chose the name The Start-up Lawyer because it summarizes who I am exactly: A constant start-up, an avid lawyer, and defender of life as we want it, not as we have it.

Businesses are evolving, so make sure to read and listen to advice and kickstart your business as soon as possible. You are the result of a few decisions you make on certain days and at certain hours.

Relationships are changing, so treat your cofounders like friends, your employees like cofounders, your investors like your partners, and your customers like members of your warm, loving community. Treat your wife/husband like the human being they are. Understand they have needs; they want excitement, passion, they want to attract and be attracted to, and most importantly, they want to be on top of their game so let them be. I am a big fan of Libertarian movements, and I will be writing quite much on Libertarianism and openness in relationships to reach relationship 2.0 personally, as much as on the professional level.

Finally, you are ready! Yes, you are ready to go and launch your market or improve it. Remember, this is a community; the Akylles community is here to help you, and we are here to interact together and make it the most amazing community out there. We are winners; remember, you are a winner, you are a friend, you are a partner, and we will be very harsh with those who try to stop us and hinder our path to success.

I will mention one last thing about humanity and evolution. As we know it, information is electrical impulses where every cell knows and talks to every other cell; they exchange thousands of bits between them per second. These cells group together, forming a giant group of communication, which in turn forms matter. Cells get together, take on one form, deform, reform, and it's all the same. We consider ourselves unique, so we have routed our whole existence on the idea of uniqueness. All social systems are a mere sketch of each other, $1+1 = 2$. We have codified our existence to bring it down to human size to make it understandable. We have created a scale so we can forget its unfathomable scale. So, you will ask what is then the unit of measure? And why should we know all this?

Film any object speeding and speed up the image faster and faster; you will see that the object disappears. Well, my friend, it is time. Time gives legitimacy to its existence, and it is the only real unit of measure and gives proof to the unit of matter. Without time, we do not exist.

Cells in time have one goal and one goal only, and it has been there since the beginning of time: to reproduce to pass information and knowledge from one cell to another.

Transpose this theory into your life. As you are growing and evolving, you will encounter many people, situations, and events that we will call cells. These cells will interact with each other, share information, and work together. So, each cell's nature will affect the others and create a web that will conclude to be either positive, neutral, or negative to your success. The famous book "The Secret" discussed this energy concept but did not dive into what makes energy.

Energy is concretely cells interacting together and reaching a particular outcome. So, transpose this theory into your start-up life or even your everyday life. Say you have a negative person or a negative situation in your surroundings. You think you control this negativity from head to toe, and all is under your supervision. Well, think again, and think really hard because you are not in control of anything. It is quite the opposite; it is in control of you. You are under an illusion that you are in control while, in the meantime, the situation is getting worse by the second. It is getting worse with every exchange of bits in between cells. The negativity in one will continuously transpose into the other, and vice versa, the positivity in the other will try to reach the first one, and so it continues. The caveat, and this is a personal opinion, not research, is that negativity moves at a pace that is much faster than positivity. Its life span and velocity are much higher because of two primary fuels:

1. Fear,
2. Time.

We are all fearful of many things in life, and we are all aware of time.

Negativity will spread much faster, is fuelled by much more circumstances, and can be very destructive. On the other hand, positivity is a far bigger challenge, a further goal to reach but a much more consistent situation once achieved. You will find that once you have reached a high level of positivity and, most importantly, you think you deserve this positivity, you will find a much happier person.

The last point I want to make before I can close the first part of the journey comes down to mindset. I struggled a lot with mindset, and you probably will too. When you decide to take the path of change, impact, and passion, you will face many obstacles that will make you doubt your direction, but there comes a moment, a night, and a shooting star you follow with your gazing eyes that guides you to your destiny, that guides you back to your journey's goal. There comes a person that says just a few words, and somehow everything makes more sense. I am sitting looking at the amazing horizon, sun rays warming my gazing look. I sit back waiting for what it has to offer, what narrative will shadow a combination of cells forming what was, is and once will be. I go back to my coffee, slide my fingers on the keyboard, and here we go again.

www.ingramcontent.com/pod-product-compliance
Lightning Source LLC
Chambersburg PA
CBHW060316200326
41519CB00011BA/1752